Manhood on the Line

THE WORKING CLASS IN AMERICAN HISTORY

Editorial Advisors
James R. Barrett, Julie Greene, William P. Jones,
Alice Kessler-Harris, and Nelson Lichtenstein

A list of books in the series appears at the end of this book.

Manhood on the Line

Working-Class Masculinities in the American Heartland

STEPHEN MEYER

UNIVERSITY OF ILLINOIS PRESS

Urbana, Chicago, and Springfield

Library of Congress Cataloging-in-Publication Data
Names: Meyer, Stephen, 1942–
Title: Manhood on the line: working-class masculinities in the
    American heartland / Stephen Meyer.
Description: Urbana, Chicago, and Springfield : University of
    Illinois Press, 2016. | Series: The working class in american
    history | Includes bibliographical references and index.
Identifiers: LCCN 2015035920| ISBN 9780252040054 (cloth :
    alk. paper) | ISBN 9780252081545 (pbk. : alk. paper) | ISBN
    9780252098253 (e-book)
Subjects: LCSH: Automobile industry workers—United States—
    History. | Working class—United States—History. | Sexual
    division of labor—United States. | Women employees—
    United States. | Discrimination in employment—United
    States. | Ford Motor Company—History.
Classification: LCC HD8039.A82 M4659 2016 | DDC
    331.7/6292220973—dc23
LC record available at http://lccn.loc.gov/2015035920

To:
Graham, Liam,
Stella, and Theo
As you grow older, may the world
become a nicer and fairer place

Contents

Preface   ix

Introduction: Forms and Meanings
of Working-Class Manhood   1

1   Lost Manhood: Mass Production
    and Auto-Worker Masculinity   12

2   Reclaiming Manhood: Shop Culture,
    Industrial Unionism, and the Derogation
    of Women, 1920s and 1930s   33

3   "Rats, Finks, and Stool Pigeons":
    The Disreputable Manhood of Factory Spies
    in the 1920s and 1930s   58

4   Fighting to Provide: The Battle to Organize
    the Ford River Rouge Plant, 1930–1945   82

5   Fashioning Dense Masculine Space: Industrial
    Unionism and Altered Shop-Floor Relations, 1935–1960s   112

6   The Female "Invasion": Women and the Male
    Workplace, 1940–1945   141

7   The Challenge to White Manhood: Black Men
    and Women Move to White Male Jobs, 1940–1945   165

Conclusion: The More Things Change, the More
They Stay the Same   192

Abbreviations   211

Notes   213

Index   241

Preface

This book has taken too long to come to fruition and began many, many years ago. Much to my regret, some of this book reveals an underside of labor and union history—the rough and sometimes regressive aspects of working-class and union culture. When I began thinking about this subject in the mid-1980s, the American labor movement had begun a dismal decline resulting from a decade of management policies of de-industrialization and de-unionization. Around that time, I had a split appointment in history and labor studies with the University of Wisconsin–Parkside and the University of Wisconsin School for Workers.

At the School for Workers' mainly white and male union training sessions in Madison, I noticed few African American and female workers at the sessions for local union leaders. At the time, female and black workers were social groups that surveys indicated had the strongest desire and support for unions. From these gatherings, troubling images come to mind: for example, steelworkers would spend the evening at strip clubs, and then the next morning at breakfast, a lone woman had to sit and listen to her union colleagues talk about the previous night's foray and stories of stuffing bills into g-strings or to the machinists whose chief concern was connecting with Madison coeds on State Street. In the midst of a major crisis of union decline, the absence of black workers for leadership training or sexist male behavior of men isolated those who most desired unions.

This was not the situation for all workers and all unions. I recall attending UAW leadership training in 1988 at its Family Education Center at Black Lake. The UAW certainly had its problems with race and gender in the previous decades, but by then it had come a long way in the transformation of its union culture. The weeklong Black Lake session was diverse in its gender and racial composition and involved the full participation of its male, female, and African American workers and their families. Its evening social functions were socially and culturally mixed. By this time, the UAW had learned from its earlier problems with female and black workers of the 1960s and 1970s.

Subsequently, I began wondering about how the negative elements of male working-class culture emerged and developed over time in the industry that I knew best—the American automobile industry. Though I consider some sectors of the American labor movement as constituting a major progressive force in our society, I have here written a work that explores more than the heroic struggles of workers and their unions in their quest to bring social equity and justice to their workplaces. The men who built unions used their masculine culture in its rough and respectable forms alike. Unfortunately, in their battle to build unions, they had to rely on its rough elements, and these became embedded in the industrial unions and the shop cultures they created. The white males who engaged in the initial struggles devised institutions that reflected their rough cultures and values and proved inhospitable to those who did not share them.

Research for this book began too many years ago when I had a yearlong fellowship at the Reuther Library at Wayne State University in the mid-1980s. While doing research for an earlier book, I had a wonderful opportunity to delve into the library's vast collection of the records of the UAW, auto workers, labor scholars, and social critics. I discovered that some materials, especially grievance records and shop newspapers, provided windows into the workplace, into the day-to-day lives of ordinary working men and women. As a side project, I began collecting materials on sometimes odd or quirky topics around the themes of gender and race. Several hundred oral histories of auto workers from libraries around the Midwest complemented the evidence I found in the grievances and shop newspapers. These items later formed the basis of early papers on the subject this book addresses.

Schooled as I was in the social and labor history of the late 1960s and early 1970s, my historical work has always attempted to examine "history from the bottom up" (rather than the top down) or the "history of the inarticulate" of those who left few formal records of the past. Within this context, my prior work represented a sometimes-odd mix of cultural and labor history. *The Five Dollar Day* focused on how Ford officials attempted to transform the social and cultural lives of immigrant workers and to force them to adapt to the rigors of assembly-line mass production. *"Stalin Over Wisconsin"* explored the workplace culture of opposition of a militant and leftist UAW local in the building of the strongest and largest industrial union in Wisconsin at the Allis-Chalmers firm.

The present work, *Manhood on the Line*, delves more deeply into workplace culture to reveal how densely masculine the culture of automobile industrial workers actually was. It interrogates autoworker male culture in several ways: in relation to the newly evolving industrial technology; with regard to the relationship of workers to their managers and supervisors; in their relationships among other workers with different skill levels, racial backgrounds, ethnic identities, and political convictions; and in their interactions with women workers. Analytically, I probe working-class masculine culture within the context of its two polar opposites, its rough and its respectable dimensions and the blending of the two. While I examine both elements, I must confess that I emphasize the rough ones, since they have not been fully investigated elsewhere. So this is not solely an investigation of the heroic workers in their struggles with an oppressive management. Nonetheless, that struggle was important because it shaped the workers and the culture of their unions.

I want to acknowledge the aid and assistance that many have provided over the years. First, three journals have granted permission for the republication of materials or parts of items previously published. I do wish to thank:

Peter Stearns for allowing a revised and modified version of "Rough Manhood: The Aggressive and Confrontational Culture of Male Auto Workers during World War II" in the *Journal of Social History* 36 (2002): 125–47, to constitute an important portion of chapter 6, "Fashioning Dense Masculine Space";

Michael Kimmel for allowing parts of "Work, Play, and Power: Masculine Culture on the Automotive Shop Floor, 1930–1965," *Men and Masculinities* 2 (October 1999): 115–34, to be scattered through the last chapters of this book;

Leon Fink, editor, and Diane Grosse (Duke University Press) also for the use of partortions of "Workplace Predators: Sex and Sexuality on the Automotive Shop Floor, 1930–1960," *Labor: Studies in the Working-Class History of the Americas* 1 (Spring 2004): 77–93, in the last chapters of this book.

Funding for *Manhood on the Line* came from several sources: a Rockefeller Foundation Humanities Fellowship in residence at the Walter P. Reuther Library at Wayne State University (September 1985–June 1986), a research fellowship from the National Endowment for the Humanities (September 2000–June 2001), and several short-term fellowships from the University of Wisconsin–Parkside and the University of Wisconsin–Milwaukee.

This book's long period of gestation means that I owe thanks to far too many more people than I can remember. I want to thank especially the chairs, commentators, and audiences of many conferences and seminars in the United States and Europe. These venues, where I began working through my ideas on working-class manhood, include many sessions of the North American Labor History Conferences at Wayne State University; Social Science History Association conferences; European Social Science History Conferences; British Association of American Studies conferences; an Organization of American History conference; an International Conference of Labour and Social History meeting in Linz, Austria; several thematic conferences, including two Laboring Feminism Conferences in Toronto and Stockholm; the "Boys and their Toys" Conference at the Hagley Museum; the "Car in History" meeting in Toronto; and various seminars at University of Warwick, the Tamiment at New York University, the Newberry Library, and the DC Working Class History Seminar.

Some people deserve special mention. The two reviewers for the University of Illinois Press offered wonderfully detailed comments and advice to my original manuscript submission. Though I may not have followed all of their suggestions, I greatly appreciated all of their thoughts. I know that Alice Kessler-Harris was one reviewer who sent me her copy of the manuscript with insightful comments, including precise edits of my sometimes horrendous typing and proofreading. She also offered public encouragement at various academic settings. I wish I knew the other reader so that I could offer my public appreciation. At the university press, Editor-in-Chief Laurie Matheson encouraged my work for years and made me realize the value of completing it; copyeditor Julie Gay assiduously read the manuscript, corrected too many typing and spelling errors, and greatly improved its writing style. Two other people were also very helpful: Ava Baron offered useful written comments regarding two early presentations on this subject. Liz Faue offered conversation, wisdom, and encouragement in many discussions at the North American Labor History and Social Science History Association conferences.

I cannot forget the staff and the many researchers I met at the Reuther Library at Wayne State University; my often-more-than-yearly visits made this my archival second home since the early 1970s. My thanks go to archivists Mike Smith and William LeFevre and many others on the library's archival staff, especially the student aides who wandered the stacks to pull materials and later to staff copy machines for me. I wish also to express my appreciation to the archivists and staffs of the many libraries and manuscript collections I have visited for this research.

Finally, I can never offer too much thanks to Margo, who connected with a rough guy in graduate school, had faith in him, became his life-partner, and softened some (but not all) of his rough edges. For this and many other things, my debt to her is enormous.

Manhood on the Line

Introduction

Forms and Meanings of Working-Class Manhood

In recent decades, historians of women have pressed other historians, especially their male colleagues, to consider gender as an important category of social and cultural analysis. Consequently, a growing body of important and suggestive work on the history of men *as* men has resulted and has emphasized the history of masculinity and manhood.[1] Although these works examined men as men, they did not focus on men as workers. Ava Baron has forcefully reminded us that "the history of working-class masculinity has yet to be written." In order to write this history, she added: "We must understand men's and women's efforts to construct and to defend a collective gender identity." Also important, she asserted, is "the significance of gender regardless of women's presence or absence."[2] Within Baron's context, this book is an effort to consider automobile workers through much of the twentieth century and to examine how auto workers in different situations and settings generated, fashioned, and nurtured their masculine cultures at the workplace and in their industrial communities, how they made and remade that culture, and how that culture functioned for them on the automotive shop floor.

Discussing the "vigorous subculture" that existed among "working-class youth," Peter N. Stearns cited an anonymous worker who recalled the broad outlines of his youthful and rough manhood: "When I was eighteen I knew it took four things to be a man: fight, work, screw, and booze."[3] Except for fighting, the young Frank Marquart, an auto worker and later labor radical and activist, seemed preoccupied with these rough masculine traits in his early work years. Recalling how he "became increasingly conditioned to the ways of a young factory hand" in the 1910s, Marquart wrote about his youthful "peer group" at the Detroit Metal Products Company. From work, they went home to eat and then later congregated at a bar, Premos on Jefferson Avenue. Though still a minor, Marquart was proud to look old enough for the bartender to serve him. "In the saloon," he recalled, "men gathered in groups and usually talked shop. Each tried to impress the others with how important his particular job was, how much skill it required." On Saturday, "the *big* night," the young workers played a few games of pool at Curley's Poolroom, "went downtown to take in a burlesque, either the Gaiety or the Cadillac," and then went to the Champlain Street "red-light" district. For Marquart and his circle, manhood meant work, especially skilled work, daily drinking, and the weekend foray to what they nicknamed "Joy Street."[4]

Though other forms existed, Marquart described the masculine culture of the young production workers in the new automobile industry. To be sure, notions and ideals of manhood varied with age: the young often engaged in the rough culture of fighting, screwing, and boozing; as some grew older, got married, and had families, responsibility and respectability sometimes became important factors; as others matured, irresponsibility and roughness may have persisted; and as many aged and became slower, more fragile, and less agile, their masculine identity through work became questionable and shifted to other areas of their lives.

Working-class masculine identity had many roots. The relations of social class, gender, race, and ethnicity influenced and shaped male attitudes, values, and behaviors. Young working-class boys learned to become men from their families at home and in their relations with other people—women, men, girls, and boys—in the larger world. Generationally, fathers taught their sons, craftsmen their apprentices, senior workers their younger workmates what manhood was and how to become and be men. Most important, boys becoming men, young men, and adult men fashioned and refashioned their manliness in a variety of all-male settings—in the schoolyard, on the playground or the athletic field, or in the locker room, on the hunting field, in the army barracks, in the saloon or tavern, in work camps, and, of course, at the workplace.[5]

Certainly, other personal relationships and other social institutions softened the rough edges and mixed up the meanings of masculine identity. Also important were the home, the church, the classroom, the fraternal society or lodge, and the union hall. As well, whenever and wherever men came into contact with women, they had to negotiate and to renegotiate their manhood, sometimes in positive and sometimes in negative ways.

The workplace was central to the forming, nurturing, widening, and deepening of this masculine culture. Stan Gray was a Westinghouse worker in the early 1980s. He was also a progressive and a sympathetic witness to what he labeled the "female invasion" of the shop floor. He described the workplace as "the last sanctum of male culture." The male world of the shop floor, he observed, was away from the world of women, away from responsibility and children and civilized cultural restraints. In the plant, they could regale in the rough and tumble of a masculine world of physical harshness; of constant swearing and rough behavior, of half-serious fighting and competition with each other, and more serious fighting with the boss. For Gray, this was a world "full of filth and dirt and grease and grime and swear—manual labor, a *manly* atmosphere." The shop talk was "vulgar and obscene" and often "about football and car repairs."[6]

Generally, this working-class masculine culture has surfaced in two distinct forms—a respectable culture and a rough one. Though analytically quite discrete, these two contradictory forms might result from either personal disposition or social position. Yet they sometimes coexisted with, overlapped with, or blended into each other. Some men certainly carried elements of both the rough and respectable cultures within their individual masculine identities. On the one hand, the respectable masculine culture corresponded with the attitudes, values, and behaviors associated with the craft traditions of skilled workers. David Montgomery, perhaps unwittingly, inaugurated the historical discussion of working-class manhood when he described the aggressive and respectable "craftsmen's ethical" code that demanded a "'manly' bearing toward the boss," connoting "dignity, respectability, defiant egalitarianism, and patriarchal male supremacy." On the other hand, the rough masculine culture correlated to the rough values of unskilled laborers and certainly countered the respectable ones of the craft tradition. The rough laborers' world formed a "life-style" that, Montgomery observed, "made a mockery of social reformers' efforts to promote habits of 'thrift, sobriety, adaptability, [and] initiative.'"[7] Clearly this rough masculine culture contrasted sharply with both respectable middle-class and working-class virtues. Embedded in the structure of the working class, the rough and the respectable male cultures reflected the life experiences of the unskilled common laborers and the highly skilled artisans of the late nineteenth and early twentieth centuries.

Often rooted in unskilled labor and lifestyles of newly arrived immigrants, the rough culture mirrored the unsteady and insecure world of common laborers, who often worked in a number of jobs in various industries, such as steel mills, railroad, or canal building. Laborers inside factories rarely lifted or hauled raw materials of finished work. "These tasks," noted Andrea Graziosi, quoting from a 1915 Immigration Commission report, "were performed by laborers: 'in a machine shop a laborer sweeps the floor, carts material about the shop, removes the finished products and performs other general work of like character.'" Even in highly industrialized industries and societies, such labor constituted a significant proportion of the workforce. Graziosi discovered that American steel mills at the turn of the twentieth century employed many Southern and Eastern European laborers, constituting 10 percent to 20 percent of their workforce, which included Italian, Polish, Hungarian, Bulgarian, Slovenian, and Slovak workers. They worked "in gangs, under the authority of a gang boss" and under a "driving" foreman responsible for "hiring and firing" them. A common laborer was hired "solely for his physical strength, his brute force, to carry, pull, push, turn, just as a horse would do."[8] About "indispensable" hobo laborers, Frank Tobias Higbie observed: "The dominant social discourse marked laborers as dirty, lazy, and degraded outsiders."[9]

Whiting Williams, a respectable middle-class migrant to the world of the common labor, described his experiences among common laborers in his journalistic account, *What's on the Worker's Mind*.[10] He waited at the hiring gates with laborers, worked alongside them, lived in their boarding houses, and ate in their restaurants in steel-mill, coal, ship-building, oil-refinery, and iron-mining towns of America. As Graziosi observed, the world of the common laborer involved the "continuous changing of jobs," the "uninterrupted search for jobs," the "enormous mobility," and the "instability of work conditions." When workers engaged in collective actions, they exhibited a "'rude' materialism" and expressed demands for "more money, less hours."[11]

For common laborers, such a brutal existence generated a violent and rough culture. As he examined the rougher masculine culture of mid-twentieth-century construction workers, Joshua Freeman found an "aggressive, crude masculinity," or what he labeled a "swaggering masculinity."[12] In his discussion of Canadian steel workers and bush workers, Steven Maynard added that the "dangerous conditions . . . reinforced a rugged masculinity."[13] Peter Way's study of antebellum canal workers outlined the basic elements of rough manhood and suggested its deep roots into the North American past—the rough work world of mainly Irish unskilled manual laborers who built canals. Much like immigrant workers Graziosi described, these unskilled laborers, Way noted, were "a swearing, drinking, brawling, hurting, dying mass" shaped by a harsh climate, difficult toil, meager economic resources, and a social life of heavy drinking.[14] Through the nineteenth and into the early twentieth century, gangs of unskilled Irish laborers often literally fought their way into the better jobs and then a modicum of respectability against African Americans and other Southern and Eastern European immigrant groups.[15] These crude male communities were characterized by their religious and ethnic identities, vice and violence, alcohol and drinking, brawling and roughhousing, physical prowess and risk taking, sport and gambling, female dependence on and subordination to men, and strong egalitarianism and stiff opposition to employers.[16]

Searching for a laborer's job in a steel mill, Whiting Williams described a "whole roomful" of job seekers, "about seventy-five laborers of every conceivable nationality and of every degree of respectability—or lack of it." When finally hired, he went to an employment office occupied with a "coughing, swearing, smoking, ill-smelling gang of fifty representatives of all the known races, including Mexicans, negroes, Indians, and Turks." About the steel-mill common laborers, Williams wrote: "The only thing in the world these 'boys' have to give, or are asked to give, is their physical strength." After a long and hard day's work they imbibed in the "local and highly familiar celebrity known as the 'whiskey-beer.'" Half of them took "a 'large small' glass of whiskey" and then downed "a big beer."[17]

Almost everywhere Williams went, he found illicit masculine activities. In another coal town, the unskilled common laborers spent their leisure time drinking at "all-day sessions in the licensed clubs" and in "the boarding-houses of the foreigners" or at "the crap games and drinking feasts on the hills near the towns." When Williams visited an iron-mining town, he discovered "supposedly dry saloons openly selling whiskey, with chuck-a-luck and other gambling games going on everywhere." For Williams, a "considerable part" of the laborer's "vices, especially their drinking" was connected to the absence of "individual manliness and value" in their work lives.[18]

In 1920, Williams described the rough culture of his work group of steel workers: "They're very husky and seem trained to the bone." Their profanity was "a goulash of blasphemy, obscenity, and filth." Speaking about women and marriage, one oil-refinery worker stated his preference for manly pursuits: "They make me sick! Give me a good boxin' bout or a cock-fight. I used to belong to a club that had swell affairs of that sort. Sometimes they began at one o'clock in the mornin.' That's the life!"[19] Around the same time, Carlton H. Parker described the socially dysfunctional character of a rough American lumberjack: "He cannot marry, for he cannot take his wife to the camp." Moreover, if he became "a 'regular' lumberjack he is not fit for married life; he drinks, fights and leads an immoral life."[20] The rough work world often made these men unsuited to the tame domestic life.

In stark contrast, the respectable masculine culture emerged from the work skills, social pride, and economic security of the craft tradition. For more skilled construction workers in the late nineteenth-century, Freeman asserted, "manliness meant independence, mutuality, and pride in craft." This form of manhood also contained a "political construct" that rested on "respect, manhood, and citizenship." In contrast to common laborers, craft workers' exclusive monopolization of skilled work through their unions provided for their economic security and economic independence, "which was seen as the fruit of skill, hard work, sobriety, and organization." For this reason, the craftsmen's social and cultural construct of "manliness was firmly attached and even subsumed to ideas of respectability and domesticity." Though "not immune from the temptations of drink, gambling, and extra-marital sex," these respectable workers "sought to temper themselves, to control such impulses, and thereby disassociate themselves from the 'rough working-class culture' dominated by less-skilled, more poorly-paid workers."[21] In his investigation of early-twentieth-century Canadian auto workers, Wayne Lewchuk suggested that through their monopolization of skilled work, the respectable craftsmen socially and culturally established and constructed their manhood through "social norms that identified control, independence, and the ability to make decisions as inherent masculine traits." If the laborer's sense of crude manliness emerged from the roughness of physical strength and dangerous work, the respectable craftsman's manhood arose from refined values of control, skill, autonomy, and independence.[22]

The essence of skilled-worker manhood resided in the control he exercised in the workplace. Control was often a central concept in the many forms of American manhood. Among autonomous craftsmen, this control was deeply embedded in their shop traditions and cultures of work and shaped the broader contours of their social lives. From this craft control, the skilled worker earned relatively high wages, conducted himself in a manly way, exhibited personal and social pride, maintained an aura of dignified respectability, and exercised patriarchal authority derived from the family wage.

Among autonomous craftsmen, this control was deeply embedded in their shop traditions and cultures of work. The idea of respectability separated these skilled workers from the rougher, poorer, and cruder common laborers and from the less knowledgeable specialists and handy men. At the turn of the century, for example, machinists often arrived at their workplaces dressed in suits, white shirts, ties, and sometimes bowler hats. In the all-male shop, they would strip down to their work clothes and labor at their often oily and greasy machines. At the end of the day, they often demanded additional time to wash up, dress for the street, and leave for the male camaraderie of the tavern or the domestic propriety of the home.

In the late 1870s, Terence V. Powderly, the future leader of the Knights of Labor and then a young Machinists' and Blacksmiths' International Union leader, penned a verse that illustrated his vision of the high status of machinists. The occasion was a machinists' resolution to keep the rougher boiler makers out of the MBIU. Powderly favored the exclusion of boiler makers from his union, but the his fellow union members endorsed their inclusion. Powderly's verse emphasized the privileged social position of highly skilled machinists: "Aristocrats of labor, we / Are up on airs and graces. / We wear clean collars, cuffs, and shirts, / Likewise we wash our faces." In their "airs and graces," in their dress, and in their cleanliness, the highly skilled machinists distanced themselves from the rougher boiler makers and revealed their high regard for themselves.

In the mid-1890s, P. J. Conlon, a veteran organizer of the International Association of Machinists (IAM), recalled his early wandering years as an organizer for his union. Conlon remembered that he "traveled in box cars and lived in boarding houses on the hospitality of our members, while trying to do organizing work." Since the young IAM could not afford to pay full-time organizers, he and other organizers had "to bum and borrow because of a lack of necessary funds." Some IAM lodges, he added, "had the nerve to write headquarters, complaining of our appearance, because we appeared in their midst wearing blue flannel shirts and corduroy trousers." Reflecting on his ruder past as a young union organizer, this 1920s "baron" of labor normally dressed in a suit, white shirt, and tie evidently felt some mild embarrassment at the absence of his suit, his uniform of respectability.[23]

In the late 1920s, Hyacinthe Dubreuil, a machinist and an officer of the French Confederation of Labor, traveled to the United States and worked in several automobile plants and machine shops. Upon arrival he purchased a khaki-colored "overall suit," which he thought Americans wore at work. To his surprise, American machinists did not wear such clothing. Instead, he discovered that "almost everybody works in shirt sleeves, even in winter, for the shops are generally well heated. In street trousers and vest, the skilled workman protects himself only with an apron of blue or white canvas." To protect their hair, American machinists wore cloth caps. Much like those of white-collar office workers and accountants, these caps sometimes had "transparent visors of green celluloid." Other less-skilled, less-fastidious, and less-status-conscious workers dressed quite differently. Typically, Dubreuil's less-skilled shop mates dressed "almost any old way for work."[24]

Another emblem of the skilled machinist's status was his tool box. Dubreuil also noted the importance of the tool box for American craft traditions. The

American machinist, he observed, "even preserves craft traditions that we have lost: he has a genuine love for his tools." Each skilled worker "carries with him wherever he goes, through all his changes from one factory to another, an elegant little case of tools, fitted with drawers, the like of which is unknown in our country." Carried like a suitcase, this tool chest "contain[ed] a good two hundred dollars' worth of those precise and ingenious tools to be employed even by us . . . that every worker takes pride in gradually accumulating in this precise box." Without a tool box on his first job, Dubreuil said that he "suffered in advance in the estimation of my neighbors." But Dubreuil quickly corrected its absence and purchased an American-style tool box. For some time, his chest contained no tools. He confessed: "It contained almost nothing, for my means were limited, but at least I had a box. Appearances were saved."[25]

Like many other craftsmen, the ownership of tools signified their proud independence from their employers. If the employer provided the work tools, the worker depended on the boss to perform his labor. In this sense, the possession of a tool chest signified manly independence. Often, during a strike, machinists would pack their tools and march out of the plant with their tool boxes on their shoulders, ready to head for another firm if the strike was lost.

The all-round machinist was the prototypical craftsmen in the formative years of the emergent auto-industrial age. The skilled machinist often served a five- to seven-year apprenticeship where he learned the varied and multifaceted mental and manual skills that constituted the arts and mysteries of the craft. He learned the reading of blueprints, the various uses of multiple-purpose machine tools (drill press, lathe, planer, milling machine, and the like), the bench work of filling and fitting of components for other machines, and the assembly of the varied components into the final product. The measuring and the marking of rough castings transformed ideas from two-dimensional blueprints into three-dimensional parts, often meeting exact standards. Based on years of experience, a skilled machinist often judged the feel, the smell, or the color of the metal being cut to assess the progress of work on the machine. In the assembly process of an automobile engine in the early years, for example, the skilled machinist effectively put together the many parts of a three-dimensional jigsaw puzzle. Sometimes parts needed to be filed and fitted in order to complete the assembly process. The skilled machinist made many small decisions about how to produce and assemble the final product, and he dexterously manipulated the tools, the parts, and the machines.[26]

At the end of the nineteenth century, a new and important category, often labeled the semiskilled worker or factory operative, intruded into the social structure of the American working class between the laborer and the craftsman. In time, Taylorism and Fordism would transform the semiskilled operative into a barely skilled or unskilled production worker. This occurred most dramatically in the automobile industry, where such workers became the preponderant group in the workforce.

This new configuration altered the social boundaries and ultimately the cultural possibilities for working-class men and their sense of manhood. As Maynard suggested, the newly emerging industrial and economic system "not only altered class relations, but also shifted gender relations, precipitating a crisis in masculinity."[27] Moreover, this crisis of masculinity saturated an industrializing American culture, as indicated by the social creation and construction of the late-nineteenth-century immigrant and labor problems. In turn, these social fears fostered assertive and aggressive middle-class male identities.[28]

For working-class men, Maynard said, "the 'crisis of the craftsman' was . . . both a crisis of work *and* masculinity, of class and gender." For the skilled and the unskilled worker alike, the crisis of masculinity undermined the fundamental bases of their work, both the manual dimension of the unskilled laborer and the mental one of the skilled tradesman. Effectively, the social and cultural forces of the mass-production revolution emasculated both the physical and the intellectual bases of working-class male identities. They broke, Maynard suggested, the "very explicit connections" that working men made "between their work and their gender identity as men."[29]

For unskilled workers, these forces undermined the rough masculine identity through the elimination of brawn and strength in favor of material-handling devices from unskilled work and subverted the respectable identity through the removal of independence and control from skilled work. For skilled workers, work reorganization, line production, and automatic machines diluted their trades and undermined their pride of craft. "All the hallmarks of masculinity at the workplace," Lisa Fine wrote regarding American auto workers, "were eradicated by automation, machines, time clocks as well as new management practices, repressive and paternalistic."[30] Removing the male traits of brawn and brain from workplace skills, Taylorism and Fordism redefined skill as the ability to endure repetitive and monotonous tasks and to perform them with speed and dexterity For both craftsmen and laborers, their work became less manly.

This book details how the dual crises of industrialism and of masculinity prompted working-class and other men to re-masculinize their work and male identities. To a certain extent, the newly forming masculine culture of semi-skilled mass-production workers blended and merged elements of the rough and the respectable manhood. In automobile plants, male workers maintained some of their masculine identity through a boy-like playfulness on the shop floor and displayed some of the rougher side of masculine culture—drinking, fighting, gambling, and confrontational opposition to management. At the same time, for production workers, a relatively high wage permitted a small degree of economic stability and independence away from the workplace, feeding the respectable aspect of working-class male culture. Moreover, at the same time, automotive employers also attempted to fashion and reshape masculine identities—either through creation of a male fraternity that glorified hard work at higher wages or by fostering a competitive and loyal male culture emphasizing respectability and cooperation.[31]

In addition to the blending and mixing of the rough and respectable cultures, the new working-class idea of manliness in the age of mass production most likely took on more explicit sexual connotations. "Within the craft tradition," Freeman declared, "manhood apparently did not have an explicitly sexual meaning." Yet moving into and through the twentieth century, working-class men remade and reconstructed their manly identities, derogating and demeaning those who appeared to threaten them. For construction workers, manliness took on a "decidedly male idiom" characterized by "physical jousting, sexual boasting, sports talk, and shared sexual activities"[32] that consciously operated to exclude and debase women. By the 1970s the sexualization of the automotive workplace was rampant. John Lippert recounted the full import of such male behavior in an Ohio Fisher Body plant:

> Many men are completely unabashed about letting the women know that they are being watched and discussed, and some men are quite open about the results of the analysis. Really attractive women have to put up with incredible harassment, from constant propositions to mindless and obscene grunts as they walk by.[33]

The re-masculinization of the shop floor often resulted in the general degradation and dehumanization of all women.

This study is about the transformations of male cultures and identities of production workers primarily in automotive workplaces on the shop floor and to a lesser extent in their local communities. Although mainly about automobile workers, it might well describe workers concentrated in all-male industries, such as the mining, iron and steel, or construction, or in mass-production industries with all-male shops departments, such as the electrical or meat-packing industries. Through the twentieth century, male workers vacillated between the rough and respectable cultures as their situations shifted. They were rough in their resistance to technical change and managerial domination and against others who posed perceived threats to their security and prosperity. They were respectable when they strove to create unions in order to alleviate the rigors of the factory regime and to provide a living wage for their families.

As the first to labor under mass production, automobile workers lost their earlier notions of manhood as Fordist mass production unmanned and emasculated them on the job, especially in the 1910s and 1920s. They attempted to reclaim their masculinity through the creation of a rough and controlling male shop culture and through the derogation of women at work and on the streets of Detroit. At the same time, they longed for the formation of unions, especially industrial ones, to attain respectably as generous providers to their families. For union-oriented men, factory spies, often labeled rats, finks, or stool pigeons, presented a negative and disreputable form of manhood in the 1920s and 1930s. Their rough and physical manhood, set against these minions of management, and the militant struggles to build industrial unionism constituted another means for the reclamation of their manhood through the 1930s and into the early 1940s. The muscular union campaigns in Detroit, Toledo, Flint, and elsewhere, and especially the Ford battles at the River Rouge plant in Dearborn, were telling examples of the manly struggle to build unionism. Ironically, the industrial contests for respectability rested on the rougher dimension of male culture.

As a result, once established, the new industrial unionism offered the opportunity to reshape the shop floor, to fashion it as a densely masculine space, and to dramatically alter and transform shop-floor relations through the 1930s to the 1960s. During the World War II years, men faced challenges to their male work space: first, women "invaded" the shop floor to perform traditionally male jobs, and, second, African American men and women challenged factory racial boundaries and began to occupy positions formerly reserved for white men. Through the early postwar years, the success of industrial unionism provided decent living wages and union mechanisms for the resolution of disputes between management. Under the pressures of automation, de-industrialization, and de-unionization, the rough underside of manhood reared in the racist and sexist attitudes of working-class white men from the 1960s through 1980s many new changes and challenges. White male dominion over the automotive shop floor persisted into the 1970s.

1

Lost Manhood

Mass Production and Auto-Worker Masculinity

In the mid 1930s a Detroit physician testified at the Automobile Labor Board hearings in Detroit and described how work in an automobile plant threatened and undermined auto-worker health and safety, destroying any sense of worth, dignity, and manhood. Dr. I. W. Raskin characterized automobile plants as a huge, human sausage grinder. He recalled his reading of Upton Sinclair's *The Jungle* long ago and remembered how he "was horrified to read of a luckless worker who, in the process of making pork sausage, fell into the machine and was incorporated into the product." Practicing medicine among auto workers since the early 1920s, Raskin testified: "There is many a luckless worker today whose limbs and blood and sanity is part of that shiny car on the Boulevard."[1] Over the course of thirteen years, he witnessed a dramatic change in the physical and mental health of his working-class patients. They now, he observed, suffered from a "high percentage of neurosis and psychosis," which he attributed to "the speed-up of the production line and the keenness in the competition in getting jobs and particularly in keeping jobs." The "high tension of work," Raskin added, "has broken down other portions of the human system." After listing several similar cases, Raskin concluded that these and many other workers were the American auto industry's "human INDUSTRIAL SCRAP."[2]

From the nineteenth century through the first decade of the twentieth, the American System of Manufactures evolved into a new system of mass production.[3] Numerous academics touted mass production's unique importance to the modern industrial economy. As sociologist Ely Chinoy noted, the Ford assembly line "has been a dominating symbol of modern industrialism."[4] The new automotive production technology was indeed the dominant paradigm for modern industrial technology for most of the twentieth century. As business historian Peter Drucker proclaimed, "The automobile industry stands for modern industry all over the globe. It is to the twentieth century what the Lancashire cotton mills were to the nineteenth century: the industry of industries."[5]

Charles R. Walker, the director of the Yale Technology Project and deeply familiar with mid-twentieth-century American industrial life, understood the social and cultural importance of the automotive shop floor. Though speaking of the steel mills that he knew best years ago, he emphasized that factories were unique settings that created their own special social and cultural worlds. "Persons unfamiliar with mills and factories," he observed, " . . . often remark on visiting them that they seem like another world." He added: "This is particularly true if . . . both tradition and technology have strongly and uniquely molded the ways men think and act when at work." The traditions of people and the forces of technology blended to refashion social and cultural workplace life. Even the new or "green" worker realized how this other world constituted a special and unique space in terms of its "social classes, folklore, ritual, and traditions."[6] Factory workers spent the major part of their lives in their workplaces. All workers profoundly knew and understood its social and cultural context for working-class manhood. In the first decades of the century, auto-worker traditions were embedded in the skilled metal trades and its craft production technology. Especially after the innovations of Frederick W. Taylor, Henry Ford, and numerous anonymous engineers, work reorganization, more automatic machines, and assembly lines transformed auto-worker shop traditions. These certainly remade and refashioned how workers thought and acted at work. For male workers, these also reshaped their social and cultural attitudes toward their maleness.

Although work tasks, work situations, and work routines varied considerably from automobile firm to automobile firm and from one shop or department to another, the work of assembly line workers was the simplest, most boring, and most degrading. Though the assembly line was the predominate image of the modern factory, numerous other work tasks and routines bore similar traits. In a modern automobile plant, Chinoy noted that no more than 18 percent of auto workers were classified as assemblers, but many auto factory jobs, such as "paint sprayers, polishers, welders, upholsterers," and others, "have been subject to the same kinds of job experience as those engaged in assembly."[7] In other words many, many others worked at machines whose rhythms and cycles shaped and determined their work tasks and work pace; most important, it reshaped their workplace social and cultural life.

Modern automotive mass production began in the Ford Highland Park plant in the 1910s and gradually spread through most other firms in the 1920s. The industrial technology of the American automobile industry had its origins in the American System of Manufactures that evolved through the second half of the nineteenth century. In many ways, the new mass-production technology that evolved in the Ford Highland Park plant from 1908 through 1913 represented a culmination of this unfolding technical system. Ford managers and engineers achieved the new forms of control through the stricter supervision of workers, the design of new machine tools, and the major innovation of line production. Under traditional craft production, the skilled craftsman often supervised himself and the helpers and laborers who worked with him. The years of apprenticeship and the pride in craft re-enforced the self-discipline and self-supervision as to the amount of output and the quality of the product. To be sure, craft notions of equity in the amount of effort and the amount of pay might inhibit management expectations for excessive overwork. In contrast, at the Highland Park factory a large contingent of foremen, straw bosses, inspectors, and clerks directly supervised and monitored Ford workers and their output. Foremen and straw bosses encouraged the men continuously to hurry up and work faster. The inspectors and clerks also assured that the quality and amount of work met supervisory expectations.[8]

At Ford and later other auto plants, the design of the machines also defined the specialized machine operator's work routine and work pace. A drill-press operator, for example, neither measured and marked the places for holes in a piece of work nor located the work on the table of the machine, judged the proper feed and speed, or gauged the proper depths of the holes. Instead, he picked up the piece of work, attached it to the machine's fixture, and threw a switch. Then, a multi-spindled drill automatically made all the necessary holes in the right place to the proper depth. The machine operation redefined the drill-press operator's work routine. It now required virtually no judgment or thought. Moreover, the machine established the pace and rhythm of the machine operator's work.

For the skilled and specialized craftsmen (who constituted most of the early male auto workforce) and others, the mass production workplace was a singularly different world. A most common metaphor for it was a mad, absurd, and irrational place, a bedlam not connected to their prior work or industrial experience. A newspaper reporter who visited the Ford Highland

Park factory used the image of the asylum to convey his impression of the new industrial system in 1914. For Julian Street, it meant just one thing— "delirium." The Ford plant was "a Gargantuan lunatic asylum where fifteen thousand raving, tearing maniacs had been given full authority to go ahead and do their damnedest."[9]

Slightly more than a decade later, E. McCluny Fleming, one of a group of Yale students[10] who worked in the Ford River Rouge plant during the summer in the 1920s and early 1930s also described the insanity of his work environment. "Alice in Wonderland could have no stranger sensations than I, as we hurried down the enormous, shrieking room," he wrote.

> Machines everywhere,—acres and acres of them. Gigantic, clumsy, elephantine ones; small whirling, sputtering ones; punch presses, drills, conveyor motors, overhead trollies,—all clanging, and buzzing and roaring and pounding;—a deafening background noise against which occasional rivet guns and blow torches would emit piercing staccato screams. Everywhere a dizzy tangled jungle of flying wheels, whizzing cogs, jerking belts; clattering pinions, teeth, levers, flywheels, chains, gears. And buried amidst this mechanical bedlam hundreds of grease-covered, bored-looking men, moving hands and legs as in an awful dream. Would I be able to do my job? Did I know enough about machines? Could I ever stick it out? My God, would I ever come out of there alive?"[11]

In the late 1920s a union correspondent who hired into the River Rouge plant objected to the monstrous conveyor system. "This new mechanical monster," he observed, "with its tributaries of chains, belts and slides binds practically the whole plant together and automatically adjusts the speed of every worker." In the crazed rush to produce, if a worker could not "keep up with the belt," then "the work piles up and the line gets clogged." Frantic to avoid such assembly-line pile-ups and supervisory recriminations, many workers pushed themselves to match the pace the mechanized monster. Ford workers "in their blind submission to the Ford machine drive each other on in a mad insane orgy of production, and the belt drives them all."[12]

Many who labored on the lines or at machines resented becoming mindless automatons, laboring at their specialized small tasks. A union correspondent decried the loss of craft skills: "Mass production eliminates skill. Each laborer is assigned to a single operation. He repeats this over and over again and for all he knows he will continue to do so until the end of time. . . . John Doe, for instance, who spends 48 hours a week tightening nut No. 17, in the course of time becomes a nut himself."[13]

An Illinois college student in the Ford plant noted "a deadening effect, particularly upon a man's mental life" and "the repetitive nature or monotony of his work." He added: "You cannot get interested in screwing screw number 6421 into some housing or doing some similar job over and over, hour after hour, and day after day."[14] For many workers, the loss of control over work tasks and routines, an important feature of craft production, was the most disconcerting feature of the new industrial system. One machine operator rhetorically asked journalist Robert Cruden: "Am I bossed around? No, I don't need to be. The machine I'm on goes at such a terrific speed that I can't help stepping on it in order to keep up with the machine. It's my boss."[15]

Noise was another unsettling feature of the madhouse of mass production. Two of the Yale students commented on the insidious influence of the dreadful noise in the huge machine-filled Ford plant. Sawyer Brockunier complained about the horrible volume of noise of the Ford River Rouge Plant: "In many buildings, the roar of machinery is terrific." Even after a long night's sleep, he added, "when I got up, my ears would still seem muffled two or three hours after that."[16] Everett Davies, an African sociology student at Yale, worked a stereotypical job for black workers in the foundry and expressed a similar sentiment about his work. "Without exception," he stated, "the noise of the machines is simply distressing." He complained about "the nauseating noise resulting from the operation of these machines." In order for one worker to speak with another, "one must put his mouth directly to the other's ear and then talk as loud as he can. . . . [E]veryone tries to talk by signs."[17]

The Yale students all discovered that the machine- and line-paced work was repetitive, monotonous, mindless, and continuous. Davies described how his work in a Ford foundry "dwarfed" his mind. "The trained mind and the skilled hand," he wrote, "once in the sole possession of the worker are now being transferred to machines." While the modern machines eliminated "man-power," he added, "they are also displacing mental keenness and alertness, and arresting mental development." All that the worker did was "simply to remove what the machine has made."[18] Another student, Kemper Dobbins operated a Gleason press at Ford. Though at first impressed with the "wonderful precision" and the "automatic adjustment" of the machines, he quickly learned his "series of seven physical movements—absolutely automatic in character." Soon, he realized: "I was on a tread mill—producing-producing-producing-getting nowhere." Finally, he concluded: "Compared to the work of the machine, mine was worth nothing."[19]

In his 1929 assessment of the automobile industry, Phil Raymond, treasurer of the early Auto Workers Union, highlighted the impact of "new machines and industrial processes" on auto worker skills. "Many new machines," he observed, "have been introduced, displacing skilled workers by unskilled." He mentioned two machines specifically—the polishing machine and the striping machine. These machines eliminated skill and sped up the work of the metal polishers who smoothed and prepared auto bodies for painters and of the stripers who added the final detail to the paint jobs. Due to the "slave-driving system of the Ford plant, plus the piece work and fake bonus schemes in other plants," he noted, "the workers are literally burned up in this mad orgy of speeding production."[20]

In addition to its massive size, frenetic activity, and deafening noise, the new mass production system contained two technical innovations that transformed the work regime into Bedlam. Each undermined or removed the workers' ability to control their work situations and regulated and controlled the pace and rhythm of brutal labor regime. These were the semiautomatic and automatic machines and the conveyor belts that characterized the new production system. The new special- or single-purpose machine tools removed the machine operator's discretion of judgment in its operation. The cycle of the machine determined the pace of loading and unloading. If a worker had idle time, the foreman typically assigned a second machine. The new conveyor systems, where each operation followed the previous one and set the limits of the next one, similarly controlled the pace and rhythm of production at the workplace. Each operation depended on the other. Moreover, the conveyor line controlled how much time an auto worker had to complete each operation, over and over. The speed of the conveyor set the work pace. In a similar manner such machines arranged in line according to consecutive tasks also set the workers' pace. Machine operators and assemblers neither thought about nor controlled their work. They no longer determined the tempo or rhythm of their work in the factory. This loss of mental skill and control greatly diminished and eroded their sense of manly accomplishment.

The speed-up, or the technical acceleration of machine and line speeds and the insidious incentive schemes (in other words, individual and group piece rates and other systems), increased work effort and sapped human strength and endurance, especially as the Great Depression deepened and workers strove to match ever higher work quotas and levels of production. For labor journalist and researcher Robert W. Dunn, the speed-up was one of the most pernicious evils of the modern production system. "Speed-up of man and machine," he reported, "rules the Detroit automobile industry, piling up workers on the job market in long queues of the unemployed, even in the busiest seasons." This speed-up occurred in many ways, he added:

The assembly line may be screwed up a little faster. The stop watch men may observe that workers, by sweating more, can turn out more per hour. The task is then increased. The rates may be cut so that the worker has to move faster to equal his former wage. The steam may even be turned low in winter to keep the workers a bit chilly and hence in the mood to move faster at the machine.[21]

When Frank Marquart first encountered auto work as a young man in the late 1910s, the transformation to mass production involved much more than the "new and faster machines" and included the dramatic reconfiguration of "assembly operations." Former "motor builders" now worked at conveyor-paced assembly lines where each worker performed "a single task" over and over again. Under the new work regime, he added: "The emphasis increasingly was on speed, speed, speed."[22] The speed-up physically wore auto workers out. It refashioned the age profile of the workforce and favored the young and vigorous worker and not the older and slower one. Moreover, it produced abusive foremen and straw bosses who drove workers to produce more and more and ultimately undermined worker health and safety.

Some Yale students recalled their frequent struggles to perform their work tasks and to pace their work at their frenetic work stations. On the Ford assembly lines, Fleming remembered his constant fumbling while trying to learn his simple work tasks. The basic problem was the consistent and relentless pace of his work, which never seemed to slow down or stop: "The infernal machines didn't wait! With a merciless, cruel persistency they would glide irresistibly by; and to take a fraction too long to the job meant getting in the way of the man to the right,—only to find a shortened interval for the next machine." Often, too much work passed him without completion. This, he said, "shook my morale, destroyed my self-confidence, and harassed my conscience." The result wore him down physically and mentally. "Fingers," he wrote, "were soon cut to pieces, patience worn out, nerves frazzled. Sweat streamed down my eyes, and the corners of my mouth, tasting brackish and dirty."[23]

Similarly, C. N. Li, a Chinese student, also worked on the conveyor lines of the Ford motor assembly department. He worked two summers in both the Highland Park and River Rouge factories in the mid 1920s. For Li, the central issue was control—how line production and the minute subdivision of labor regulated the rhythm and pace of his work. "Each man," Li reported, "is allotted only a limited amount of time during which he must get his job done accurately and rapidly." If the worker could not complete the task, he disrupted the entire assembly line. "If he lags behind," the Chinese student noted, "the whole gang has to stop and wait for him. . . . Nobody can be lazy even if he wants to."[24]

For Everett Davies, the man-killing work in the mechanized foundry was "a hard, incessant, hot, and killing job." With a long rod or fork, he removed his piece of work from a conveyor as it emerged from a foundry furnace. "The Ford motor parts just out of the fire come past along on conveyors," the Yale student related, "and every man is supposed to get his part out." Sometimes, when Davies had difficulty with the large number of pieces, the boss harassed and hounded him to keep up. Paced by the conveyor, he "must never allow any of it to pass." According to Davies, his first day in the foundry "was one of the hardest days of my working life. I was tired and sore and almost fagged out."[25]

These temporary migrants to the auto plant were fortunate, since as students they would leave after their two- or three-month stint with mass production work. Oliver M. Zendt claimed: "Several students remarked, that if they had to work on the production line all of their life they would commit suicide. The jobs are mechanical, monotonous, non-creative and mechanistic."[26] For some of the Yale students, their summer interlude in Detroit's automobile factories and plants deeply affected and even radicalized them. After an especially difficult day's work that offered him the grim pride of feeding his machine, Kemper Dobbins concluded: "This machine driving pride is really an expression of hatred for the machine, the foreman, the capitalists, for 'the whole damned works,' as the Ford workers put it."[27] Davies complained, "Every day left me more and more bitter and opposed to the whole industrial system. I felt that I could join any revolution, no matter what its platform; just so it was a revolution against the whole industrial system." After he finished his stint in the Ford factory, Davies concluded, "I came out of industry feeling that the only way out was revolution."[28] George Zalkan, concurred: "Karl Marx was no fool when he admonished the workmen of the world to unite."[29]

A University of Chicago college student, Andrew Steiger, concurred with such sentiments. He too labored in Detroit automobile plants in the summer of 1927 and also condemned the absence of control in modern factory work. "The workers," he observed, "are just a mechanical unit in a production process over which they exercise no control. The worker is valuable as long as he performs a given set of muscular motions upon a regular schedule—so many number of seconds per piece."[30] Such a work regime went against the essential elements of skilled-worker manhood.

For those skilled and specialized workers who labored in the modern automobile plants and factories, their manhood was effectively destroyed, was embedded in craft ideals of autonomy, independence, and control in the performance of their work tasks and in their relations with their supervisors. In the mid-1920s a veteran machinist rued the devolution of his trade. "It was a few years ago," he lamented, "that we machinists were looked up to. We had 'some' trade and we were proud of it. I might also add that we looked down on the other fellow." Consequently, he said, "we are far from the lofty position we once held."[31] In the mid-1930s, to the applause of other workers, a Pontiac worker described the loss of his manhood in the factory, which he portrayed as "a penal system in the shops in which men of spirit, men who would be expected to have spirit have to hang up their citizenship and their manhood and their self-respect on the gate when they go into these places of employment."[32] A few years later, Walter Ulrich, a young worker who toiled in Buick and Chevrolet plants, concurred: "A man cannot work long in an automobile factory and retain his self-respect." The reason was a loss of his manly dignity: "A man in the factory does not count as a man but loses all rights of self-expression or determination in his work."[33] At the Packard plant, a "young married polisher" told Robert Cruden, "You have to see that the boss gets nothing on you, and if he does, you just let him bawl you out."[34] Years later, David Moore, an African American Ford worker, remembered the oppressive control of the production system and the indignities of the Service Department in the River Rouge plant. If you worked for Ford, he recalled, "You had to give up your manhood, your dignity, your pride."[35]

John Leheney, a former railroad worker, described the suppression of manhood in the "inhuman system" of the Milwaukee Nash plant. After a brief stint at Nash Motors, he found "the spiritual degradation of labor manhood" and "the docility that meekly accepts dictation." Under the strict discipline of a "'bucko' foreman, or superintendent," he added, the "manhood" of Nash workers was "crush[ed] utterly. The price men paid for their Nash job meant the "surrender of manhood, relinquishment of independence, and the abandonment of every employee right to a say in the regulation of the relationship between them and the company." A fundamental premise of the management system was "to weed out spirited employes." When they became soon disgusted, the "most independent workers" quit; the "less spirited" hung on "until [among] those who persevere there are only a few who are not devoid of spirit." For Leheney, the elimination of the "spirited" workers creates "a docile, servile working force."[36]

As Dr. Raskin observed, the automotive mass-production regime literally wore down and physically destroyed those who toiled in the different plants and factories. Managerial indifference exacerbated their awful situations. Many accounts of auto workers described their utter physical exhaustion after a punishing and speeded-up day's labor at their machines and assembly lines. Yale student Fred Wolff described Ford workers who left the River Rouge plant: "Those parking spaces reserved for workers are alive with dirty, tired figures. . . . They seem to move mechanically; there is no true life in them. They walk or push or stoop automatically, not with any real thought about what they are doing."[37] The *Auto Workers News* invited those who wanted to view "how mass production affects the workers" to "board a [street]car filled with Ford workers returning from work. That the cars are packed to suffocation is to be expected." Most important, "due to the great fatigue these workers a suffering under," such an observer would notice "that many of them, including some that are standing on their feet, are sound asleep five minutes after boarding the car."[38] Dobbins reported: "The production workers were so tired after each working day that they would often break their lines and stampede through the street car doors for seats." In a mad scramble for seats, "every man would fight like an animal to cheat the one next to him out of a seat." Sometimes, in kindness, they would "crowd themselves to make room for an old fellow left hanging on the strap." But they were dreadfully exhausted with "livid and healthless" faces. "Often," Dobbins concluded, "they ride past their stops they are so tired."[39]

For many auto workers, management also seemed genuinely indifferent to the safety and health of the men and women on the shop floor. Years later, one Fisher Body worker recalled seeing a fellow worker who "dropped dead right in the middle of work." Management's response? "They called the fellows with the stretchers to take him away, and the superintendent he came over to the foreman and he said to him: Write a requisition for another man. That was all they cared—write a requisition for another man."[40]

More maddening than the pace of machines was the callous indifference of managers and supervisors who created and allowed a degrading work environment. An affront to dignified manhood, the humiliating and dehumanized work resulted in threats to worker health and safety. For Davies and others, the relentless pace of the machines wore them down mentally and physically. In the foundry, hot flying embers and red-hot castings often caused minor and major injuries to workers. One day, Davies lamented, "I had thirteen burns on my fingers, arms and neck to take care of."[41] Similarly, Dobbins remembered such frequent and disconcerting injuries: "Not knowing how to handle steel with bare hands, I soon had my fingers pretty well cut up after feeding a few axles into the 'Gleasons.'"[42] Fred M. Wolff, another Yale student, complained about having been left with a "rotten wrench" which caused work problems and resulted in physical injuries: "My hands are so full of steel splinters that I can hardly take up a spoon or a paper." Despite his damaged hands, he could not "wear gloves on account of having to put washers on the bolts at the beginning of every operation."[43]

These dangerous conditions constantly reminded auto workers that they were barely human and that managers did not even consider them men. The relentless speed-up, the abusive control, and the intimidated workforce threatened the health and safety of auto workers. Harassed by foremen and straw bosses, nervous, anxious, and exhausted auto workers often failed to attend to the details of their sometimes-dangerous work, and they suffered consequences. Accidents and injuries were routine.

Men who worked on machines lost fingers or even limbs. Managers frequently disabled or neglected safety devices at machines since they slowed output. Some workers themselves also disabled such mechanisms in order to maintain production quotas and to avoid the harassment by shop foremen and straw bosses. One Ford Rouge worker who operated a punch press, the *Auto Workers News* related, "lost four fingers while trying out a die in the gas tank department last Saturday." With no aid station and no hospital nearby, "the worker nearly went mad in an attempt to get any attention and it took some time before he was given any attention." In order hide the evidence of the industrial accident, a Ford serviceman "picked up the fingers and threw them into the garbage can." The union newspaper concluded: "This atrocious act is a result of the mad rush for production that the Ford plants are famous for."[44]

Another *Auto Workers News* correspondent described an abusive foreman, cowed workers, and the loss of fingers in the huge River Rouge facility. A press operator, he reported, "had just lost the small finger on his left hand." Since Ford managers needed the parts produced by the press to maintain production elsewhere in the Ford factory, no one checked the machine to see whether or not it was defective. "Another man," the reporter continued, "was immediately put to work on the very same press. This man had not turned out more than a dozen pieces, when he lost the thumb of his right hand." Obviously, the two accidents generated much attention among the shop workers as they "congregated around the machine talking about the accidents." But shop supervisors "came rushing over, yelling, 'Back to work, back to work.' The men sullenly obeyed, production went on as usual."[45]

Despite two serious accidents on this machine, the Ford foreman "called another man over and brusquely ordered him to go to work on the same press, which had just mutilated two workers." With wisdom gained from the recent experience of his two shop mates, the man looked at his ten fingers. Next, he looked at the machine. Then he told the foreman that if he was in a hurry to get the parts turned out by this press, that he had better go to work himself. He went on to say that he liked his ten fingers and intended to keep them; besides, he thought the machine would enjoy the foreman's fingers as much as his. Before the foreman could gather his thoughts together to tell the man that he was fired, this worker told him that he quit.[46]

Roy Speth, a Wisconsin auto worker, took pride that he had all his fingers after twelve years working as a shaper hand. This, he said, "was an unusual thing at that time." One Chevrolet worker proclaimed: "One week of this nightmare convinced me that I better pull out while I still had ten fingers."[47]

No wonder that novelist Erskine Caldwell labeled Detroit the "eight-finger city." Writing about a Detroit tour as the Great Depression began to ease, he attributed an increase of worker accidents to the speed-up that manufacturers instituted in the mid-1930s after the creation of the National Recovery Administration. "Workers," he wrote, "arrived at their plants to find their machines geared up to a higher speed, with no warning given, and they were unable to adjust themselves overnight to the new tempo." In the L. A. Young, Hudson, and Dodge plants, many workers suffered serious accidents at these faster machines. "In working class Detroit," Caldwell said, "you are known by your hands." Fingers signified the status and competency of a worker. "If you have all your fingers intact," he wrote, "you are neither an automobile worker, or a new automobile worker, or an exceptionally lucky automobile worker. If you have one finger missing, it serves as an identification device. But if two fingers have been torn from your hands, you are an outcast." When hired, employers took into account "the state of your hands before they look at the color of your skin." He concluded: "Eighteen or forty, it does not matter what the age may be; if you are eight-fingered, you are done for in Detroit."[48]

One Yale student witnessed a much more serious industrial accident that revealed managerial indifference in the River Rouge plant. "Old 'Horse-Face,'" he reported, "lost all the fingers on his right hand this morning." While cleaning a chain drive, the unfortunate worker's fingers got caught "between the sprocket and chain." The Yale student claimed that because it took too long to remove the chain, management believed it was "better, in the long run, to let the hand go round the whole wheel, and then rush the fellow to a 'first aid.'" About the misfortunate worker: "If he's lucky, he'll get $200 apiece for his fingers, and an easy job as janitor."[49]

The AWU leader Phil Raymond blamed the "continued pressure" to achieve higher rates of production at lower costs for "the increased number of accidents and poor health conditions prevalent throughout the industry." Poor health and susceptibility to accidents often made workers feel less human and less manly. At Cadillac he reported "a 30 percent production increase came at the expense of a 100 percent increase in accidents." In 1927, General Motors reported sixteen worker deaths, 293 amputations, and sixteen lost eyes. The automobile industry also had many "health destroying occupations such as duco-spraying, sand blasting, grinding, acid dripping, etc." A survey of eighteen thousand Ohio auto workers revealed that from 5 percent to 10 percent "contracted tuberculosis as a result of their occupation" and a "large percentage . . . had lead and turpentine poisoning."[50]

Ken Bannon, the future director of the Ford UAW Department, remembered his degraded and agonizing labor at an automatic machine and that management had absolutely no concern for his health and safety. When he first entered the automobile industry in the mid-1930s as a worker at the Ford River Rouge plant, Brannon was assigned to operate a complicated production machine, one of the Bullard Multiaumatic and Continumatic lathes—marvels of the specialized machine revolution in the late 1910s and 1920s. These indexed machine tools performed multiple and sequential operations on foundry castings of automobile parts such as pistons. The task of the machine operator simply involved loading and unloading the machine. Brannon's particular machine handled castings for steering-gear housings. He processed "thousands of castings each day." The castings, he related, "are very rough, and after a few hours on this job your fingers would begin to bleed. They would bleed from the beginning of the week really until the end of the week." At no time would Ford supervisors allow Brannon to wear gloves, since they considered them a "safety hazard." Consequently, Brannon recalled, "we would get cloths and make bandages out of them and wrap them around our fingers and from the dime store buy a package of rubber bands and put a rubber band around the bandage so that it would hold on our fingers. This way we would try to save our fingers." Nonetheless, he and others were "always fearful of a foreman coming by and seeing us with cloths on our fingers, for which we were subject to discharge or some type of penalty." The Bullard lathes used an alkaline solution, "soda water, a white milky water." This wreaked havoc on the skin of machine operators. For manufacturers, the Bullard was a miraculous cost- and labor-saving device; for workers, it was hellacious misery.[51]

Similarly, one worker described the running sores from handling cylinder blocks in the Hudson plant. "Almost all the workers who handle the cylinder blocks from the time they are hardened until they reach the washing machine have running sores all over their hands and legs. This is caused by the chemicals in the hardening process."[52] Often, American-born workers refused to perform such miserable work, so managers assigned foreign-born immigrants to it. In time, immigrant workers also declined such assignments- which later became one of the package of "man-killing" jobs designated for black workers.

A serious challenge to manhood was the transformation of the age profile of auto workers, from the craft tradition where age and experience mattered to one where youth and speed were more important. Under the mass production regime of speed, older workers found it difficult to keep up the frantic pace needed to match production quotas. Workers who could not keep up would not be rehired after a seasonal layoff. The men lost the ability to provide a family wage, and the patriarchal and responsible component of his manhood diminished considerably. For manufacturers, youthful workers possessed an added advantage—the young men that auto manufacturers desired also did not carry the restrictive cultural baggage of skill and unionized craftsmen. By the mid-1920s many manufacturers believed that at age forty, or even younger, a man was too old to bear the rigors of auto work at automatic machines or on mechanized assembly lines.

Many observers noted and discussed the youthfulness of the automobile work force in the early years of mass production. One observed that increased mechanization brought in more young workers: "In Detroit particularly we notice an increasing number of young workers in the auto industry. This is largely due to the new 'improvements' in machinery." Another noted that in the early 1920s, a "comparatively small number of young workers" worked in auto plants. By the end of the decade, "simplified production" resulted in "more young workers" and more women in male jobs. The older men faced layoffs, and "boys and young girls fill[ed their] places." Robert Dunn described the age profile of auto workers in the Ford Highland Park plant in the late 1920s. It employed 44,500 workers; 34,200 were under age forty. Generally, it was "almost impossible for a man of 40 to get a job" in a Detroit auto plant. At the end of the decade, the AWU president reported: "In some plants from 10 to 15% of the employees are under 21 years of age." These youthful workers filled the less-skilled production jobs and worked as "machine operators, laborers, helpers in the foundry and the core-rooms, truckers, drivers, etc." He discovered also that "the lowest proportion of young workers is to be found in departments where skill is required."[53] As the American economy grew in the late 1920s and headed into the Great Depression, auto work speed-up favored the vigorous and young worker and was no longer suited for older workers.

Wyndham Mortimer, a Cleveland White Motors worker and future UAW leader, depicted the awful consequences for older men in the generalized speed-up in the late 1920s and early 1930s. "The old workers," he testified at an Automobile Labor Board (ALB) hearing, "unable to stand the pressure of high speed production, are pushed out on the street where, after their most vigorous years are spent, they are forced to live on charity, or to be a burden to their already overburdened children." The older man, government investigator Harry Weiss noted, saw a very early end to their working careers. "The situation of these men is terrible," he wrote. "They are doomed to idleness. . . . [They] have fifteen to twenty years of life ahead of them in many cases."[54] In addition to the human indignities of the work regimen, these still capable, though older, men were unable to function as responsible providers for their families.

For many auto workers, manufacturers considered them much too old to work when they reached forty or fifty years old, an age when the repetition and speed of their work tasks resulted in innumerable aches and pains to their beaten bodies. Until unionization the normal workday might be nine or ten hours, not counting possible overtime, the normal workweek five and a half or six days. During the seasonal rushes for production, longer workdays and longer workweeks were common. Although Social Security would not come until the mid-1930s, many older auto workers would have been too young to collect it and would have been condemned to low-wage underemployment in their later years.

A fifty-seven-year-old Toledo worker told the ALB of his grueling experience on the shop floor: "I work at the Chevrolet [plant], and in regard to working there, it is speeded too fast." He admitted, "Of course, I am an old man, but it is too fast for a man to keep his health. It is more than a human being can endure." Reflecting on his father's shop experience in the 1930s, Indiana auto worker Joe Meszaros commented: "Forty-five or 50 was an old man." At Dodge, personnel managers "refuse[d] to hire men over 45"; at the many General Motors plants around Flint, "workers [were] scrapped at 40." A "Ford personnel man," Dunn related, "has openly stated that the company does not hire men over that age." The auto worker Harry Ross recalled, "When you got to 40, you had it. . . . You were old at 40." He believed that "it was humanly impossible at that age to keep up with the conveyor lines." Robert Cruden, a reporter for *The Nation*, stood in the employment lines at several other auto plants. Though he "had never been inside a factory," he was amazed when Packard hired him, "while men whose hair had whitened in the service of motor kings were turned away with a shrug." In American automobile factories in the 1920s, an older auto worker was indeed a relatively young man.[55]

At the ALB hearings, one of the major complaints the auto workers made was how the speed-up quickly aged men out of the automobile factories. An Overland foreman described how the speed-up system destroyed the working lives of men in his plant. "After these men have served ten years in this work," he told the Toledo ALB hearing, "they are burned up. . . . Therefore, a man who is 40 years old is beyond the age of earning." An Oldsmobile worker from Lansing told a Detroit ALB hearing that they now "put 18 years in the automobile shops." He was forty-six years old, with twelve of those years "in the Olds Motor Works." "I am living," he said, "on borrowed time, a man of 46." Many workers had more than the fifteen or twenty years that Harry Weiss claimed lay ahead of them after their work lives in auto factories. In the late 1920s one worker even claimed, "This inhuman speeding up of work accounts for the great numbers of workers who are thrown on the scrap heap before reaching the age of 35."[56]

The new technological system clearly favored the young, but even they had problems keeping up with mechanized production. "The youth of the land," Yale student Zendt asserted, "are the only ones who can stand working on the tedious production line. Thus older and worn out men must give place to the younger and fresher ones." Auto-industry researcher Dunn observed: "Personnel men say that the policy is to hire young—after 8 or ten years when they have given their best it is hoped that they will shift to something else." Even the youthful worker quickly aged out of the factory. A South Bend worker described the twenty-one- to twenty-eight-year-old Bendix Products workers who labored at the automatic molding machines to produce castings for carburetors. "Now," he told the ALB, "the men that are operating these machines are most all young fellows. They have to be, because I don't know whether the old men could stand it, . . . and they all have reported that when they came in there to work that they had lost from 10 to 50 pounds."[57]

With the stiffer competition for any existing jobs, the Great Depression exacerbated the situation of the older worker. In December 1933 an "Auto Worker Correspondent" describe the travails of a worn-out Buick auto worker. Hired into the firm in 1922, he worked successively as a steamfitter, a production worker, a repairman, a shop foreman, and finally trained as a die repairman. After ten years of employment, Buick laid the "poor fellow off on the flimsy pretext: 'reducing forces,'" and he went on welfare in Flint.

Since he had a wife and seven children, he received a meager grocery allotment of $6.88, along with a "miserable supply of clothes, shoes, etc." In addition to working one day a week for the city, he spent much time "waiting, stalling around in lines," and going to and from his brief weekly job. His job search occurred three or four times a week, sometimes all day, "in all sorts of weather. The family lost their home, purchased from General Motors." Unable to perform adequately the role of family breadwinner, he suffered a loss in his patriarchal identity. Subsequently, "the wife grew exceedingly irritable and there was no seeming end to the quarrels and domestic friction from this source." Ultimately, the family disputes reached "an acute stage" and his wife called the police. They immediately arrested him, and he received a 30-day sentence in "the filthy Flint City jail."[58]

The dreadful experience emotionally and psychically ruined the Buick auto worker. The correspondent concluded: "The man represents a picture of utter mortification, broken down in spirit, listless and terribly aged." Although he was relatively young, the auto worker "has deep furrows all over his face, a pity to look upon." This case was one of hundreds of "similar cases" in the Flint area that suffered from General Motors' "insatiable greed for ever increasing profits."[59]

With their physical vigor undermined at the relatively young age of forty or forty-five, auto workers lost an important component of their manhood. No longer employable at age forty, a male automobile worker lost his ability to earn a decent income and serve as patriarchal breadwinner for his family. Without these, they were less than men and felt themselves emasculated.

The speed-up further added to these humiliations and indignities of the auto workers' sense of their manhood and worth. It created and fostered angry, aggressive, and abusive foremen who wanted to get out production at all costs. Prior to the mass-production regime, the proud skilled tradesmen refused to cower before any shop supervisor; they bowed down to neither the plant superintendent nor the shop foremen. In the words of labor historian David Montgomery, they asserted their "manly bearing." Any effort at intimidation prompted a swift worker response. If a supervisor dared watch a skilled mechanic at work, the mechanic would immediately stop until the shop supervisor left the work area. Only then would he resume production.[60] Production workers on automatic machines or at assembly lines did not have such independent traditions to protect them. They often grudgingly and meekly accepted the intimidation and coercion of their shop superiors.

Many auto workers complained about another assault on male dignity—the abusive, driving, and cursing foremen in the 1920s and 1930s. A Chevrolet worker complained about his rapid line speed and his abusive foremen: "The speed of the assembly lines is so great, it makes nervous wrecks out of the men, because the foremen walk up and down the line and yell at the men, and sometimes even curse them and tell them that if they don't go faster, not to come back tomorrow, and all that sort of thing." A Briggs worker decried both the pace of work and the cursing of foremen: "The pace on the line is maddening. Still we heard the cry, 'Step on it! Step on it!'" The shop supervisors "were yelling, cussing, swearing." The treatment of workers was exceptionally humiliating and demeaning, the writer added: "This was the first time I ever saw a foreman actually kick a man to get him to speed up."[61]

Other workers, too, condemned their awful treatment and belittling abuse. Charlie, "a modern 'Simon Legree,'" the *Auto Workers News* reported, "stands about 300 feet away from a person and yells at him like a dog." And when he yelled, "there is lots of other choice language but it is simply not fit to print." Mass-production workers did not have the opportunity for a prideful and manly response to supervisor's humiliation or intimidation. "It is bad enough," the worker said, "that the men must work like horses all day long without being obliged to listen to his growling, cursing and foul language all day long." A union reporter also criticized the sanctimonious hypocrisy of a Packard foreman, "a tall, lanky chap who swears like a trooper and teache[s] Sunday school." A Milwaukee auto worker did not like foremen "cussing the men, talking to them as though they were animals rather than human beings. They will cuss them and call them what is fighting talk, I would call it."[62] Since workers might face dismissal and would or could not react to such "fighting talk," this supervisory abuse and intimidation frequently made normally proud men meek and docile. A manly response to fighting words would result in immediate dismissal.

Other humiliations were even more egregious. Possessing the authority to determine transfers, promotions, wage increases, layoffs, and even dismissals, foremen established a workplace world of petty tyranny and corruption. In order to avoid layoff on one assembly line, the foreman conducted three profitable raffles and demanded that workers purchase tickets. "The first time," an auto worker reported, "it was an automatic shotgun, the second time, a tent, and the third time a wrist watch." He added: "It was made obvious to the workers, that if they wanted to hold on to their jobs, that they had better not refuse to buy at least one raffle ticket on each of these occasions." And the foreman pocketed the income from the raffle. In order to retain the supervisor's good graces, many auto workers offered the foreman a box of cigars, a bottle of whiskey, a case of beer, labor for innumerable services, or even work at the supervisor's home. When asked about the allocation of wage rates in the 1930s, a Flint auto worker answered: "The top man happens to be a fellow that goes out to the cottage, paints the boss's cottage and his house, goes to parties, lets the boss play with his wife and all that stuff." John Anderson also remembered a similar situation for men during the Great Depression: "It was common talk around the shop that if a man wanted to hold his job he often had to respond with his wife or his daughter to the wishes of the foreman. He would visit the home or he would take them out. But that was common knowledge in talk around the industry during those years."[63] Nothing demonstrated the loss of manhood more intensely than the loss of control over the women in his family, the need to offer a wife or daughter to keep his job.

But other daily humiliations devalued the personal worth and sense of manhood of auto workers. Before unionization in the late 1930s, the inhuman and inhumane shop environment involved many forms of physical and psychological degradation. The filth of the workers' worlds was indescribable and indefensible: the human body perpetually coated with industrial fluids, oils, and paints, or the absence of decent sanitary facilities. The demeaning and horrid shop conditions of auto workers demonstrated that they were less than human and not real men. Though a few men may have reveled in the rough and crude shop environment, others made it a source of constant complaint and uttered plaintiff appeals for their dignity and humanity or for their proud sense of being men. Frequently, human needs did not mesh with the industrial needs. Ordinary biological needs threatened line speeds and efficient production. Shop floor supervisors and foremen resisted a workers need to get a drink of water, have a toilet break, or leave a work station due to illness.

In the pre-union era, the difficulty of getting relief from their work to get a drink of water or to go to the toilet especially rankled auto workers. A Chevrolet worker's line speed ran so fast that he needed relief to get to "a water fountain less than 15 feet" from his work station. He also deplored the sorry situation of a sick workmate: "A man across the line from me was sick to his stomach. The foreman told him that he couldn't get him the relief man and the man just worked and vomited and worked and vomited and didn't dare leave his job." A Flint Chevrolet foundry worker complained, "They treat you just like a dog, you know." If a worker needed "to go to a rest room or the toilet you had to ask 'em and they'd pull the watch on you to see how long you were gone." Ken Brannon recalled going to the restroom at Ford's in the early 1930s. When permitted "to go to the washroom, it was not unusual for a serviceman to come in and want to know what you were doing, how long you were there and also to ask you to stand up if you were sitting down to see if you were lying or not."[64] In the Ford plants, workers were expected to produce both on the line and in the toilet.

The wife of a worker bemoaned the problems of her husband who labored in the Fisher Body paint shop. In the Flint plant, she said, "they didn't have enough relief men [so] the men couldn't go to the bathroom when they wanted to. Sometimes in order to relieve themselves they just urinated on the floor because the administration wouldn't stop the line for them." Another Flint Fisher Body worker described the urinals in the body-sanding department. "And as far urinals in there," he disclosed, "they had a trough right along the wall there." A St. Louis Chevrolet worker, who had a work stint from 7:00 A.M. to noon, needed to go to the toilet, as such a long work spell often prompted the call of nature. He said, "You know during that time a fellow would have to go to the toilet." When he "asked the supervisor one time for relief," the reply was, "If you can not wait, by God, do it in your pants. That is the only way I can let you go."[65]

Serious illness also revealed managerial indifference to important human needs. A St. Louis Chevrolet worker related an incident when he was sick and needed to go to the toilet for a "running of the bowels." The ailing worker told his foreman that he did not feel well and wanted to go home so that he could go to the toilet. The foreman noted that Chevrolet policy did not allow him to leave his workplace unless someone relieved him. After being relieved a couple of times, he again asked for relief. The foreman said, "I haven't got time." The ailing worker replied: "All right, bring a slop jar or bucket and if the rest of the men are satisfied to put up with this, put it down here and I will stay on the job." Finally, he said, late in the morning, "I went home and I was home thirty days sick in bed. . . . Those were the conditions under which we worked."[66]

Generally, the deplorable sanitary conditions of the shops revealed managerial indifference to the basic health needs of auto workers. A "young worker" at the Peninsular Metal Products plant griped about the condition of the washrooms: "To the initiated, the shop is one of the worst for sanitary conditions. True, there were provisions for workers to wash after work—but soap and towels were conspicuous by their absence."[67] A Hudson worker, who described himself as "ONE OF THE COGS," wrote: "In the Essex cylinder block division there is but one small toilet for several hundred men and facilities for washing and dressing are unknown."[68] Another auto worker reported, "There is no consideration for sanitary conditions. There are no washing facilities. Some men wash their hands in the toilet bowls."[69]

Sometimes, the workers themselves were a source of the filthy conditions in the auto shops. Since employers banned smoking in auto factories, many auto workers chewed tobacco to satisfy their craving for nicotine. H. Dubreuil, a French machinist who labored in American plants, could not resist commenting on this unique American habit: "The 'sport' of chewing and spitting tobacco is practiced with so much activity that even the floors of the workshops bear many unfortunate traces of it." He could vividly remember the "wall decorations" of his machine shop. A Hudson worker also complained how tobacco fouled his work: "The oil used in lapping the cylinders is used over and over again, with its ever increasing loads of filth consisting of tobacco expectorations, oil mopped up from the floors, etc."[70]

The mass-production work regime and the aggressive supervision of work all devalued and undermined an auto worker's sense of dignity and manhood. The brutal technical system established a highly controlled work environment of monotony and degradation. For skilled workers and those who aspired to such positions, the desired autonomy and control so essential for manly independence no longer existed. For others, the vicious speed-up, the endless fatigue, the absence of concern for health and safety, the abusive foremen and supervisors, and an uncivilized work environment all revealed lack of concern for human and manly dignity. Auto workers responded, individually and collectively, positively and negatively, to reframe and to reclaim a sense of their manhood through their sometimes retrograde shop floor behaviors, their efforts to fight back through union representation, and their general devaluation of women at work and in their local communities.

2

Reclaiming Manhood

*Shop Culture, Industrial Unionism,
and the Derogation of Women, 1920s and 1930s*

In the first decades of the American automobile factories, auto workers resisted the oppressive work regime and inhuman management policies
individually and collectively. They reached back to older forms of protest and
created new shop cultures of resistance as well. Often they relied on what
political anthropologist James C. Scott characterized as the "weapons of the
weak,"[1] those individual, everyday, and subterranean practices that alleviated
intolerable work situations or even avoided them. From automotive mass-
production's origins to more recent times, such traditions and resistance have
been commonplace and a means to contain and control onerous work conditions. Worker absenteeism and labor turnover continuously plagued auto
foremen and shop supervisors and offered a break from rigorous assembly
line routines. Auto workers shirked and soldiered on the job and covertly
restricted their output to ease the tiring work pace. Some stole a trade bit
by bit, and day by day, to gain the skills required for more prestigious and
more rewarding work. Hoping to acquire the autonomy and independence of
skilled craftsmen, these workers were not fully aware of the profound technical changes occurring around them. As they gained collective consciousness,
others attempted to form either craft or industrial unions to assert control
over their work situations and work environment, and to achieve a family
wage. For some who feared the loss of their manhood at work, a common
practice was also the generalized demeaning and sexualizing of women in
the workers' everyday words and behaviors on the job and in their communities. They relished and asserted their manhood also through the demeaning
of African Americans or other despised ethnic groups. Through the 1920s

automotive workplaces became densely masculine spaces inhospitable to the presence of women and difficult for minorities and others who deviated from prevailing white male norms.

During World War I the new profession of industrial management began to seriously address two labor problems that had previously been the concern of industrial engineers—absenteeism and labor turnover.[2] At the dawn of automotive mass production, these problems severely plagued the efficiency of modern and integrated methods and techniques of production. For example, after the creation of Ford line production for machine and assembly work, absenteeism averaged 10 percent over the course of a workweek. The number was routinely higher on the first days of the week, since workers often received their pay on Fridays. This meant that an average of one in ten workers was not at his assigned place in the highly synchronized and integrated manufacturing system, and so the anticipated output fell dramatically. To have replacements to fill the vacancies, the Ford Highland Park plant in 1913 needed to hire a daily average of about fourteen hundred additional workers to guarantee output, a very inefficient and costly endeavor.

Similarly, annual labor turnover, or the quit rate, bedeviled the automobile industry's early industrial managers in the new age of mass production. Though not as technologically sophisticated as Ford, the Packard firm had a quit rate of 200 percent in 1913. For the innovative Ford Highland Park factory, the rate of labor turnover reached an astonishing 360 percent in 1913, a figure that meant that the firm had to hire about fifty-two thousand workers each year to maintain its 13,600-person workforce.[3] Such a continuous stream of new hires was a costly operation that inhibited the technical efficiency of the modern factory.

For auto workers, the root causes of such behavior varied. Absenteeism often represented a short break from monotonous, wearying, and mind-numbing work routines. Some absented themselves to look for more satisfactory work or slightly higher-paying positions. Others, mainly from rural agricultural regions of the United States and Europe, did not know or understand the requirement for persistent and consistent work in their new industrial settings. They did not possess the needed work or industrial discipline and maintained their pre-industrial rural habits of life and work.[4] Still other workers entered the Ford facilities and other modern plants with the expectation of entering at the bottom rung of skilled work in the metal trades and progressing up the working-class ladder of mobility. In an era where industrial change was so rapid and so extensive, such hopes often proved futile and needed to be abandoned. Moreover, some firms were not so thoroughly modernized that dreams of acquiring skilled status could be gained in the less innovative establishments. Many of the quits represented the search for different and more satisfying work, jobs where workers might achieve slightly higher pay, more satisfying work, or even the possibility of eventually acquiring craft skills.

Either individually or collectively, the withdrawal of work effort was another mechanism for coping with and resisting the modern world of mass production. Even before the beginning of the new century, soldiering and output restriction—the two serious industrial sins—were a means to protest and to assert some control over unpleasant work situations as a rapacious industrial capitalism advanced. These practices were connected to the nineteenth-century labor and union tradition of "a fair day's wages for a fair day's work." The central issue was the different interpretation of "fair" by managers and workers. In his classic early-twentieth-century work on industrial management, Frederick Winslow Taylor repeatedly railed against the "the greatest evil" of "the working-people," their lackluster effort and performance on the job. "Underworking, that is, deliberately working slowly so as to avoid doing a full day's work," or, as Taylor called it, "soldiering," was "almost universal in industrial establishments." For Taylor, "natural" soldiering involved an individual worker's tradition of exerting the least amount of effort in his daily work tasks. Much more insidious was "systematic soldiering," or what later generally became known as output restriction; it occurred when workers banded together and collectively conspired to limit production, arose "from more intricate second thought and reasoning caused by their relations with other men."[5] Much worse, Taylor said, was that systematic soldiering was "almost universal under all of the ordinary schemes of management," arising from "a careful study on the part of the workmen of what will promote their best interests."[6] Whether paid by day rates, piece rates, or still other more complicated incentive schemes, American workers practiced output restriction and knew how to use it to their advantage. This advantage rested on notions of fairness and equity, of assuring the availability of work for all members of the trade, and of maintaining a work pace that insured safety and good health.

In the late nineteenth and early twentieth centuries, manufacturers and industrial analysts believed that only skilled workers organized into craft unions were capable of limiting production or restricting output.[7] Through the late 1920s Stanley B. Mathewson and six others engaged in participant observation and conducted interviews of unorganized workers in slightly more than one hundred modern industrial settings, including machine shops, automobile factories, and parts plants. Funded by the Social Science Research Council, the project resulted in the publication of *Restriction of Output among Unorganized Workers*.[8] Mathewson's research team collected and examined 223 detailed accounts of output restriction. Contrary to conventional wisdom, the Antioch College industrial sociologist discovered that even unorganized and less skilled workers widely practiced and engaged in numerous and diverse forms of output restriction. The reasons for output restriction varied: the pressures from workmates not to work too fast, the "boss-ordered" restrictions to avoid layoffs and the breakup of work crews, the attempts to maintain equity of effort and pay under incentive schemes to raise productivity, the efforts to defeat time-study men and obtain favorable job times, the fear that overwork would result in unemployment, and the personal grievances against supervisors and management policies.[9]

Mathewson's main conclusion was that unskilled production workers followed the craft-union ethic of workers' control. "Restriction" he argued, "is a widespread institution, deeply intrenched in the working habits of American laboring people." His other important conclusion noted that scientific management "failed" to improve the "spirit of confidence" in labor management relations. "Underwork and restriction," he claimed, "are greater problems than over-speeding and over work." Management efforts to speed up workers failed because of "the ingenuity of workers in developing restrictive practices." Managers, he believed, paid "only superficial attention" to worker productivity and failed to convince the worker that he could "freely give his best efforts" without suffering penalties instead of rewards for his hard work.[10]

As an illustration of one worker's attitude toward output restriction, Mathewson included a poem titled "Harmony?" he had found posted on a machine-shop bulletin board. The anonymous worker/poet began: "I am working with the feeling / That the company is stealing / Fifty pennies from my pocket every day." But the aggrieved worker had a strategy to cope with and to resist his exploitation. For every penny the firm got, "They will lose ten times as many / By the speed that I'm producing, I dare say." He was "disgusted," so his speed was "adjusted" and "nevermore will my brow drip with sweat." When they wanted him to "hurry," he would let another "rush and worry." "Till an increase in wages, I do get." In the past, he concluded, he had stupidly over-exerted himself. "Nearly three years I've been working / Like a fool, but now I'm shirking—/ When I get what's fair, I'll always do my part."[11]

Arthur E. Morgan, the Antioch College president and an engineer, wrote the conclusion to Mathewson's book. Appalled by worker attitudes on restriction to production, he observed: "In some degree restriction of output is part of a half-conscious class struggle." Some workers may well have been fully conscious of the struggle with their bosses. Their subterranean struggle relied on a classic weapon of the weak: covert yet highly organized output restriction, covert because managers possessed the power to impose serious sanctions for such oppositional tactics on the shop floor.

In an unpublished draft "Introduction" for Mathewson's book, Morgan also discussed the implications of the loss of creative work to working-class notions of manhood. "A man of virility and self-respect," the Antioch president wrote, "craves to express himself by creative work. In fact, his work is the measure of his life. Take away his capacity for creative expression and you take away his very life. Compel him to do what has no importance, significance or value, and you rob him of his chance to be a man."[12] For this college president and engineer, craft skills and control over the workplace formed an important basis of working-class manhood. For unskilled workers, underwork, or soldiering and output restriction, represented an effort to reclaim their control and their manhood at work.

Auto worker Frank Marquart discussed some of the ways automobile workers reasserted their control in their workplaces. In the late 1910s he detailed how he and others bested the intrusive efforts of the time-study men. "When the time-study man stood over me," he wrote, "stopwatch and clipboard in hand, I slowed down every motion I made without seeming to do so deliberately." Even though his task involved bench work, "the simplest kind of operation," Marquart managed to get a good "price" on the job. "Once the price was set," he wrote, "I had no difficulty 'making out,' as the workers used to say." The deception created small bits of time that allowed him to earn a higher wage and still avoid serious over-exertion. Marquart concluded: "It was similar with other jobs: those of us who worked on the bench could find all kinds of shortcuts—ways we never revealed to the time-study man."[13]

Marquart also criticized the shop rate busters who exceeded a work group's production norms and who caused management to re-time the operation and lower the piece rate. At Continental Motors, the "unwritten law among cylinder grinders" was a dozen six-cylinder blocks for a work shift. He and his co-workers knew that if they exceed this limit, "management might cut our premium rates." But some workers did not agree with the notion of restricted output. Such workers were labeled "'hungry bastards,' who were so greedy for extra pay that they turned in fourteen or fifteen blocks." When this happened, management re-timed the jobs and cut the pay. The result: "We had to turn out extra blocks to make the same pay." The rest of the shop resented the "hungry bastards." The collective male shop culture ostracized and refused to talk with them. "Every time one of them went for a drink of water or to the washroom," Marquart recalled, "the belts on his machine were cut, the grinding wheel was smashed, his personal tools were damaged, the word 'RAT' was chalked on his machine in block letters." Treated as a "scab" by workmates, two such "speed kings" eventually quit Continental Motors.[14]

For many auto workers, "stealing a trade" was another means for coping with the rigors and uncertainties of mass production. For some, it meant regaining the manly virtues of the autonomous craftsman, namely, the autonomy and independence that came from a skilled trade. Labor historian David Montgomery noted that, before mass production, "for many young men in the late nineteenth century, one or more repetitive, specialized tasks in a factory . . . served as stepping-stones to a skilled craft."[15] Later, this shop tradition continued. Not fully realizing the dramatic import of the technical changes in their midst, many auto workers continued to hope to gain work in the well-paid and highly respected metal trades, and they viewed work in the new automobile industry a pathway to opportunity. The specialized work contained limited elements of skilled craft work. But under the Fordist work regime, specialized mass production offered only unrewarding and repetitive unskilled production work. Still, some hoped that a stolen trade in the remaining skilled positions might offer the possibility of security in skilled work. For others, stealing a trade simply offered the prospect of a higher wage or an opportunity to gain entry to and employment in an automobile plant. This was especially true during the Great Depression, when auto firms attempted to hire and hoard skilled workers in hard times. For auto workers, both possibilities allowed them to be the patriarchal providers of a decent wage for their families.

Many workers recalled their efforts to obtain more lucrative and more skilled work with a stolen trade. John Anderson, a veteran and leftist union activist, observed: "If you didn't have a trade you bluffed your way into a job by claiming experience in any job you thought you were able to do."[16] At the hiring gate, the worker would lie his way into a skilled position. Once hired, he fumbled at his work routines and acquired some skills but often did not last in the job. Slightly more skilled, he repeated the process several times until he could finally hold the job.

As a young man, union activist Marquart used this process to obtain a skilled job as a tool grinder. He hired in as a grinder in a small Detroit tool and die plant but lasted only "for about two weeks," he said, "before the foreman told me I was too slow and he'd have to let me go." Marquart worked in a dozen or so small shops before he "acquired enough competence to perform any grinding job in the tool room, whether external, internal, or surface grinding."[17]

In 1923, Stan Coulthard, a British immigrant to Detroit, stole a trade at Chrysler. Though he didn't know what a milling machine was and had "never worked in a machine shop before," he heard that Chrysler was hiring millers, applied for the position, and was hired the same day for the evening shift. "As soon as I got in," he related, "I was asked where were my tools?" He lied and said that he "had no time to go home to get them." When he got to his machine, Coulthard "didn't even know how to switch it on." He fumbled about and tried to look busy until the foreman left. A fellow worker sympathized with his need for a job and introduced him to the basic operation of the milling machine. "After a while," he recalled, "he said that the stock I was making was scrap, that there was some good stuff in the pan behind me and to let on that I produced it." Often, skilled workers "banked" completed work so that, if needed, they could later take it easy and lay back on the job. Later that day the foreman passed the donated pieces of Coulthard's work. For the next couple of days he continued until he "got the hang of things." Coulthard had "no qualms" about the "cheating," since, as he said, the Chrysler firm "got it out of my hide before I'd finished."[18]

During the Great Depression two Flint workers, Joe Fry and Irving King, similarly managed to obtain needed work. Fry applied for a trimmer's job at Fisher Body. When asked if he had experience, he lied and claimed to have worked at an upholstery firm. The suspicious foreman then said: "Well, if you worked down there, you must have the tools." Fry responded that he still had his tools. The foreman stipulated that if experienced, Fry's tools would have been used. Fry concurred, and the foreman told him, "You bring them tools tomorrow morning at seven o'clock. And if you got the tools to be a trimmer, you got the job." Now Fry needed to acquire quickly a used set of tools for the trimmer's trade. He convinced his brother, a trimmer at the other Fisher plant, to bring home his used tools. In exchange, they went to the hardware store and bought the brother a complete set of new tools. Fearing calls to his alleged former employer would unmask him, he returned the next day. The foreman hired him and immediately sent him to work. When he got there, Fry said, "I all I had to use was a Yankee screwdriver, puttin' the screws in the bottom of the corners of each one of the doors." He never used or needed "none of them damn tools" from his brother. Despite his costly investment, he borrowed such a screwdriver from a new workmate.[19]

During the Depression, Irving King lied that he was a metal finisher (someone who took flaws out of metal bodies) to obtain his job. When he arrived at work the first morning, he said, a new workmate "was scared to show you a job because he didn't want you to learn his job because he was in jeopardy then." Assigned to work opposite another worker, "to finish the back fender," he "knew nothin' about it." When he went to get his tools from the tool crib, King said, "Give me everything a metal finisher needs. And he give me a tool tray with files and emery cloth and so forth in it. I didn't even know how to use it." He watched those working around him and tried imitating them. But it didn't work: "The foremen walked up and says, 'You never metal finished in your life, did you?'" Caught, he confessed that he had not. The foreman had him return his tools and reassigned him to a less skilled job.[20] Despite the hard economic times, his deception got him through the factory gate and onto a job.

Unionism offered another opportunity for men to gain control at the workplace, obtain higher wages, and become better providers for their families. More than simply another means to control, union membership offered a pathway to respectable and responsible manhood. This was the perception conveyed distinctly in the auto-union press of the 1920s and 1930s. In 1915, for example, W. A. Logan, future leader of the Auto Workers Union, wrote a short piece on "the union man." To his mind, even if a man had "a union card in his pocket," that did not "always make him a union man." A union man was someone special. For Logan, the "REAL union man" subscribed the mutualistic labor ethic of helping brother workers. The genuine unionist belonged to the union as "a matter of principle," since he knew that "the entire union movement is consecrated to the uplift and betterment of workers." Despite employer efforts to encourage labor troubles and violence, the real unionist worked to organize and to hold the labor movement together. And in an acknowledgment of union women, Logan added, "The real true blue union men and women stood firmly for their convictions of what they considered was right even in the face of prison, death, and starvation." Most of all, real unionists acted. "It is actions that count in this world," he concluded. "Certificate of membership means nothing without actions to back it up."[21] And action meant fighting back and resisting the predations of managers and owners.

In another essay, the *Auto Worker* emphasized the "union man's duty," chastising those who would not build up union membership, those who would allow others to perform the difficult work of organizing and increasing membership. "Human endurance," it noted, "has its limit. Human energy its end. It cannot be expected that the few ardent, faithful workers will keep up their efforts forever." Young unionists needed to step forward and do more than simply pay their union dues. "Do your duty and do it well," the union journal urged. "Act the manly part, come to the front. Take hold of the helm. Steer clear of the difficulties you can. Encourage your fellow members to do likewise." The duty of the union man was to act and to build the union: "Get out," it exhorted, "and 'organize' and 'organize' and 'organize.'"[22]

In the late 1920s, an *Auto Worker's News* editorial titled "What Is Manhood?" asked a rhetorical question about "the most priceless possessions still retained by modern man." The answer: "Manhood is that quality in a man which gives him his self-respect, his independence, his feeling of equality with all men." Moreover, a man's paternalistic "duty" was "to fight for his family, to fight for the improvement and against the lowering of their standard of living." These attributes reached back to the patriarchal craft notion of manhood, the masculine figure of the skilled worker who exerted control at work. Without organization and common striving, men could not fight for higher wages and dignity and against wage cuts and longer hours. In the absence of organization, the union paper asked, "Can the man whose little tots have to run around ragged, whose older children are forced out into the streets to sell papers when they should be at school, who can offer almost no advantage to his family besides the barest of food clothing and shelter, can he be said to have much self-respect, responsibility, or independence?"[23] Such manly traits formed the basis of the respectable provider role.

Similarly, the leftist labor newspaper questioned the manhood of the unorganized worker: "What about THEIR manhood—their backbone?" A renewed manhood would emerge from organization and unionization.

> "Would you be a MAN—free, proud, independent, POWERFUL? Then get together with your fellow worker, ORGANIZE YOURSELF, and you will be in a position to proudly look into the eyes of foreman, straw bosses, and all the world and say: "I AM A MAN!"[24]

Such a militant and muscular notion of manhood predated the 1960s images of the black Memphis garbage workers who bore signs that read, "I AM A MAN." Union manhood would reinvigorate the sapped virility of the men who worked the new monotonous, demeaning, and repetitive work on mass-production assembly lines.

In its visual imagery, the labor press presented its ideas on aggressive, muscular, and militant union manhood. Scanning through the labor press one finds many union cartoons that present images of the muscled worker in overalls and the corpulent manufacturer in tuxedo and top hat. In 1920 the *Auto Worker* published a front-page cartoon of a fat-cat "capitalist" profiteer and a muscular organized worker. Dressed as an acrobat, a fat profiteer stood precariously balanced on teetering letters that from top to bottom read "profits." Next to him in working clothes stood a brawny worker labeled "organized labor." In his hands, he wielded a large club labeled "co-operation," an allusion to the post–World War I cooperative movement that intended to cut into profits. Poised to make a mighty swing, the worker intended to whack the unbalanced letters and knock the profiteer to the ground.[25]

The reclamation of manhood rested on a combination of both respectable and rough features: the union man needed to be a provider but also a fighter. In the late 1920s a Packard worker denounced the unmanly behavior of two rats who refused to participate in a wildcat strike brought on when a worker refused to break in a new man at a lower-than-customary wage. The two men refused to resist or fight back at what unionists believed an unreasonable supervisory demand. A foreman and his assistant ordered the worker to instruct the new worker, who would lower the wage rate for the job. "In other words," the Packard worker related, "he threw out a challenge at the men which was very promptly accepted." A "hurried canvass" was undertaken of the union men in the shop, and everyone was prepared to walk out. As the men left the shop, "most of the men busied themselves with turning in their tools and when they arrived at the time clock they discovered two men shy." These two "yellow curs" were friends of the foreman. In the eyes of his shop mates, the two who opposed the walkout demonstrated their unmanly behavior. The writer praised the he-men, the manly men, in his shop: "There was a five-year man that walked out with the bunch that was very much against it and another man that was very much against it, but they were both he-men and were for the right."[26]

These attitudes expressed in the 1910s and 1920s persisted into the late 1930s as the United Automobile Workers consolidated its position in the midst of an array of union competitors. In a 1939 poem, a Hudson worker criticized the Hudson Industrial Association, the pre-UAW company union, and praised the real unionism of the United Auto Workers. "They claim I belonged to their union," it began, "Which they called the 'H.I.A.,' / But as long as I have my manhood, / I want my kids to say: / 'MY FATHER WAS A MAN.'" The Hudson worker equated CIO industrial unionism with responsible and combative manhood. This vision of manhood also contained a sense of a militant collective solidarity with his fellow workers. The poem continued: "We represent the MEN to the Bosses, / Not the bosses to the men" and represented them "In a militant, fighting manner," unlike the earlier company-dominated union. He asked his fellow workers to consider where they stood. "Just ask yourself: 'Will my children say, / "MY FATHER WAS A MAN."[27]

For many men, the reassertion of their manhood took on negative connotations in their sexualized conversations about women, in the general demeaning of women in their workplace conversations, and in their attitudes and behaviors toward women at work and beyond the factory gates on Detroit's streets. Though the historical record is not rich, sex has always been present in the workplace wherever men gathered together and especially when men and women shared the same space. At Lowell in the 1820s, textile manufacturers established their "moral police" and boarding-house system to protect women from the sexual advances of male supervisors. Wherever women worked, supervisors and workers preyed on them. But all-male work settings often involved men who sexually demeaned women in their boastful conversations and their aggressive behaviors.

In the late nineteenth century, David Montgomery noted Alfred Kolb's account of "the male ambience" of a bicycle factory machine shop. Kolb described his all-male shop:

> A Monday morning in the factory. Brr! Many stand at their places, worn out, with rings under their eyes, and try to pull themselves together with their work, as well as it goes. The overseer looks in, hung-over; his voice is husky. There is more chatting than usual: about Sunday naturally. A new acquaintance, a pick-up tried without success, some overheard lovemaking, a couple of coarse jokes. Even the married men joined in and in naive cynicism raise the curtains of their marriage beds.[28]

Montgomery also mentioned a 1913 *Iron Age* editorial that "commended 'a large manufacturing plant' for banning all pictures, postcards, and calendars from its walls." The editorial observed: "The men do not always make a proper choices of subjects."[29] Similar incidents and behaviors existed in automobile factories.

But these sexualized conversations and behaviors became much more visible in auto shops among young and unskilled auto workers in the automobile factories of the 1920s and 1930s, and later. This was the era of the "New Woman" and the more sexualized popular culture. These men asserted and reclaimed their manhood through their sexualized preoccupations in their day-to-day behaviors at work. If a woman, either a member of the secretarial staff or of a tour group observing the wonders of mass production, walked through a plant, auto workers exploded with hoots, howls, grunts, and catcalls. Even without a female presence, male automobile workers possessed a feral, almost wild and manic demeanor as they labored and toiled at their degraded, monotonous, and routinized work tasks. They often literally howled to maintain their sense of sanity in the mad world of metals and machines.

The Flint Autoworker editor asked a Fisher Body worker, "We would like to know the reason for the Tarzan yells from the Duco spray line? How about it Brother Somers?"[30] Another worker explained one reason for such primitive shop-floor howling. Gene Richards, a twenty-three-year-old musician and temporary auto worker, observed: "Men about me are constantly cursing and talking filth. Something about the monotonous routine breaks down all restraint. . . . We work on and on with spurts of conversation. Suddenly a man breaks forth with a mighty howl. Others follow. We set up a howling all over the shop. It is a relief, this howling."[31]

For Richards, this wild and feral howling on the shop floor bore a deeply sexualized component. As he discussed his daily work life, the aspiring musician recounted many workplace conversations about his co-workers' sex lives. Coming from different social and ethnic backgrounds, the auto workers were almost strangers in their non-work lives and had "little in common." Since their work did not "absorb the mind," they felt a compulsive need to communicate with each other. A sense of "isolation" led "to the assurance that his confidences will never escape" the frantic and noisy shop floor. A co-worker on the line, "without a trace of conscience," talked about "his more intimate relations with his wife." As the frenzied workday approached its end, Richards related how they screamed and howled their anger and frustration. "We slip into some pretty childish ruts sometimes," he added. "We are so completely dulled by our work that trivial and boyish pranks amuse us." He concluded: "We take to hollering [as the shift is ending] to build up a morale which will help us to lick the last hour."[32]

The middle- and upper-class Yale students who spent summers in Detroit's automobile plants also experienced this constant cursing and talking filth as they encountered the working class. As in other industrial cities, the Motor City contained a large working-class "bachelor culture"[33] of young, single men and also older "bachelor" married men who lived and worked far from their spouses. Their sexual conversations and behaviors were an almost-constant shop-floor occurrence. Morris L. Marcus, who worked for the Chrysler Corporation, described the rather raucous "gang" of workers who worked with him in the "pit" under the assembly line. The gang in front of the pit often indulged in "lewd talk and obscene pranks." Two co-workers near him "were telling smutty jokes." Tired but curious, he "listened in of course." "Needless to say," he admitted, "the jokes, the experiences and tales of the workers are not genteel enough to put down in writing." To Marcus's mind, such behavior made the workers less "machine-like." For these young assembly-line workers, their "wrestling, horsing, jostling, [and] joking" was "the only means of varying the monotony of work aside from climbing out of the pit for a drink or lunch." Generally, he observed that "the workers' thoughts and conversation" concerned such issues as current shop production, the expected workday, the next day's work, recent purchases for their cars, and "sex, obscene language, smutty jokes." He concluded: "Altogether, sex pervades the conversation."[34]

Other Yale students shared similar workplace experiences. Divinity-school student Thomas Mimms worked with both an American and a Canadian worker. "Tobacco juice and profanity," he observed, "were in abundance." The Canadian "entertained" the small work group with tales of his Sunday sexual escapades. "He told of the woman with whom he spent Sunday, the good wine she had and of his ability to triumph over women generally." Mimms also recalled another man, characterized as one of the "unstable element" of the Ford workforce. The nine-year Ford worker had a dangerous encounter the previous summer. Discovered with another man's wife and chased around town, the worker "dodged his pursuers and left the woman at her home." The husband soon found him and attempted to shoot him three times and missed. The worker "seized the pistol and thus saved his own life." The Yale student concluded: "The man seemed to shiver as he told me this story. 'Man I thought sure as hell, the next day they'd be saying, "Don't he look natural."'"[35] Such a titillating tale and deathly image surely sobered the less-world-wise young Ivy League student.

E. McCluny Fleming described a French co-worker who "had a wonderful sense of humor." This worker, the Yale student wrote, "confided to me his nightly amours with his landlady and a certain young widow." Another co-worker suffered the "childish" discipline of the Ford servicemen. He was "a handsome young Italian fitting camshafts opposite me [who] was sent home for smiling at one of the girls passing thru the plant." After he left work, Fleming preferred not to "sit all evening on the front porch listening to the radio, reading the tabloid, or motoring about the city." But he did enjoy some of the other pleasures of bachelor sociability. He "shot billiards," "went to the free-for-all dances," discovered "prohibition is a myth," and learned the "enormous role" that sex played in the "daily thinking" of Ford workers. Still, Fleming complained of his after-work world:

> [A] greasy drabness, an unventilated crampedness, a sort of frowsy, dusty wearisome monotony about this $25 a week world of eternally dirty fingernails, lurching trollies, smoke-laden poolrooms, Sunday morning movies, clock-work routine, green tabloids, listless front-stoop gossip, installment-plan agents, and the be-all and end-all of the bi-weekly check.[36]

The divinity student Oliver M. Zendt made reference to Whiting Williams's book *What's on the Worker's Mind*. His fellow Yale students "think they can answer that question in one word, namely sex." And, he added: "Most of the workers talk about nothing but women in a vulgar sort of way." Ernest Ackley blamed "the effect of this industrial system on the minds of the workers" and on the male preoccupation with sex and sexuality, which he attributed to their meaningless work: "He may think on the level of low amusement, sex and self gratification, largely because the work he is doing deadens the ability to think on a higher level."[37] For these workers, this lewd sex talk—though derogating women—offered an escape and reaffirmed their sense of manhood.

The young Yale students readily intermixed with and blended into the large bachelor subculture of working-class Detroit. When they searched for a boarding house, they found the cheap ones where the young working-class migrants of the "suitcase brigade" stayed for their first nights in the Motor City. A YMCA investigator described such a boarding house: "It is difficult to find clean beds. Conditions in some houses are revolting to the extreme." The new arrivals, he added, were "subject to severe temptations."[38] In the mid-1920s, Mimms, who worked at the River Rouge plant, asked about finding an inexpensive rooming house near work. One local resident's reply emphasized the dismal living arrangements: "You'll not want to stay out there. . . . Nobody lives near there 'cept 'wops' and 'Hunks' and 'Spicks.'" In another instance, a rooming-house landlord mentioned the drink habits of his Prohibition-era tenants: "Yes I got a bunch of [Ford] men here and I can't keep 'em sober, but I do keep 'em quiet or put 'em out." Fleming described the male-oriented embellishments to the room he rented in a working-class boarding house. After passing through "a shadowy, old-fashioned drawing room containing radio and Victrola," he went "up a narrow flight of stairs to an unpretentious room with good air and light. Its sole mural decoration consisted of a 'Havana Smoke Shop' calender of an extremely artificial nude woman in a rococo interior. Two other rooms were similarly beautified."[39]

Divinity student Ernest Ackley worked at the Fordson tractor plant and described the summer interlude in Detroit that he shared with twenty other Yale students. He described his neighborhood as "fairly respectable" where "the men had regular jobs." But it bore some of the rougher elements of working-class male culture and had "a few slight disturbances" during his summer sojourn. The police "raided a store up the street for booze," and two Italians got into a knife fight. He also described the vigorous bachelor culture: "The workers frequented pool parlors, went to movies, sat in their coffee houses, played diverse kinds of music in their houses, or sat on their front steps and talked."[40]

Another Yale student, C. N. Li, also was in contact with "various types of workingmen—the skilled and the unskilled, the native and the foreigner, the conservative and the radical." The Chinese student wrote about the "recreational activities" of Detroit's working class. He mentioned walking, socializing, driving around, and attending movies with his fellow auto workers. The average workman, he observed, "takes great interest in neighborhood gossip in pool rooms and drug stores." The unmarried worker, Li added, "goes once or twice a week to concerts, burlesque, vaudeville, photoplay, or public dances." Most of his young co-workers "frequent[ed] parks, theaters, and dancing halls." The prudish Li expressed his uneasy concern about a "rather perverted way of recreation"—the young workmen's visits to "the so-called 'sporting houses' of which, I am told, Detroit has an enormous number—greater than most of the big cities in the United States." And while Li also "visited their pool rooms and watched them dance at evening parties," this straight-laced Asian student drew the line at "drinking whiskey and visiting prostitutes."[41]

Apparently, some of the Yale students were not so prudish and actually participated in the underside of the bachelor culture. According to Ackley, a subgroup of his fellow Yale students "investigated the conditions regarding prostitution, turned in a report that frankly faced the fact that in an industrial community there seems to be a rather large recourse to this practice." The city authorities, their report concluded, did little to eradicate the social evil and simply tried to "limit certain more dangerous aspects of it" and "to use prophylactic measures in the practice in general."[42]

Recalling their early years in Detroit, auto workers remembered their encounters with and fascination for prostitutes and brothels. Charles Madison, a former auto worker, recalled his naive young manhood in Detroit, earning money by selling newspapers and shining shoes. Like many other youths, the fourteen-year-old Detroiter sold newspapers on Sunday mornings. But around 10 o'clock in the morning he would abandon them: "[I'd] go with my shoeshine kit to the back doors of saloons where I had most success in finding customers." Although a shoeshine normally cost five cents, some of the generous "drinkers would give me a dime," he said. "For two hours or more I would go from saloon to saloon and solicit the men standing at the bar." One Sunday he asked a mixed-race woman, who had apparently earned eighteen dollars the previous evening, if she wanted a shoeshine, and she consented. "I was startled," Madison recalled, "when she gave me a half dollar and told me to keep the change." Her male companion told her that she should not "squander" her hard-earned money. But the woman "maintained laughingly that the 'kid' no doubt needed the money more than she did." The naive young Madison hurriedly thanked her and ran out of the saloon, feeling somewhat "ashamed" about his "illegitimate" good will. Later, when he told some of his older companions about his "windfall," they informed him that "she was a prostitute and had many men that night." At the time, the fourteen-year-old shoeshine boy felt "both repelled and ashamed," he recalled, "prostitution being to me a degrading and ugly activity."

Although Madison initially felt repulsion and shame for these women, he gradually became "more tolerant toward them during that summer." In 1909, Champlain Street, where he worked as a clerk in a small factory, had "a concentration of brothels." Although he wondered how and why the young women became prostitutes, he often performed small errands for them, earning "a dime for the service." In time, he felt that they were "no different from other young women." Though more tolerant and sympathetic, Madison retained contradictory emotions, since he both "felt sorry for them" and "condemned them for taking what must have seemed to them an easy way out." Nonetheless, despite his shame and pity, he enjoyed youthful and illicit male pleasures. He "did not mind joining the factory men who crowded the windows on Friday afternoons to watch the girls on the back porches sitting scantily dressed and drying their hair."[43] As noted earlier in the introduction, labor activist Frank Marquart also recalled his early experiences as a young man deeply engaged in Detroit's bachelor culture on "Joy Street."

The commercialized and often sexualized institutions of the bachelor culture aroused the concern of the more moralistic manufacturers, such as Henry Ford. In 1908, a specific concern of Ford's was over what the *Ford Times* described as the "dude employe." This was the young worker who wore "a higher priced hat than his boss," who was "immaculately neat," and who "looks like a fashion plate." Always in debt, this reprobate worker spent "his evenings in cafes" and "dodge[d] out to look at the racing form and smoke a cigarette." He stayed up late and spent his earnings "in the gay life."[44] At the time, this dude employee was often a young and fairly skilled worker with plenty of cash to spend, one who left work to enjoy the commercial amusements of the Motor City.

When Henry Ford instituted the famous Five Dollar Day, he was especially concerned about the lifestyles and habits of young, single, male workers with money in their pockets. For these workers the requirements for the high wages were much more stringent than for more stable and responsible older and married workers. In 1914 the Ford Sociological Department demanded and defined "proven signs of thrift," by which they meant that "the employe shall not be addicted to the excessive use of liquor, nor gamble, nor engage in any malicious practices derogatory to good physical manhood or moral character; shall conserve his resources and make the most of his opportunities that are afforded him in his work."[45] These were stern proscriptions against the youthful excesses of the male bachelor culture and clearly chastised youthful male sexuality. When Ford sociological investigators discovered these workers' excesses, they lost the high wages and saw it halved.

And Ford was not the only one to recognize the transformation of the young, male, working-class culture. In 1920, Myron Watkins, a labor economist, offered an assembly-line version of Ford's dude employee. In his commentary on working-class fashion, he observed that "workingmen no longer like to be marked off as a class by their dress." When they emerged from the factory gates, the young auto workers no longer wore blue jeans, khaki overalls, or visor-less caps to mark their class positions as manual workers. The young working-class man, Watkins wrote, "goes to and from work in the garb of other folk, somewhat more soiled usually, but that, the only difference, is an unavoidable one." Often these working class dandies wore "a stiff straw or a Panama hat, a collar and necktie, a light-colored shirt occasionally of silk, a dark suit of street clothes and polished shoes." And such dress represented "the rule and not the exception for the young fellows who flock to the machines and benches in the automobile shops." These young men, Watkins concluded, "are proud—but not of their work!"[46] As they left the shop gates, these dandily clad workers headed for the wide array of urban venues for working-class bachelor amusement and entertainment—the saloons, pool rooms, burlesque shows, and brothels.

In his autobiography *Hard Stuff*, former Detroit mayor Coleman Young described an African American version of the dude employee prevalent during his youth in Detroit's Black Bottom in the 1920s. Young remembered that, for young African Americans, there were two role models at the time: "the hustlers, with their flashy clothes and money clips, and the Ford mules, as they were called, straggling home from work all dirty and sweaty and beat." He described the hustlers, often recent migrants from the South: "All over the streets you'd see black guys with their pants neatly pressed and their fingernails manicured and their yellow leather shoes shined so bright it made you squint." Their goal, Young declared, "was to remain unsullied by hard labor, and the young smartasses of Black Bottom seemed to have it knocked. Naturally, I aspired to be one of those fine gentlemen." A common theme in African American oral histories described Ford workers as too worn out to satisfy their wives or women when they came home from work. Young recalled: "They were so brazen as to taunt the Ford men about having their wives while the husbands were off bolting bumpers." He concluded: "To this day, it amazes me that I became a labor man."[47]

When the dude employees, "bachelor" auto workers, and even the Yale students walked through the factory gates after their long day of monotonous labor, they often had money in their pockets and encountered a vibrant and thriving world of commercialized leisure. Much of this world revolved around establishments offering sexual encounters with women. Detroit in the Prohibition era, Fleming noted, had "cat houses, blind pigs, speakeasies, and gambling houses," was a city "notorious for its smuggling, bootlegging, and sexual irregularities." The Yale students worked with the men who constantly cursed and talked filth on the shop floor and frequented Detroit's vaudeville houses, dance halls, brothels, and sporting establishments. Mimms, who worked in the Ford Rouge plant in the summer of 1925, testified to the attraction of these commercial amusements to Detroit auto workers. Although he found few of his workmates in the dance halls and in the "better class" movie houses, he discovered them at the vaudeville shows and burlesque houses. In front of the burlesque theater, he noted, "the entire group looked like factory workers. In the midst of the assembly of prowling men was a newsboy yelling; 'Buy a "Sunday Star" (a paper). It tells you where to go and how to get it.'"[48]

As the automobile industry expanded in the 1910s and 1920s, Detroit became a wide-open town for what then was described the "social evil." In a 1910 YMCA survey, investigators focused on the impact of the "social evil" on Detroit's working-class adolescents and young men. They spent time "on the streets in the 'red light' district observing those entering known houses of ill-repute, but no conversations or interviews were held there." They claimed that about 20 percent of the visitors to such establishments were young boys ages fourteen to seventeen. They found it "significant" that 60 percent of those seen entering such establishments" were between ages eighteen and twenty-one. In other words, they reported, amazingly, that fully 80 percent of the brothel visitors were boys and young men under twenty-one years old.[49]

Other YMCA investigators also uncovered the sleazy underside the Motor City's bachelor culture. One focused on the commercial amusements, the theaters and penny arcades. The burlesque theaters, he wrote, were "suggestive to the extreme," adding that the new small motion picture theaters were even "more suggestive." The penny arcades in the amusement parks showed "pictures in these [arcade] machines" that were "so vile that they would leave their influence on the strongest of characters or the purist of minds." Another investigator added that Detroit also possessed several publishers of obscene literature, pictures, and post cards that were "vulgarly suggestive and a menace to public morals." The local saloons and cigar stores often exhibited and sold these items.[50]

The amusement parks, with their the beer gardens, also contributed to moral subversion of boys and young men and of girls and young women. Attracted to "the crowd, electric lights and gaudy display," young onlookers eyed "the penny slot machines, filling their minds with nude pictures" and listened to music at "the dancing pavilion where hundreds of young fellows were 'picking up' girls to dance with, who were there for that purpose." "Beyond question," the investigator noted, the amusement park "was a feeder of the houses of prostitution and the immoral rooming houses." At a nearby 420-table beer garden and vaudeville show, "a large percentage of the young men were under twenty-one and at that period of life when the opposite sex is a large factor in their pleasure." The young women "gathered here were largely waitresses, shop and factory girls, and in a number of cases, they were older than the young men." The investigator witnessed the role models for the younger boys that the association targeted the "older boys by the scores meeting young girls and 'picking up' acquaintance with them on the streets and in the parks."[51]

Prostitution flourished in the Motor City to serve the sexual needs of large numbers of unattached men of the suitcase brigade from around the nation and from distant lands. If these men thought about and talked about sex on the shop floor, many others acted on their sexual conversations and fantasies when they walked the streets of Detroit. By the mid-1920s the Rockefeller Foundation funded two different American Social Hygiene Association investigations of prostitution in Detroit. Its reports labeled Detroit "the American Mecca of prostitutes" and the "blackest hole of crime and vice in the United States."[52]

In the early 1930s, the sociologist Glen S. Taylor summarized the evolution of prostitution as the automobile industry became embedded in the social and economic fabric of Detroit. During and after World War I, he said, "the vice situation assumed tremendous proportions as Detroit's pattern of industrial expansion brought on an influx of women from all parts of the country."[53] At the time, Detroit possessed a semi-official system of prostitution with a core red-light district within the central business district and adjacent the immigrant and African American neighborhoods. This was the location of many brothels and parlor houses, sexual venues that operated under "Dixon's regulations," named after the director of the Detroit Board of Health clinic. It was a regulatory system that applied "mainly to the regular 'houses' with their continuous inmates."[54]

The Detroit Health Department considered prostitutes "as spreaders of disease," and its "methods" were "designed solely with this end in view." According to Taylor, health officials "have no interest in suppression of prostitution, no interest in reforming prostitutes, none in seeing them sent off to prison or chased out of town." Instead they wanted to protect the families of men who visited and used prostitutes for their pleasure, to "recognize its existence and attempt to minimize its effects and provide temporary relief by keeping prostitutes clean for the sake of decent wives, mothers, and children."[55]

In January and March of 1926 three Rockefeller investigators covertly conducted two surveys of Detroit's sexual climate. The investigators found 269 venues operating openly and 134 operating clandestinely. In the two surveys, the number of women investigated was 1,932. "The rapid growth of Detroit and the failure of its police department to enforce laws against prostitution," the investigators reasoned, "have attracted prostitutes and pimps from all over the country." Subsequently, they surmised that "underworld characters have accepted Detroit as a sort of haven where they can operate flagrantly, and without much fear of coming in contact with authorities."[56]

Detroit, they reported, was "unusual" because "prostitution flagrantly flourishes within a mile radius of Cadillac Square, an area which embraces one of the main business sections of the city." In this area, prostitutes occupied "house after house," and "street corners were gathering places for street soliciting prostitutes." At night these streets were "also crowded with men who loiter about either to be accosted by streetwalkers or to enter the houses of prostitution which are nearby."[57]

The investigators reported that a Romanian official, known only Dr. R., visited the United States to survey social conditions. "Detroit," he concluded, "is the most wide-open town of any visited by me in the United States. Prostitution seems to be openly tolerated. Prostitutes were observed to be openly soliciting on the streets and from the houses." The "large number venereal cases" reported to the Health Department "impressed" him. Some immigrant men evidently could not recognize the subtle social and cultural cues that separated the New Women of the Jazz Age from actual prostitutes and streetwalkers. He added: "The attitude of men on the streets toward women is different than elsewhere. Men make indecent proposals to women who appear decent."[58] In some instances, the appearance and dress of the New Women sometimes resembled prostitutes. A German student who also toured several major American cities, including the industrial centers of Chicago, Pittsburgh, Cleveland, Milwaukee, Schenectady, and others, to study "industrial conditions" concluded that Detroit was the most vice-ridden of cities. The student, who apparently did "a great deal of personal investigating," added: "The girls run wild in Detroit, in fact it is the most open town [I have] seen in this country or in Europe."[59]

For the most part, working-class men seem to have been the principal visitors to Detroit brothels. One of the Yale students observed: "In the parks and on the streets where there were houses of prostitution, working men seemed to predominate." The Rockefeller investigators reported: "All types of customers can be seen entering and leaving the houses. One may see young, middle-aged, and in some instances, old men. Some appear to be foreigners, others natives. The majority, however, are men of the manual laboring class, along with youths who appear to have just started to go to work." Helen McGowan, who called herself the Motor City Madam, came from Chicago to Flint and then to Detroit in the 1920s and operated several parlor houses there over the course of her career. She focused on her working-class clientele in the 1920s and 1930s, asserting, "I am a working man's madam." To be sure, some of her clients were professionals, but "the majority of callers are from the working class. . . . I charge a fair price, well within the means of the lonely employed worker."[60]

The growth of prostitution in Detroit corresponded with the growth of the automobile industry with its well-paid young bachelor auto workers. Glen Taylor observed that after the mid-1920s, "the fortune of prostitution paralleled those of the Motor City as a whole. When Detroit boomed, so also did prostitution." Embarrassed by the findings of the Rockefeller investigators, Detroit mayor John W. Smith added: "This is a boom town even today and that must be remembered. It is practically a mining town in some ways. It lacks many of the facilities which would help young persons to keep straight." Taylor believed that "Detroit was passing through a period of more than merely a prostitutional boom."[61]

In the 1920s, Detroit prostitution took many forms—street walking, call flats, larger buffet flats, and parlor houses or brothels. Other methods to attract customers included "the time-honored custom of 'window-tapping'" or the hotel prostitute who worked with a bellboy or from the referrals from taxi drivers, restaurant owners, pool room operators, and others. As the "car culture" arrived in the mid 1920s, observers noted a new form—automobile prostitution, where women drove to Detroit hotels to find customers and bring them to their apartments. Though some of these methods appealed to middle-class men, streetwalking and accosting workers on streets was the most common form of Detroit prostitution, with call flats and parlor houses distant second and third options. Detroit's buffet flats were the naughtiest and raciest venues, offering women, drinks, and bawdy entertainment. Some parlor houses catered to the poorest clientele. In the "cheaper houses," the German student reported, "the men will just stand in line waiting their turn, at least this is so on Saturday and Sunday." These were called "'week-end' or pay-day houses." The cost was two dollars. He related: "They are disgustingly dirty."[62]

Many native-born and foreign-born rural migrants to the Motor City encountered an alien urban world in the Roaring Twenties, the age of the New Woman and the flapper. As they wandered the streets in search of female sexual companionship they often missed the subtle social cues and received mixed signals about the women they saw on the urban streets. The new styles of dress and appearance often confused them. Especially in the vice districts, the "respectable women," the Rockefeller investigators reported, "do not want to be seen in and about these streets during the day or night." When men met a woman, any woman, they often propositioned her. "Nowhere else in this country have [the investigators] seen men approach women so boldly who seem to be respectable," the report said. "They seem to expect every woman to be a prostitute." This happened even in Detroit's more respectable neighborhoods. "Men seem to be constantly roaming the streets," they reported, scouring the faces of women—'looking them over,' in the vernacular—apparently looking for the type which most appeals to them."[63]

Some Mexican migrants to industrial Detroit spoke about their difficulties in understanding American urban women. In the late 1920s, one noted: "It certainly is terrible the way these American women dress. It is nice yet it is quite a temptation to a man." Another said that when his friends went to "a cheap burlesque and movie," he never went along: "I only go in to see the movie, I can see the leg show in the streets." A third related the social dilemma of the recent migrant: "Often the Mexican cannot judge the American girl right. Sometimes he thinks she is a good girl when she isn't and sometimes he thinks that she is a prostitute or a loose living girl when she isn't."[64]

The prostitutes were mainly underpaid working-class women who simply could not live on their low wages, or they were working-class women of the Jazz Age who thrived on the high times and gay life that prostitution offered. During the Great Depression, Glenn Taylor interviewed eighty-five prostitutes in the Detroit House of Corrections and developed a social profile of them. He discovered that the jailed prostitutes were adult women and not young girls; only two were teenagers. Their median age was twenty-seven, their ages ranging from nineteen to forty eight. They were also urban-bred women. Almost 80 percent of the interviewees, Taylor noted, were from the city, 20 percent from the country.[65]

Moreover, the Detroit prostitutes tended to be American-born women. Though public opinion blamed immigrant women for "all manner of evils" and in the recent past immigrant women were "the popular American buga-boo," Taylor noted that "the *nationality* of our sample of prostitutes shows no undue proportion of the foreign-born." White women "of Irish extraction predominated," and other major groups were "German, French, Scotch, Polish, Dutch, and Spanish" women. African American women, mainly from the South, were often the targets of police, were probably overrepresented, and were "more frequently picked up by police officers."[66]

For Taylor, many of these women became prostitutes, because "the lot of the working girl was no easy one." He cataloged a long list of abuses: "Small salaries, long hours, little choice of occupations, limited opportunities for advancement, irregular work, exploitation by employers, and demands of sexual favors on threat of discharge by foremen."[67]

The twenty-eight experienced women who "worked the racket in other cities had mixed opinions on Detroit's desirability as a hustler's town." One claimed it was "the best in the union." A second said that "the cops are tough but the Johns are plentiful." A few others felt that Detroit was a "lousy" place. "Incidentally," Taylor concluded, "all agreed that Detroit was at least superior to her neighbor, Toledo—invariably characterized as a 'fifty cent' town." One young cynic told Taylor: "Sporting girls will exist as long as men and women do. If it weren't for us girls men would die or go crazy masturbating. They ought to have licensed houses though—to protect other women."[68]

Auto workers often formed central characters as a backdrop in some of these women's lives. One woman "hustled" before she married and continued after she married. "Her husband," Taylor reported, "works nights at Ford's and she works nights at home." The Ford worker did not mind his wife's hustling, "for his own wages are no more than enough than to support his mother and her three small children." Another woman worked as a waitress and had her first "sex experience" with an auto worker who apparently propositioned her at work. The Hudson worker came to eat where she worked and "she went to his room with him."[69]

The dreadful economic situation of working women often pushed them to the more lucrative field of prostitution. The most common previous occupations of the women Taylor interviewed were domestic labor, waitressing, clerical work, and light factory work, all low-wage positions. Their main reasons for leaving such jobs were "just tired of it," low pay, a lay off, a failed marriage, and the "lure of prostitution." Taylor noted that a frequent comment from the women related to an economic factor: "I'll quit in a minute if you'll find me a decent job that's just as easy for the same pay." The most frequently stated reasons for becoming a prostitute were economic hardship and the influence of friends. A few of women said they were in the racket for fun, the desire for pretty clothes, and the high life.[70]

During the Great Depression, the social situation for all Detroit women further worsened as unemployment rose and men lost their source of income. Working-class men could no longer be adequate providers for their families. In 1935 the novelist Erskine Caldwell toured the United States to assess the impact of the Great Depression on ordinary American men and women. He found Detroit to be one of the more dismal places for women and children. Since the city was about automobile production, the "mothers, the children, and the wives" were not important. He believed that "these persons are the trimmings, the shavings, the waste of automobile production."[71] Much in the same ways the 1920s physically and psychologically injured working men of Detroit, their wives and children were unneeded and became industrial detritus or scrap.

For the young working-class women of Detroit who could not find jobs, things were even more grim. With high levels of unemployment, male workers did not want the competition of women and drove them from the automobile shops and factories. With Detroit's legacy of semi-official prostitution, Caldwell claimed, "the city is taking care of the daughters" by allowing them to engage in the sex trade. Detroit, "with its customary graft," he suggested, was "in the red light business. Girls may ask for and receive a very insignificant-looking [health department] permit that is used by them as though they were certified public prostitutes." For young women from ages sixteen to twenty-five, prostitution, Caldwell maintained, was a means for the reduction of welfare rolls, and the Detroit Health Department was "blindly cooperative in spirit."[72]

As bad as this was, it was even worse for the youngest homeless girls. Those children between the ages nine and fifteen, he noted, "can be seen in downtown Detroit, slipping in and out of beer parlors, hovering in the shadows in the alleys, and whispering in the all night movie houses of Woodward Avenue." For these children, Caldwell related:

The few pennies they are able to earn are tossed to them on the floors of beer joints, crap rooms, and vacant buildings. Most of them are too young to be prostitutes with a health department certificate, but in the empty houses and apartment buildings they are taught to circumvent their ages for pennies, nickels, and dimes. In the back-room beer-joints they strip off their clothes, go through a few childish motions of dance routine, and reap a fistful of copper money from the floor. In the crap rooms, their buskings take the form of any type of entertainment called for.[73]

The sleazy and seedy world of debased male sexuality undermined and destroyed the lives of many young girls.

After mass production undermined and assailed their manhood, auto workers attempted to reassert or to reclaim it in numerous ways, some positive and some negative. They relied on shop traditions, some old and some new, to regain control over their working lives. They looked to and worked to build unions that would provide dignity, a structure to resist hated changes, and a family wage to enhance their personal and economic situations. They reveled in the sexual dimension of manhood in their ribald conversations on the shop floor and in the commercialized and sexual venues of the bachelor culture. As the Great Depression arrived and deepened, they would return to industrial unionism to mitigate the worst of the managerial abuses and would build a dense white and male culture at the workplace.

3

"Rats, Finks, and Stool Pigeons"

The Disreputable Manhood of Factory Spies in the 1920s and 1930s

In 1906 an early auto union used a typical union invective against the vile men who were the factory spies. Its journal reported on a union informer uncovered in a wagon shop, describing the corporate agent as a "cheap Judas." This man, it noted, "would for a few dollars" through "his lying treachery betray" his fellow workers. The company operative "would prevent his fellow workers from getting better conditions."[1] Two decades later the angry and vicious vilification against industrial spies continued. In the mid-1920s, one machinist excoriated "these leeches and blackmailers." These anti-union men were "blackmailing and sneaking renegades" and "treacherous ex-pickpockets, ex-porch climbers, and degenerates."[2] Earlier, such angry language was reserved for scabs and strikebreakers who stole another worker's job and livelihood. The industrial spy, who betrayed his loyalty to his class, genuinely represented the negative case for the auto workers' notions of exemplary manhood, of real union manhood, of the manhood of the fighter for unionism or the breadwinner of a family.

This army of industrial mercenaries included many individualistic and anti-labor figures—union supporters called them rats, stool pigeons, finks, sluggers, thugs, goons, scabs, and strikebreakers. They were the union movement's negative examples that separated the honorable and respectable manhood of union men from the dishonorable and disreputable spies and thugs. Often violent men from the underside of urban America, these mercenaries of the class war spent several decades battling industrial unionism.

From the earliest years, the places where auto workers labored have been plagued by the insidious activities of factory spies. Except for the investigations of the La Follette Civil Liberties Committee, the documentation of industrial espionage is scattered and fragmentary, but it can be pieced together from a variety of sources. Harold Cranefield, an attorney and La Follette investigator, characterized industrial espionage as "a shabby and nasty business." While working with the new National Labor Relations Board, he observed: "We were sure from interviews with people who had been trying to organize the plants under the NIRA [National Industrial Recovery Act] that the use of undercover agents was widespread." This spy system, he added, "had been very effective." An effort at unionization "would start out with much enthusiasm. Then the men would observe the discharge of their leadership for patently false reasons and would fall away in terror of losing their jobs." The spy system revealed "some tragic personal experiences," involving workers who informed on their workmates. Displaying "scorn and pity" toward shop mates who "sold out their neighbors" for several extra dollars each week, union members often shunned and sometimes physically assaulted these traitors to the union cause.[3]

In 1936 Heber Blankenhorn, an industrial economist working for the NLRB, attempted to estimate the extent of industrial espionage in American industry in the 1930s. He told the La Follette Committee that "over 200" industrial espionage agencies existed "in every part of the country and in every industry." Although the precise "number of operatives" was "unknown," he said that, "minimum estimates [suggested that] . . . there are at least 40,000 paid operatives and stool pigeons regularly employed in labor groups by employers in these organizations."[4] Industrial spying in America originated in the 1870s as unions grew and dramatically increased during the World War I era into the 1920s and 1930s. These agencies often drew their supervisors and agents, both organizers and spies, from the seedy netherworld of urban America. "Gangsters," he reported, "sometimes 'come up' through strikebreaking, and as heads of political gangs often retain an interest, sometimes vested, in strikebreaking for a section an industry or of a city." According to Blankenhorn, the number of local unions "broken up or emasculated" by factory spies was "very high."[5] Sometimes a majority of local union officers and board members were actually paid agents of the espionage firms.

For automobile workers, spy systems existed from the very origins of the automobile industry. For example, in 1903 the Carriage and Wagon Workers' Union, an early predecessor to auto unions, published a copy of a solicitation letter of the Thiel Detective Service Company. This letter to manufacturers suggested that the best way to obtain information on the workforce was the "placing of one or more detectives among them as employees, whose duty it was to investigate thoroughly as to existing conditions and report in detail therein." In this manner, the management would be "fully posted as to any dissatisfaction or agitation." Aside from possessing "a large force of detectives skilled and experienced in this class of work, carefully selected from the various nationalities, professions, and trades," the Thiel service was also, in the event of a strike, "prepared to promptly furnish guards, as well as to recruit and deliver workmen of the various trades required." Its "experienced operatives" could also "collect evidence in connection with the perpetration of any acts of violence . . . for the purpose of criminally prosecuting such persons." The union journal labeled such people "spies, scabs, and cutthroats." The rules of "Capitalist class," it added, "are based on the grossest injustice imaginable and it gathers in the lowest, meanest, vilest element to be found in the present world of civilized cannibalism."[6]

In 1906 the same union also warned its members to "Beware of this Spy," George Miller, who worked in the Muessler wagon shop. A member of one union local, Miller was "a smooth-talking individual, but an enthusiast for the union." During impromptu shop discussions on negotiations with the wagon shop, he was the agitator "invariably in favor of a strike." When the local finally did go on strike "to enforce demands for a closed shop agreement," Miller requested "immediate" assignment to picket duty. "He never advocated open violence," the union reported, "but in a surreptitious way, by hints and innuendos, suggested action that would lead to overt acts [of violence]." Although arrested during the strike with two other union members, the provocateur "developed a case of blood-poisoning in his foot" while in jail. A "mysterious stranger" paid his $5,000 bail. Just before his trial, he skipped town and disappeared. Apparently, the union noted, Miller was "getting $100 per month[7] as a spy for Corporation Auxiliary . . . the secret spy bureau of the Manufacturers' Association." The union published his photograph and warned other carriage and wagon workers to beware of his insidious activities.[8]

As the new era of mass production dawned, the Ford Motor Company used such disreputable spies to inform on fellow shop mates who might be slackers, radicals, or union advocates. As early as the 1910s, William C. Klann, the head of Ford's engine assembly department, directed about three hundred workers. The engine assembly foreman recalled: "We always had spies or agents to get information on the union." He added that even S. S. Marquis, later the head of the paternalistic Ford Sociological Department, knew about the spies. Klann reported, "I had twenty-five fellows working for me." In other words, he had about one spy for every dozen workers in his assembly department. The spies worked in and reported on the different operations of engine assembly. "We didn't get written reports from all these fellows. They were all verbal."[9]

Sometimes Klann would utilize the subterfuge of shop spies to detect and to dismiss recalcitrant and disgruntled workers. If he heard that a department planned to "lay down" on the job, he would assign a man to monitor the department. This man would be new to the particular job and also a Ford subforeman. The undercover spy would work fast and "then we'd see what they would say to him." When one of the shop workers tried to convince the "new" worker to go slow, his name would be sent to Klann, who then passed on the offending worker's name to the employment office, where they would create an excuse to fire him.[10]

Though industrial espionage emerged in the late nineteenth century through the early twentieth, it genuinely flourished during World War I and later into the 1920s and early 1930s. In the automobile industry, no firm exceeded the Ford expansion of its spy system, which eventually evolved into Harry Bennett's infamous Service Department with its full array of gangsters, plug-uglies, and thugs. In the production-oriented war years, fears and concerns about slackers, immigrant radicals, pro-German saboteurs, and even union activists caused the paternalist Ford firm to slide into the outright repression of shop-floor dissidents. In addition to conventional factory spies, networks of American Protective League patriots, Detroit employer-association agents, and military intelligence officers all reported to Ford officials on the supposed illicit activities in the plant and in the local communities. After World War I the brutal Service Department supplanted the more welfare-oriented Sociological Department at the Ford firm.[11]

Near the end of World War I, Edmund Leigh, the chief of the War Department's plant protection program, later denounced the Ford Motor Company's use of hired industrial spies. "Henry Ford," he reported, "is accustomed to employing criminals in his plant." This, Leigh believed, was "hardly to be considered the best selection of tools." It was not "a good or safe policy to go to the criminal classes to seek good and faithful men." He also criticized the industrial espionage firms, since "the proportion of ex-convicts employed by Detective Agencies is exceedingly large."[12]

Leigh also strongly disapproved of the wartime role and function of private detective agencies, since the profit motive often shaped the nature of their reports. With private detective agencies, the "value of information" thus obtained was "practically worthless"; the war served as "merely the opportunity to increase their revenue by working upon the fears of manufacturers and

introducing their operatives into the plants." Defending his turf of governmental plant protection, he noted that his organization was "imbued solely
by the question of loyalty in the performance of their duties," whereas the
private detective agencies were "imbued solely with the mercenary spirit."[13]
Nonetheless, the wartime counterespionage program fostered the increased
use of shop-floor espionage in the postwar years. In the early 1920s the U.S.
War Department's plant protection program's tradition of shop-floor surveillance morphed into War Plans White, a government program that spied on
leftist workplace radicals in an effort to insure against domestic security in
the face of feared Soviet-style insurrections.[14]

The rapid rise of the automobile industry made the 1920s the heyday for
industrial espionage throughout the industrial Midwest where auto production
predominated. For example, after a 1919 strike, factory spies apparently began
to appear in an Akron machinist's lodge. Two years later, S. L. Newman, the
lodge business agent, described the Akron "vicinity" as "infested with spies"
and condemned the injury to union members who lost their jobs. Recently, his
union had uncovered several spies, some who even served in union positions.
These "dicks" were "despicable creatures" who carried out their "nefarious"
and "contemptible" work in his machinists' local. Two spies even served as
trustees of the IAM lodge—one was an "experienced spy" and another posed
as "a revolutionary member of the working class movement." The latter even
managed to serve as recording secretary for the local Akron IWW organization.
Newman urged fellow IAM members to "lift the veil that has been covering
our eyes and clouding our brains and view our employers in their real light
. . . willing to pay men to become traitors to their fellow workers."[15]

Auto worker unionists often challenged the manhood of these anti-union
mercenaries. In early 1920s, W. A. Logan, an early Auto Workers' Union
leader, criticized the unmanly behavior of those who might favor their employers. "In every shop and factory," he observed, "there are to be found those
who fawn on the boss and curry favor." Such workers, he added, "lack the
moral fiber of those who face the world squarely and who can be depended
upon to stand up for their rights." These workers "meekly bend their necks to
the yoke and submit to any conditions without protest." In Logan's eyes, they
were "weak, servile, and submissive; they make ideal tools for the employer."
Simply put, these fawning and meek anti-union workers did not demonstrate
or display the independence and control of a skilled worker. In a word, they
were unmanly.[16]

The industrial spy system expanded rapidly with the growth of the automobile industry through the 1920s. John S. Martin, an early AWU organizer,

recalled the widespread systems of industrial espionage that appeared in Detroit at that time. "It was common practice in almost every automobile plant in America," he wrote to Edward Levinson, "to maintain 2% of their employees as industrial detectives whose chief job it was to see that no union got its chin above the water line." He listed several major national firms— Corporations Auxiliary, Pinkerton, Railway Audit and Supply, and Sherman, as well as "hundreds of little outfits." So extensive was spying that the early AWU organizers "naturally took it for granted that every Local Secretary was a dick and generally found that the entire set of officers was also." Early membership meetings always had a "fair crowd," because "the Detectives never missed" a union meeting.[17] Another early union organizer, Nick DiGaetano, believed that the early Auto Workers Union "almost succeeded." The auto union "was a new union coming up, and it meant to organize all auto workers on an industrial basis. But there was too much dissention created by stool-pigeons."[18] Industrial espionage delayed automotive industrial unionism until the mid-1930s.

The espionage firms and detective agencies expected a lot from their agents and spies and often provided detailed suggestions for the people who wrote their reports. These suggestions revealed the full range of issues that concerned their corporate clients. In 1922, *The Auto Worker* published an excerpt of the rules taken from "the instruction book furnished to labor spies by one of the large detective agencies." Emphasizing the necessity for "the utmost secrecy," these instructions emphasized that the main office would supply a special "code name" to the spy. The rules told the new factory spy to "sign all reports and communications with this code name, and do not at any time use your full name." They also advised making many friendships, both at and after work, and "upon leaving the premises," the book prompted, "try to gain their confidence and accompany them to their various places of entertainment and amusement."[19]

When the novice agent first appeared at the job, the instructions urged him to learn his new environment and his new job. It advised not "to do a whole lot of secret service work during the first days of your employment, but observe closely your surroundings and the employees, and familiarize yourself most especially with your own line of work on the premises, thus enabling you to do your work capable and well." Once he accomplished these, the factory spy could then devote himself to his main task, watching and reporting on shop-floor activities and potential problems.[20]

Specifically, the detective agency desired to know the sentiments of the workers, their dissatisfactions, the possibilities for job actions, and any activities of union organizers. A new agent's report should cover "all questions which may be discussed among the employees as to whether or not they are dissatisfied with the working conditions, the number of hours employed, the amount of their earnings . . ., etc." Moreover, it should provide "in detail all matters of agitations regarding strikes and any other labor troubles of that kind." If the spy encountered a "secret" union organizer or "any agitator who may be attempting a 'walkout,'" he should immediately get in touch with his handler at the detective agency.[21]

Nothing was too mundane to include in the report. The labor spy should "cover clearly [the] entire daily routine and operations" whether or not the details appeared to be of "importance," since this was precisely the kind of "information of most importance to us and our Client." The agency desired information on whether or not the foreman or superintendent was "unfriendly" toward the workers and even if a fellow worker was "lax in the performance of his duty" or was "turning out inferior work." The reason for this was the detective agency's desire, and probably advertised promise, to help "raise the entire standard of efficiency" for the manufacturer.[22]

Similarly, another 1929 guide for factory operatives contained a long list of 145 individual issues to be included in reports to help the novice industrial spy in his work. The list revealed the extraordinarily wide range of concerns that factory managers had about the workplace and the workforce. Some issues dealt with the improper behavior of workers. These included ringing up another's time card, arriving late, loafing, smoking, gambling, stealing, doing personal work on company time, agitating or finding fault, or espousing IWW, red, or socialist ideas while at work. In one instance, the suggestions sought out good worker behavior and wanted to know those who "deserve credit for good faithful service and work." They also wanted to know about how other workmen performed their jobs, notably set-up men, janitors, millwrights, and inspectors. The potential spy should also report on the "real" reasons for quitting and leaving jobs.[23]

The spy agency wanted reports on the "character of the employes," the "attitude of the men towards the company," the worker attitude towards unions, the causes of any labor trouble in the past, and present or future prospects of labor agitation. Many issues concerned the conditions, procedures, and operations of the plant, such as lighting, safety, machine maintenance, cleanliness, and even "instances where certain operations could be done in more economical methods." If a foreman displayed "favoritism" toward the men, the spy firm wanted to know so that such behavior could be reported to its client. Industrial espionage dealt with much more than the attitudes and activities of workers; it also focused on the overall efficiency in the operation of the client's firm.[24]

Through the 1920s factory spies could be found almost anywhere—on the shop floor, on public transportation, or even in local taverns. Their presence in automobile shops and departments was pervasive. Bill McKie, a Communist union organizer at Ford, told the Automobile Labor Board: "But you rarely find Ford men speaking to each other. The service men come along in the lunch hour and say 'move' and the men move." A Ford worker could not speak while at work or during their lunch break. The industrial spies and stool pigeons were often found scattered throughout the local communities where workers lived and gathered. "They send these service men," McKie continued, "to the streetcars and places where men congregate to hear what they say." Especially as the CIO movement grew, Ralph Rimar, a Ford agent and outside investigator, concurred: "A number of men were employed by Ford to check up on workers. They would get on streetcars and ride back and forth in order to get badge numbers." Ingvald Bjaland, a Flint Fisher Body worker, told an interviewer that if a spy really wanted information, he would not go to the plant where the men were too busy working. Instead, he would "go to the bar where all the guys from the union hang out. . . . All he'd have to do is go to the local bar somewhere where they are and he'd find out everything he wants to know. A supervisor can go with a bunch of guys in a bar and learn more in five minutes than you can in the plant in a month." Stan Coulthard, a union organizer and British migrant to Detroit, recalled a hotdog vendor who came into his workplace: "Without any warning I said to him: 'Are you working for Pinkerton or is it one of the others?' The bloke went white so I knew immediately I was on to something. I told him that he had to mid-day to get out of town or I'd set the lads on him." Fearful of union retribution, he bolted and ran. Coulthard wrote, "He never even waited to collect his money."[25]

Many UAW founders, both local and national leaders, decried the pervasive presence of industrial spies in the early years of union organization. A Saint Louis Fisher Body worker said that the General Motors "spy system" was so extensive and effective "that it would make Scotland Yard look like an amateur detective agency." Anything a worker said or did was soon known to management. "Nothing," he declared, "can be said or done but the company knows all about it. Everything that is said or done at union meetings is reported in their office by [a] spy." Louis Adkins, a trimmer in the Flint Fisher Body plant, mentioned two men in the Chevrolet plant who were GM Pinkerton spies. As machine oilers, they had free range to roam the shops.

Their task "was to be in everything. Every time you saw two people talking together, they would get in on the conversation. They were always any place wherever there was a group of people." Asked about how such spies were caught, Adkins responded, "They had nose trouble. They were too obvious, too ambitious, too eager to find out and to be into things." The Janesville unionists wreaked their vengeance on one of the two oilers when they "ransacked" his room and found out that "he was a Pinkerton man." After uncovering him as a spy, "he was taken out of the plant." Given the strong union feelings about stool pigeons and rats, his physical ejection from the plant was most likely not a very gentle one.[26]

Often the detective agencies surreptitiously managed to infiltrate and to staff the offices of the unions that represented workers. According to a La Follette Committee summary report, the "largest single industrial client" of the Pinkerton agency was the General Motors Corporation. In the mid-1930s, two hundred Pinkerton agents covered about sixty GM plants. They "held offices of varying importance," ranging from local union president down to union committeemen. Fourteen were local presidents, twenty were local secretaries, and fourteen were local recording secretaries. They often held those "positions where they were the first to learn the names of new members." The La Follette report concluded: "Thus fifty-two [Pinkerton] operatives were concentrated in the highly important United Automobile Workers Union, reporting on the organization drive in General Motors."[27]

During the 1934 unionization upsurge encouraged by the announcement of the creation of the Automobile Labor Board, Flint auto workers rushed into the new AFL Federal Union of Automobile Workers in the heart of the GM empire. Some twenty thousand workers enrolled in the union cause. But, at the time, General Motors utilized the services of fourteen detective agencies. In GM plants, three Corporations Auxiliary and two Pinkerton agents were on the thirteen-member federal union executive board. The spies included the chair of the union's legislative committee and the chair of the organizing committee. One spy was even a delegate to the UAW's founding convention in South Bend, Indiana. One GM worker told the La Follette Committee: "I thought the whole executive board were spies." By 1936, the membership dropped to 120. When UAW organizers Robert Travis and Wyndham Mortimer arrived in Flint to rebuild the union, GM even assigned a Pinkerton operative to trail them. The two organizers discovered a "community in a state of terror." So terrified were Flint auto workers that Travis and Mortimer had to conduct secret meetings in dark basements as they slowly and painfully rebuilt the union local that eventually conducted the famous GM sit-down strike.[28]

As the General Motors case demonstrated, factory spies managed to occupy critical positions as union officers in the new and expanding UAW unions. A Michigan Steel Tube Products grinder remembered one spy, "an officer in the UAW, a high officer," who was a Pinkerton agent and who interviewed new union members, took their names, and passed the information to managers. In one instance, a plant manger came to his department and spoke with the foremen. Then, the worker reported, "he went around pointing us out one by one . . . 'This son of a bitch joined the union. That son of a bitch joined the union and that son of a bitch joined the union.'" Only later did he learn that the information came from the Pinkerton spy.[29]

Another local UAW leader agreed. "In every single local union we established," he related, "several" officers "were paid stool pigeons, but we did not know it." They were often operatives of Pinkerton, Corporations Auxiliary, or the Railway Audit and Inspection firms. This body worker added: "Every imaginable kind of stool pigeon was brought into the industry to spy, and it was not very hard to find some decent people, for instance, to take on a spying job." Hard pressed in hard times to provide for their families, decent workers sometimes took these positions associated with the seedy underside of the American industrial economy to provide for their families. Most of the factory spies, Cranefield observed, were "recruited by what operatives of these companies themselves used to call 'hooking.'" The detective agencies approached "ordinary working men with no experience in undercover work at all" and offered a "bribe" to make seemingly innocuous reports to them. Once hooked, these workers obtained a privileged factory job for regular wages and earned a bit more with their reports to the espionage corporation.[30]

Once they occupied important union positions, the industrial spies had access to strategic information about the plans of unions and their organizational campaigns. These spies and their employers knew about "news of organizers coming into town, contacts the organizers make among his [the employer's] employes, the names of employes who show interest in the union, the names and addresses of employes who join the union, all organization plans, all activities of the union." With such information "readily available to the employer" it was "as though he himself were running the union." If a strike was called, "the employer is forewarned. The strike plans, the strength of the union in ability to hold, its weaknesses are intimately known to the employer."[31]

An important consequence of industrial espionage was the fear generated among ordinary workers who might consider enlisting in the union cause. Maurice Sugar, an attorney for Detroit unions through the late 1920s and into the 1930s, testified before the Automobile Labor Board in 1934. He recounted and emphasized what a Ford worker said the day before about the deep fears of many Ford workers: "The men, he says, cannot talk to each other in the factory, they cannot talk to each other on the bridge leaving the factory. They are afraid to talk to each other in the street car on the way home, and he explains that they are afraid to talk to him in their homes about what is going on in the Ford plant. That is industrial slavery." When Sugar described Ford service man as "a high falutin' name for spy," he received vigorous applause from the Detroit working-class audience.[32]

Cranefield recounted the early efforts at unionization: "Organization proceeded secretly in '33. '34, '35 in small groups." Organizers conducted "basement meetings with blankets over the windows." At these secret meetings, a half-dozen or so men would discuss how to organize their plants and to build a union. "Then the most articulate and responsive men of that group would be fired five or six days later or the next week for some trivial, trumped up infraction of some plant rule or other." After the creation of the La Follette Committee assisted in the exposing of industrial spies, union organizers would examine the names of those who were not fired and interview them. Through a "laborious" process the organizers and the government investigators made an "estimate of who might possibly been the traitor in that group." Sometimes, Cranefield recalled, "It would take weeks to isolate a man."[33]

Other workers concurred about the widespread fear in the automobile plants. A Janesville Chevrolet machinist related that it was "not healthy to let it be known that you were a [union] member" due to "their sleuths and their spies, or . . . their finks, throughout the shop." In those early years of organization, no one could be trusted. He added: "You were not always quite sure of whom you were talking to." A Flint Fisher Body worker said, "We were always suspicious. . . . We were suspicious of our best friends, practically." So deep were these fears that workers often attempted to conceal their identities as they demonstrated their union support. "I remember marching in the Labor Day parade," a Ford foundry worker related. "We had to wear masks. The Ford workers had to wear masks so that nobody would identify them." As others recalled, when workers went to a union meeting, "later two or three of the fellows were fired." No one knew who the informants were; fear bred suspicion: "Every body was getting suspicious of every one." A White Motor Company worker remembered that "in the beginning they had fears. The people that paid their [union] dues made sure that the boss did not see. There was this fear for many years." Ultimately, he said, the successful UAW campaign for unionization dispelled many of those fears. "As the union grew stronger, then the fear disappeared."[34]

Clayton Fountain, later a strong UAW supporter and activist, remembered how the fear of spies almost undermined his union activism. In 1936 he decided to join the UAW. However, he said, "I knew that this decision meant danger to myself and my family. It held the possibility of getting fired and blacklisted, so that I could never work in the industry again if the organization drive failed." He feared much more than his loss of employment and his inability to support his family: "It meant personal danger from goons and spies employed by the auto companies to resist unionism. Nevertheless, I decided in favor of the union."[35]

One local union leader described the complicated tactics that he and others employed to avoid being dogged and followed by corporate spies. "We were trailed and followed night and day by a management spy system," mainly by corporate groups such as the National Association of Manufacturers, the Michigan Manufacturers' Association, the Automobile Manufacturers' Association, the Metal Trades Association, and others. The union organizers went to considerable lengths to shake off the various industrial spies as they attempted to organize auto workers. They needed "to change cars two or three times on the way over to this guy's house or pull up in a guy's drive, go in the house, and go out of the back of the garage with another car and take a long way route to the fellow's house" to keep the spies off their trail. The union crusade to organize, he concluded, was a "cloak and dagger type of operation as far as hiding and keeping everything quiet."[36]

Three instances illustrate how the American industrial espionage system functioned. One involved the assignment of two spies to befriend Richard Frankensteen, a Dodge union activist who was rising to prominence after the formation of the United Auto Workers in the mid 1930s. A second concerned Gerald Corkum, a Plymouth worker and local union leader, someone *Fortune* magazine described as a typical and exemplary auto worker in 1935. The third revealed the hooking and uncovering of Harold D. Lewis, a Janesville Chevrolet worker and local UAW officer.

Richard Frankensteen, a UAW organizer and worker in the Dodge plant, had attracted the attention of Chrysler officials as a rising star in auto unionism. His case illustrated the pernicious nature of industrial espionage to restrict union success and growth in the mid-1930s. The Chrysler firm contracted Corporations Auxiliary to assign a spy to befriend Frankensteen. The detective agency later assigned an even more senior agent to cultivate the future UAW leader. In 1935 Richard Frankensteen, who started as a leader in the Dodge company union, organized and became the first president of an independent union at Chrysler, the Automotive Industrial Workers Association, and later became a prominent UAW leader. At the time, Chrysler officials were "confused" about Frankensteen's election to chair the bargaining committee of the firms shop representation plan and worried about why "a very desirable employee" was apparently "causing them so much trouble." John C. Andrews, a Corporations Auxiliary spy identified as L-392, eventually befriended Frankensteen, and they "became very well acquainted," so well that their two families were "fraternizing together." Over time, Andrews earned "many, many thousands of dollars from Chrysler for the purpose of espionage." When the La Follette Committee showed Frankensteen the spy's reports, the "shocked" Dodge union leader found it "inconceivable" that "a man could be as close as we had been and still do what he had done." The relationship was so close that Frankensteen's wife prepared and sent food to Andrew's wife when she was ill. In the summer of 1935 the two families spent their vacation together at a cabin on Lake Orion. There, Andrews, who earned $40 per month plus expenses, introduced Frankensteen to Mr. A. J. Bath, allegedly a rich uncle, but Bath was actually a senior Corporations Auxiliary spy. For several weeks, Bath wined and dined Frankensteen and his family. Bath and Andrews discovered that Frankensteen had attended college, been "a leader in his debating teams and in his athletic activities," and was "a very smart fellow in every respect." As Frankensteen was clearly not the ideal candidate for work on a Dodge assembly line, the espionage firm concluded "that a mistake had been made in hiring" him.[37]

When the La Follette Committee revealed the reports of Andrews and Bath to Frankensteen in early 1937, he read them and confirmed the details of his vacation with them. About Andrews, he commented, "I thought I knew him intimately." As for Bath, the union activist recalled: "I had a very splendid impression of him." Because Bath was introduced as a millionaire theater producer, Frankensteen believed that he and Bath shared a strong interest in "theatricals and the show business." During the Lake Orion vacation, the supposedly wealthy Bath "would not let us spend a penny on everything that was purchased," Frankensteen said. Andrews and Frankensteen did, however, share the expenses for their rented summer cottage and boat.[38]

Frankensteen first met Andrews in 1934 and knew him as an Automotive Industrial Workers Association union activist in the Dodge paint department. Since Frankensteen did not own a car, Andrews volunteered to drive him from one organizational meeting to another for Dodge workers. He was with Frankensteen five nights a week and on Sundays, following him in the frantic effort to organize Dodge workers into the AWIA. "Our acquaintanceship," Frankensteen said, "became very friendly. He was a nice clean chap and, I thought, a very fine young fellow." Andrews also insinuated himself into union organizational activities, apparently double dipping from both the independent union and the espionage firm for gas, meals, and other expenses. In fact he was "very intimate with all of the members of our organization, the officers." And he was sometimes allowed "to sit in on executive committee meetings." Frankensteen said, "Every movement that I made was reported to the Corporation Auxiliary and subsequently to the Chrysler Corporation."[39]

Within the labor organization, Andrews also apparently played the role of an agent provocateur. "He was," Frankensteen said, "very militant, in fact he agitated and urged us to go on strike this year." At union strike strategy meetings after the layoff of three thousand Dodge workers, "John Andrews sat at the table and urged us, using some very strong language to use force and violence."[40]

By then Frankensteen had affiliated with the UAW, and he subsequently voiced his opinion, one shared by many of his fellow Dodge workers of factory spies: "Get rid of the spies or we'll stop work!" Claiming to represent a majority of the Dodge workers, the UAW leader threatened: "We won't work in the same plants with labor spies."[41] Two months later in early March, the Dodge workers followed the example of their fellow workers in General Motors plants around the nation and sat down in several Detroit Chrysler plants and stayed until a March 24 agreement, calling for vacating the plants and obtaining union recognition a week later.

A second example of how the espionage network functioned is the Gerald Corkum case. In 1935, *Fortune* magazine characterized Corkum as the "typical" American worker. The business magazine selected and featured Corkum, a forty-two-year-old Plymouth spray painter and local union leader, as a model Detroit auto employee. It described him "as typical of the class that keeps America on wheels." Raised in Massachusetts, the young man moved to Detroit at age seventeen to become an auto worker in 1912. After his arrival, Corkum worked a variety of jobs in nearly a dozen or so Detroit plants, including Hupmobile, Hudson, Packard, and Chalmers, before he eventually settled into the Plymouth plant, earning approximately $1,200 a year as a spray painter in 1937. He worked in numerous unskilled classifications and claimed that he worked "pretty much all over the car." His wife worked for the Ternstedt Manufacturing Company, a small auto-parts firm, and earned an additional $400 a year for five months' work. "Her earnings," *Fortune* reported, meant the difference "between a measure of comfort and bare subsistence."[42]

In 1927 the Corkums purchased a home, which they almost lost during the economic collapse of 1929. But a federal Home Owner's Loan Corporation loan allowed him to save it, and subsequently he became "an enthusiastic Roosevelt man." He worried and worked in a highly seasonal industry in hard economic times, receiving a widely fluctuating biweekly pay envelope whose contents ranged from $25 to $76; he constantly feared the loss of his home. At age forty, the prospect of unemployment in a young man's industry always loomed over Corkum's seemingly secure life. The *Detroit Times* touted Corkum's commendable work habits. Henry Ford would have loved such a worker: "He is usually on the early shift and leads a sober life, retiring early and getting up at 5:30 A.M. to ride to work. . . . He does not drink or smoke." At the 1934 Detroit Automobile Labor Board hearings, Corkum even testified on the effects of technical change and the speed-up on his spray painter's job. And, revealing his conservative labor views, this typical Detroit worker had recently been elected president of the Plymouth AFL union and had subsequently affiliated his local with the Detroit Federation of Labor.[43]

But *Fortune's* ideal worker also had another, more insidious identity—factory spy. Since 1934, Corkum had directed four other spies for the Plymouth plant manager. Possibly, his fears about the loss of his home and his likely aging out of his job pushed him to seek the additional income of industrial spy. By March 1937 the Plymouth local affiliated with the growing UAW. Two months earlier, Corkum lost the Plymouth local's presidential election to William Frankowski. The new local leaders accused Corkum of being a factory spy for the Chrysler Corporation. Frankowski claimed that during the recent Chrysler sit-down strikes, Corkum "attempted to start a 'back to work' movement" and charged him with "acting like a company spy." The small size of the local under Corkum's leadership also raised the suspicions of the Plymouth unionists. When he lost the election, union membership was a mere sixty workers. Through the first part of 1937, the new leadership rapidly expanded the numbers to more than ten thousand workers. After making his charge, Frankowski, the new Plymouth union president, allegedly invited Corkum to his home, where several union men threatened to beat him. After the initial interrogation and threats, they all went to the Dodge local union hall, where the accused factory spy claimed that he was beaten. There, Corkum signed a confession and also implicated others as his assistants.[44]

In his confession Corkum said that Ray Moore, the Plymouth plant manager, hired him in 1934 and instructed him to report about union activities to the personnel director and to his foreman. Two of the other spies were Glen Walker and Joseph Shutok, who both received $50 a month for their reports on union meetings. As a result of their information, when layoffs came, a number of union men were dismissed. Corkum also confessed to leading a meeting with twenty or more conservative union members during the Chrysler sit-down strikes "to delay the strike as well as influence the officers to act more rationally regarding calling strikes." For this, he received an additional $75 for himself and the other spies. His report on "communist and radical activities" resulted in the firing of several active Plymouth unionists. Earlier, Corkum also scouted out "the set-up of the new local" in Flint at the beginning of the GM sit-down strike. He expressed his displeasure at the Flint UAW organizers who replaced the Flint locals' leaders and resisted the UAW effort to reorganize his local along similar lines.

Though Frankowski and other UAW members denied physical abuse, Corkum claimed, "I signed that paper that I was a stool pigeon because they were slapping me around." At first, he thought the "worst thing" was giving up "his home, his livelihood and his future." But upon reflection, he decided "that part of it wasn't so bad at all." He and his wife "were planning to leave after the production season ended anyway."[45]

In another instance, the unfortunate case of General Motors worker Harold D. Lewis typified the experience of the "hooked" worker, duped into spying by Pinkerton agents. Lewis was a UAW Local 121 member at the Janesville General Motors Chevrolet plant. In the midst of the rapid UAW growth in 1936, the Pinkerton Detective Agency managed to "hook" him as a factory spy. He was an unloader and an occasional checker at the General Motors plant and also a trustee for the UAW local. Between February 5 and April 19, 1936, Lewis wrote approximately thirty reports to his Pinkerton handler about the activities and events in his General Motors plant. In his union trial testimony, Lewis claimed that on an "awful blustery" Saturday night in February, a stranger rang his doorbell, "an elderly man with his overcoat collar turned up." After he invited the stranger into his home, the man introduced himself as "Parker," asking to speak with Lewis in private. They went into the kitchen to talk. The stranger, Lewis testified, "asked me some questions. He seemed to know me pretty well. I couldn't figure out how he knew my name." Parker noted that Lewis had worked for General Motors for some time and asked if he was "interested in earning a little extra money?"[46]

The UAW member responded cautiously, saying no at first but then listened to the stranger's offer. Claiming to be a GM investor, the unknown visitor asserted: "I've got quite a little stock in the Company, and I would like to know what is going on down there." He suggested that Lewis place himself in the position of someone whose father owned the plant, who was not there, and who would be reporting on conditions to his absent father.

For an hour and a half, Parker attempted to convince suspicious Lewis to accept his proposition and to write him reports on the plant. Finally, Parker placed two $5 bills on the kitchen table; he told Lewis that it would be for two weeks' work and that the reluctant Lewis could have two weeks to decide whether or not to write reports on the Chevrolet plant conditions. Like Corkum, probably financially strapped during the Great Depression, the prospect of a bit more money most likely influenced Lewis's decision to send reports to his strange visitor. Parker told Lewis he was interested in a "story" on "working conditions," just "regular shop subjects." He instructed Lewis to sign his letters with the code "XY." When asked to sign for a receipt for the money, the cautious Lewis refused. The next day Lewis received a letter from St. Paul, Minnesota, that instructed him to send his letters to a Chicago postal box. For the first couple of weeks, Lewis wrote one or two letters a week.[47]

Lewis apparently revealed items of little importance in his first letters. After two weeks, the Pinkerton agent returned to Janesville to give Lewis "a few more pointers" on how to write his letters. According to Lewis, he wanted more information on shop conditions. "Now see here," Parker chastised. "You are making these letters rather short. You aren't explaining them enough. I want a little more explanation." This time Parker left two $10 bills on the kitchen table. Two weeks later, a man, identified as Otto Liden appeared at Lewis's home. He claimed to be "Parker's son-in-law." Once again, Lewis "was a little leery," saying, "I tried to find out who gave him all the information about me." Although Lewis did not know Liden, he said that Liden "knew that I got around the shop an awful lot." When he asked how so much was known about him, the Pinkerton agent whose firm's logo bore the slogan "the eye that never sleeps" replied: "We can find out anything. We know all that stuff." The new man showed up fairly regularly, around every two weeks in February, March, and April. Then a third agent appeared, and Lewis stopped writing letters. "I told him it had gone far enough. . . . I'm a Union man and you are trying to get me to put my fellow workers on the spot. . . . I am doing no more whatsoever."[48]

Lewis's letters to the Pinkerton agents revealed his caution and his uncertainty about the people he dealt with. Speaking of his comments on union affairs, he told the union trial committee, "I revealed nothing in those letters that wasn't always published in the paper before I put it in the letters." Although he drafted the original letters, his wife typed them to be sent to the Pinkerton agents. The wary auto worker apparently did not want samples of his handwriting in the spy agency's files. A careful reading of the thirty-odd reports to the Pinkerton handlers reveals that the cautious Lewis did not want to supply much information on his fellow workers.[49] Nonetheless, he evidently appreciated the additional income from the espionage firm, since he wrote reports for three months.

The typed copies of Lewis's reports have survived and offer an intriguing contrast to what his Pinkerton agent desired and to what Lewis actually reported. Curious about the UAW's organizational plans, GM wanted to know about what the new union was doing in its plants as the UAW expanded its organizational efforts. Lewis thought that he had the ear of an influential investor and could raise issues of concern to workers. None of these letters exceeded one typewritten page, and many were less than half a page. His handlers kept insisting on more details on the labor situation in the shop. In his first letter, Lewis described the operation of the plant, the sympathetic attitude of the foremen to the men, and the plight of an older man who had trouble being rehired after his layoff. As a worker and a union member, Lewis often criticized management policies. The GM company store, he noted, was "supposed to be for the welfare of the employees" but did not post a notice of profits or of how its money was spent. He noted some problems of the workers in the GM shops. On the laid-off older worker, he made the case for rehiring the man.[50]

In his letters to Parker, Lewis believed that he was writing to an important and influential investor and that he could serve as an advocate for the men in his shop. He rarely implicated Chevrolet workers in misdeeds. In one letter he noted that the "bonus check" was "appreciated" by many of the GM employees. In another, he commented on the cold weather or cold working conditions and praised fine work the janitorial staff for the clean shops and toilets.[51]

A frequent topic was the Chevrolet plant's excessive drive for higher and higher production, especially when it operated at near-peak or full production. At one point, Lewis claimed that the Chevrolet workers straining to keep up with the increased line speed had an impact on product quality. "The boys at the shop," he wrote, "are a little uneasy. The production is going up, and that means that the lines traveling faster, and they have to keep up with the line. The work can't be done as good as if they had a little more time to do it in." In another instance, he complained about how officials managed the workforce and production. "So it won't be seen so plainly," he noted, "they are laying off a man here and there and giving you a little more work to do. Of course, you're getting the same wages as before."[52]

Lewis also mentioned the numerous critical comments of many workers about the recent expansion of plant security of the Janesville Chevrolet and

Fisher Body plants. In reaction to a 1935 Chevrolet strike in Toledo, Lewis reported that management had "erected a picket fence," a new "durable swinging gate," and a watchman's gate requiring the showing of badges for entry. This new arrangement, he related, "reminds you of a prison fence when you go in." In his next report, he criticized the increased size of the plant security force. Earlier in 1933, he noted, four watchmen were on duty all of the time. Now, he complained, the plant had a police captain and three shifts of police lieutenants with ten or eleven watchmen on each shift. "The men in the shop," he reported, "have passed the remark many times that if they would cut down some of these police and give the working man a little more money it would be a lot better." Some workers believed that "they have more police in the shop than they have in the city of Janesville."[53]

In his letters, Harold Lewis undermined the premises of industrial espionage and instead voiced the sentiments of his fellow Chevrolet workers. If he really believed that he was writing to a prominent shareholder, he most likely thought also that he had an inside track to someone who might influence Chevrolet management policies. At times, he criticized overbearing officials and supervisors. In one instance, an unhappy worker complained to the Janesville plant manager about additional tasks added to his job. The plant manager, Lewis wrote, "used abusive language" to the worker and laid him off. In another, he complained about an overbearing foreman: "He must think he is down South somewheres driving the Negroes, and can keep hollering at them all the time."[54]

In several instances, Lewis served as an advocate for workers who were unfairly disciplined or discharged by Janesville managers and supervisors. After a medical examination of a janitor with eight to nine years' seniority, the company doctor discovered that the janitor had a "bad heart" and recommended that the worker be laid off. In his report, Lewis added that the man's personal doctor said that he was all right for work, but the janitor could not get back to work. In another instance, a motor gang worker was "canned" for letting bad work pass down the assembly line. Lewis suggested that he "should have the right to come back to work. . . . He is in dire need of work and willing to come back if they will give him a chance." In still another, he hoped to reverse the "unfair" discharge of a metal polisher who let two fenders pass him on the line. "The man," he wrote, "was well liked by all the foremen and also by all of his fellow workers. The group he works with thinks he got a rather raw deal."[55]

To satisfy the information needs of his Pinkerton handlers, Lewis also included some information and comments about the union in his secret reports.

One notable feature of his reports was the absence of specific detail and the lateness of the information provided. When he reported on the new union shop paper, *Conveyor*, he remarked: "Personally, I think it is a good idea." In different letters, he mentioned the recent election of the sister Janesville Fisher Body local officers, a Homer Martin address to local auto workers, and the forthcoming UAW convention, but he did not provide any specific details. When he reported on the election of his UAW local's officers, he named the winners more than two weeks after the actual election.[56]

Since the Pinkerton agency obviously wanted information on the union, radical, and leftist politics of the Chevrolet workers, his only report on this subject certainly did not satisfy Pinkerton's requirements. Rather than reporting on radical politics, Lewis wrote very generally about conventional electoral politics. The men in the shop, he related, were "undecided" on the New Deal. One man noted that the NRA did not significantly improve the workman's condition; another said, "If Al Smith didn't stir up the soup no one else did." This was hardly significant information for an organization that desired to keep an eye on possible labor activism and militancy. In another comment on politics, Lewis mentioned worker thoughts on the Chevrolet plant manager's planned run for election to Janesville city council. Recalling worker dissatisfaction with the new security measures, one worker said, "He will have a fence around town like the plant, and appoint a few more deputies and possibly even let you wear the striped clothes." Another worker, Lewis noted, had said, "Where he belongs is over across in Germany and be another Hitler, all he is a dictator." In his final April 10 report to the Pinkerton agent, he noted that the plant manager lost the city council election.[57]

Clearly, the Pinkerton handlers were not getting the labor intelligence they required and expected from Lewis. For the Pinkerton agency, his half-hearted efforts were not worth the $5 to $10 per week that they paid him. In total, Lewis had received $120 for his reports.[58] Although weak in specific detail, the Lewis reports did touch on some of the topics and subjects that generally interested industrial detective agencies. Indeed, the list of questions that concerned these firms was quite extensive and delved into the minute details of day-to-day shop-floor life. But—Harold Lewis never connected names to the misdeeds of workers.

Several months after his initial contact with the Pinkerton agents, sometime in late June or early July 1936, an increasingly guilty Lewis finally arranged a meeting with the Janesville local president and vice president, Elmer Yenney and Mark Egbert. He confessed to them about his contacts with and his letters to the Pinkerton detectives. Lewis provided his copies of the letters to the Local 121 officers and they informed the International Union about the labor spy in their midst. In December, the local sent Lewis's letters to the La Follette Committee.[59]

In February 1937 the UAW Local 121 executive board formally requested Harold Lewis's appearance before a union trial board to answer to the "charge of conduct unbecoming a union member," specifically for "the carrying of correspondence between yourself and a representative of the Pinkerton Detective Agency."[60] Although he never revealed damaging information about his union workmates and ended his contact with the agency, Lewis did accept their money and sent reports to them. At the time, the local press revealed that the La Follette Committee would investigate General Motors industrial espionage in the Janesville Chevrolet plant. At his trial, Lewis's union interrogators wanted to know if there were additional written reports to Pinkerton, whether he had made verbal reports during his biweekly meeting with his handlers, and why he waited so long to report his Pinkerton contacts to the UAW officers. Evidently, Lewis lost his union friends with the public announcement of the La Follette spy investigation. "They just seemed to fall away," he testified. "I always thought I had quite a few friends. . . . From that date on, it seems as though everything was just as I was the worst man on earth."[61] In mid-April, the Recording Secretary informed Lewis that a majority of union members voted to expel him from the UAW local.[62]

Harold Lewis was not the only factory spy in the Janesville General Motors plants. Often the identified and exposed spies represented only the small tip of the huge iceberg of labor spies and informants spread through the automobile industry. Elmer Yenny, the Janesville local union president to whom Harold Lewis had confessed, remembered "another [union] trustee who was one of the prime movers in our organization back there, who also was a labor spy, although we never got definite proof of him." During the sit-down strike, they attempted to subpoena the other spy but he quickly left town for Chicago. "We just never did get hold of him," Yenny recalled, "but we know in our minds that he was also a labor spy for the detective agency."[63]

When exposed, industrial spies often suffered vengeful retribution from their fellow workers. As in the past, the ever-vigilant labor press often exposed shop-floor spies and urged all unionists to shun them. During the General Motors and Dodge sit-down strikes in 1937, union members sometimes gained access to corporate files and passed information and documents to the La Follette Committee investigators. Other times, the Senate committee leaked information on spies to national and UAW local leaders in order to discover and uncover those who made anonymous reports to the detective agencies. As the UAW grew and consolidated, it vigorously sought out and exposed those who spied and informed on their fellow workmates.

In one issue of the *United Automobile Worker*, a main story was about the exposure and confessions of several Chrysler factory spies. Also featured were photographs and short descriptions of a "Dodge Rat" and a "Lansing Rat" to inform and warn others of their shop-floor treachery. The Dodge spy was Carl Bennett, excoriated as a "vile stool-pigeon." He used "his hypocritically pleasant personality to win an honored place among his fellow workers." After Bennett's exposure and his expulsion from UAW Local 3 at Dodge, the UAW newspaper advised: "All honest workers will shun this rat." The Lansing "rat" was a Pinkerton stool pigeon who worked his way into the leadership of Francis Dillon's UAW National Council. The publication of photographs and descriptions alerted and warned other UAW locals to keep an eye out for these men.[64]

One reason the Janesville spy left and escaped town so quickly was the rough justice often received from the spy's fellow workmates. If union members even suspected that a fellow worker was a spy, they often would violently confront him. Nick DiGaetano remembered the public exposure of someone thought to be a rat or stool pigeon: "So, some of the guys said, 'This is the spy. This the guy who reports some of the things.'" Subsequently a young Chrysler unionist managed to pick a fight with the accused man at lunchtime. "One of the union boys," he added, "beat the living out of him on the general principle." When the alleged stoolie heard about the suspicions of his shopmates, DiGaetano recalled that "he did not come back because he got wind of it."[65] In the Chrysler union organizational campaigns in the mid-1930s, this was a common practice whenever unionists discovered a suspected spy in their midst. "Some of the younger boys we had," DiGaetano concluded, "were good with their dukes. During lunch time they would pick up any excuse to pick a fight with them, and they would beat them. The next day the guy did not show up any more. And that was the last we heard of them."[66]

According to John Zaremba, the confession sometimes brought relief to the man who betrayed his shopmates. "After admission to the fact that he was an informer," the Dodge worker recalled, "he seemed so relieved—as if a ton of bricks were taken off his chest." At the time, Zaremba remembered some union members "were ready to 'tan his hide' because they had friends that lost their jobs on account of him." But he said, "Nobody laid a hand on him." The union leaders then had a photographer take pictures of the stool pigeon, "a side left view, side right view, front view and back view of him," and they then sent the photographs to every union in the United States. Other unions sent word that the blacklisted worker had attempted to find work in Detroit, Chicago, and even Pittsburgh and could not obtain it. "That is how we protected our people from stool pigeons," Zaremba concluded, "because a stool pigeon is worse than a cobra. He does not belong among human beings."[67]

Even after a strike ended, the struggles between pro-unionists and anti-unionists persisted. Archie Jones, a Flint auto worker, described the effort to get union opponents to enroll in the UAW after the General Motors sit-down strike ceased. He remembered an "old die hard" who resisted the union campaign to increase membership after the strike: "We done everything to him." They messed with his "big box of tools." They simply "didn't want to work with the rat." Although denying his own participation, Jones recalled that "there's people got their gas tanks doctored up." Some sand or sugar in the gas tank ruined one of an anti-union worker's major investment. He also recalled the treatment of anti-union foremen. "Some guys," he said, "you gotta grab 'em by the coat when there ain't nobody lookin.'" These "were guys you had to rough up."[68]

Red Mundale, a Fisher Body worker recalled a confrontation with an anti-union worker and his attempt to get the recalcitrant worker to enlist in the UAW. When Mundale asked the man why he did not join, the anti-unionist replied: "Because you're the head of it, you son of a bitch and I don't like you." Publicly insulted, Mundale boldly replied, "All right, I tell you what I'll do. . . . I'll meet you outside tonight, right outside the door, here." The more he considered his challenge, the more uneasy Mundale became about a pending fight. He recalled: "I thought I was pretty mouthy. I should have kept my mouth shut. The more I thought of it, the bigger he got, too." When they met after work, the anti-union worker threw his "dinner bucket" and grazed Mundale's shoulder and they "tangled." Worried about fighting on company property, Mundale remembered: "I just kicked the hell out of him. And he'd try to crawl over to that railing and I jerked him back and kicked the hell out of him some more. And finally the guys said, 'He's had enough Red; he's had enough. Let 'im go.' So I said, 'Okay.'" After the fight, the anti-unionist and his friend headed for the union hall to join the local. Then a plant protection man told Mundale: "Hey, the old man wants to see you." Fearing dismissal for fighting on company property, he went to the plant manager. The plant manager said: "Goddamn, Red, you're pretty shifty." Then he gave the worker a $10 bill and said: "I didn't like that son of a bitch either." Mundale concluded that the plant manager "provided a good drunk for me and four of my buddies." They went to a local restaurant and "just got stoned."[69]

So despised were factory spies that some managers even supported union retribution against them.

Such muscular resistance also shaped inter-union relations in the factional struggles between the conservative Homer Martin and the left-center R. J. Thomas UAW factions. Speaking of the UAW AFL and UAW CIO factional struggles of the late 1930s, Fisher Body worker James O'Hara remembered: "Yes, and a lot of times you get 'em fightin' amongst themself. [I]n other words a lot of times you'd better not stick your hands in your pocket walkin' across the street. Because sombody'd nail you or you'd get right in a fight on the curb goin' across the street. When we got started we had a lot of problems amongst our own people." His co-worker, Ingvald, added: "One faction would chase you with a club or somethin' and the union halls were adjacent to one another."[70]

Over time, especially after the reconfiguration of national labor policies under the National Labor Relations Act, such violent and confrontational labor-management relations gradually dissipated. Harold Cranefield, the La Follette Committee investigator, believed the major role of detective agencies ended and when the Supreme Court ruled that the NLRA was constitutional. "By late 1937, I think that the professional espionage in the plants in Detroit had been just about almost eliminated," Cranefield said. Two major automobile firms, Chrysler and General Motors, he reported, "pulled in their horns when they realized that the National Labor Relations Act was constitutional."[71] The elimination of detective agencies and their spies and strikebreakers removed a major irritant to harmonious relations between management and labor. To be sure, much work need to be done to salve the bitter heritage of conflict, but into World War II and postwar years new rules helped forge a new and more congenial relationship. Conflict persisted, but never to the same degree as in the 1920s and 1930s.

For several years the Ford Motor Company, however, remained the outlier and renegade of the Big Three. Under the invidious leadership of Harry Bennett, a vicious system of spies and thugs of the Ford Service Department operated, intimidating and brutalizing pro-union workers until the 1941 strike. From this strike through the war years, a muscular and militant struggle between UAW supporters and Ford servicemen ultimately eliminated the last vestiges of the brutal system of industrial espionage in American plants and factories.

4

Fighting to Provide

The Battle to Organize the Ford River Rouge Plant, 1930–1945

Through the 1930s and into the early 1940s, auto workers used the rough tactic of fighting to redress workplace grievances and to achieve a decent income to provide for their families. In 1929, one Chevrolet worker suggested a connection between the two—fighting and providing. He recalled that a fellow workmate admonished him for reading a labor paper on the job and suggested that he might be caught and fired. The worker "obeyed" since he was "a married man fighting for the welfare of my family." In response to his complaints about abusive foremen, a newspaper editor suggested a different form of fighting: "The workers must learn to do some 'fighting' in their own behalf. Join the union and help us FIGHT such conditions."[1]

After the onset of the Great Depression, American workers in the automobile industry and elsewhere had reached the limits of their tolerance and endurance of the horrid conditions of their work lives. The bitter struggle for industrial unionism was a militant and masculine campaign to alleviate the conditions of life and labor in their communities and mass production factories. The struggle to build unions allowed workers to fight so that they could provide for their families.

In the late 1920s another auto worker described the challenge to auto worker male identity. He lamented in *Auto Workers News* that Detroit had become a "She-Town" as the spread of mass production, with its simpler work tasks, allowed greater numbers of women (and also youth) to work at men's jobs in auto plants for lower wages. Since men were often laid off to join the "mob of unemployed" and employers hired in women at much lower wages, "Detroit is beginning to take on the aspects of a 'she-town' in which the woman works out and the man looks after the kids." The union correspondent described a worker who could not provide for his family. He could not find work "to maintain his wife and children" and was "compelled to consent to having her to look for work." This unfortunate worker related: "So I stay home and send the kids to school to learn all about this land of the free."[2]

The Great Depression further exacerbated such unsettling conditions. Since work was a central component of male identity, the Great Depression represented an enormous encroachment on the very foundations of working-class male identity. Widespread unemployment destroyed the prospect for men to become main providers for their families. Already threatened in numerous ways in the 1910s and 1920s, auto workers deeply felt this trespass from the social and economic ravages of the economic downturn and awakened to the threats to their economic security and well being, so they moved to militant and muscular action against their employers.

In the depths of the Great Depression, auto workers reached into the rough element of masculine culture to resist the encroachments on their lives. Three bitter strikes—at the Briggs auto body plant in Detroit, the Auto Lite parts firm in Toledo, and the General Motors plant in Flint—marked the awakening of auto workers to the pressing need for industrial unionism. All three strikes were militant, violent, and predominantly masculine in their attitudes and actions and were reactions to the social and economic ravages of the Great Depression. They were organizational strikes for the unionization of American industrial workers into the UAW and the CIO. A fourth campaign, against the Ford Motor Company, revealed the ferocious resistance of one firm against worker organization. It also demonstrated the determined commitment to fight and to prevail over this tremendous employer resistance to union organization.

In its organizational phase, the UAW, Irving Bernstein noted, was "democracy run wild." Its leaders were "youthful, zestful, unruly, and incorrigibly windy." One key trait was "rebellion against authority, whether the [American] Federation [of Labor], General Motors, or the law, [it] was the order of the day." Speaking to Roy Reuther, a Flint sit-down-strike leader, Arnold Lenz, the anti-union Chevrolet plant manager said: "The trouble with you . . . and all you fellows, is that you are young and full of piss and vinegar."[3] Labor historian Stephen Norwood observed that the automobile industry tended to favor and to hire younger (below age forty) rather than older workers. Prone to militant and muscular rebellion, the industry's "youthful labor force provided the union with men eager and strong enough to fight vigorously with police and vigilantes on the picket lines and in the streets, allowing it to engage in effective paramilitary actions during strikes."[4] And, in Detroit, Toledo, and Flint, these young workers fought vigorously to transform the array of power in automotive industrial relations.

The 1933 Briggs strike[5] involved the Briggs and other Detroit auto-body firms and marked an important turning point in the auto worker conscious- ness and activism in their quest for industrial unionism and the improve- ment of their dire economic situation. Samuel Romer, a correspondent for *The Nation*, labeled it "the first major labor struggle in Detroit" among auto workers since just after World War I. After sustaining wage cuts that slashed as much as 50 percent of their income, workers experienced a deep fear that they could no longer serve their primary role as breadwinners and providers for their families. A persistent strike slogan was "Give Us a Living Wage," a wage high enough for a working man to support his homemaker wife and nonworking children.[6] At the strike's peak, as many as fourteen thousand workers, mainly auto-body builders, walked the streets, and around one hundred thousand other workers suffered layoffs from curtailed auto-body production. Though the strikers never achieved their main goal of union recognition, they did obtain modest wage increases.

The Toledo Auto Lite strike[7] involved violent street battles among strikers (along with their community supporters) and company guards, the Toledo police, and eventually the Ohio National Guard. Arousing the Toledo labor movement, the action threatened to become a citywide general strike in the late spring of 1934. Initially involving several auto-parts firms, a recently created UAW local and the Electric Auto Lite plant became the core of the struggle from mid-April through early June. The main issues were union recognition, wages, and speed-ups. The Auto Lite strike involved mass pick- eting and mass arrests, the storming of the Toledo jail, large and rowdy dem- onstrations in the courthouse, and considerable violence at the plant gates against strikebreakers, police, and the National Guard. Workers with bricks, stones, and ball bearings used huge slingshots (inner tubes tied to two trees or poles) and small slingshots as well to destroy almost every window of the factory. The following morning, the Cleveland head of the Regional Labor Board wryly quipped: "The Auto Lite is now in reality an Open Shop."[8]

When the National Guard entered the fray, they used gunfire, teargas grenades, and bombs against the strikers. The strikers aggressively fought back in front of the Auto Lite plant and in the streets of the neighborhoods around the plant. In one incident, the crowd of demonstrators numbered twenty thousand, and the enraged young guardsmen fired two volleys into the crowd in the afternoon, killing two strike supporters and wounding nearly twenty others. Through the night the incensed strikers engaged in "guerilla warfare" as they threw bricks, stones, and bottles; the guard returned volleys of rifle fire and tear gas.[9] For several days the street battles continued until the threat of a citywide general strike eventually brought in a federal mediator who resolved some of the strike issues.

In the course of the strike, the men and women exacted rough and retributive justice from the strikebreakers and those who aided them, often taking the form of sexual humiliation. In one instance, a hapless strikebreaker attempted to pick up his paycheck. A woman remembered: "They took all his clothes off and paraded him down the street with nothing but his necktie on." More embarrassing was the fact that "women" actually "stripped that man bare ass naked. They took every piece of his clothes off." The *Toledo Blade* took a photograph of the man marched down the street followed by a crowd of strikers. On the published image, the newspaper lengthened the necktie to cover the man's private parts.[10]

Women also suffered from similar rough and humiliating indignities. One Toledo worker remembered the fate of a female nonstriker: "I know of one instance, where a girl got off the bus . . . she was walking down from Elm Street . . . towards the plant and they tied her dress above her head."[11] In another case, a woman who tried to bring food to her "scabbing" husband was "stripped naked on a bus."[12]

After almost one hundred Toledo unions voted to endorse a general strike, the situation changed dramatically. This threat resulted in intervention of a federal mediator, who eventually negotiated compromises that led to the return to work of all strikers and some wage increases.[13]

The Flint sit-down strike looms large in the annals of UAW, CIO, and American labor history. This transformative strike against General Motors in the heart of its industrial empire reconfigured American industrial relations for the twentieth century, bringing millions of unorganized workers into the labor movement.[14] As with other automobile firms, General Motors reacted to the Great Depression with low wages, horrid working conditions, and sped-up work. In addition, the anti-union firm fought union organization with a vast network of factory spies and thugs who harassed and intimidated organizers and pro-union workers. Slowly and persistently, UAW organizers and union activists brought together a cadre of rank-and-file supporters. Though prematurely initiated just after Christmas 1936, the GM strike involved the innovative sit-down tactic to prevent strikebreakers from taking the jobs of strikers. In addition to the occupation of the Flint Fisher One and Fisher

Two body plants, by early January GM workers struck or sat down in other GM plants in Michigan, Ohio, Indiana, and Wisconsin.

The six-week strike was a truly classic labor-management confrontation, involving the creation of a secret union to escape the notice of GM factory spies, the several violent striker confrontations with company guards and Flint police, the self-organization of GM strikers to maintain order inside the Flint plants, the creation of a working-class women's organization that engaged in angry struggles with union opponents, the formation at GM of the Flint Alliance (a mainly middle-class community organization to oppose the strike), and the involvement of state and federal authorities in its ultimate resolution.

Two incidents, the "Battle of the Running Bulls" and the occupation of the Chevrolet Four plant, revealed the firm determination and ferocity of the strikers and their supporters. On January 11, 1937, when the police attempted to attack and to evict them, the sit-down strikers overcame two assaults with fire hoses and large door hinges and drove the police back. Facing fierce resistance, the police fired at union members, wounding fourteen, one seriously. A crowd of union supporters spent the night outside the plant to prevent the eviction of the sit-down strikers. Victor Reuther described the next day as "a battlefield of the industrial age" with damaged vehicles, broken glass, stones, door hinges, and tear-gas canisters spread on the streets in front of Fisher Two.[15]

On February 1, as the strike wore on and union morale flagged, a union ruse allowed the UAW to take the initiative and capture the Chevrolet Four plant. When strikers acted to take Chevrolet Nine, GM officials rushed its security guards to the plant. At this time, the UAW Women's Emergency Brigade, a traditional but also paramilitary strike-support organization, moved into action to defend the sit-downers as guards and police used tear gas, clubs, and other weapons in an attempt to stop the plant takeover. The militant female union supporters adopted male tactics, using clubs to break windows to allow fresh air into the teargas-filled factory building and to fight with police and guards on the streets. The battle in Chevrolet Nine held the GM security forces at bay and permitted the Chevrolet Four UAW members to win their struggle and occupy the critical engine plant. Two days later the Michigan governor called out the National Guard and refused to allow it to evict the strikers.

The UAW and GM initiated difficult negotiations that resulted in a one-page contract, which provided for exclusive UAW bargaining rights and enormously enhanced the union's prestige. In the wake of the momentous victory, UAW membership soared, and sit-down fever captured the attention of American workers. CIO unions engaged in 279 of the nation's 477 sit-down strikes.[16] From General Motors, the UAW moved on to the Chrysler Corporation, where on March 8 workers sat in nine plants until March 24. On April 6 the UAW and Chrysler signed a contract similar to the GM agreement. After the GM victory, other GM plants, Chrysler, and many smaller auto firms recognized the UAW. Ford became the next objective for the UAW—but a Ford victory proved exceedingly difficult and required a long and militant campaign for eventual success.

A bitter, four-year struggle eventually brought the UAW to Ford's industrial empire. In the late 1930s and early 1940s, Ford's mercenaries faced a growing movement of muscular unionists who resisted the force and intimidation of goons and thugs hired by Harry Bennett of Ford's Service Department.

The Ford Service Department was a major impediment to success in two Ford union drives. In the spring of 1937, after the Supreme Court upheld the constitutionality of NLRA, the major automobile firms finally accepted its legitimacy. Except in a few corporate outliers and renegades, and Ford was the major one, industrial espionage virtually disappeared from the automotive workplace. The Ford Motor Company simply refused to recognize the authority of the court and the federal government. In all branches of the Ford empire, Stephen H. Norwood noted, Harry Bennett continued with his "brass knuckle" labor-relations policy toward the emergent and insurgent United Automobile Workers Union from the late 1930s into the early 1940s. Often using "pistols, whips, and lengths of rubber hose called 'persuaders,'" Bennett's "private army ensured that Ford remained the 'citadel of the open shop' through the 1930s, the last of the major auto companies to be organized."[17]

Ford workers engaged in two concerted efforts to organize the Ford industrial empire. In the wake of the GM and Chrysler victories, the first campaign in 1937 failed to overcome the forceful resistance of Bennett's service department; the second, in 1941, was a vicious two-week battle that finally ended in a complete victory for the United Automobile Workers.

In 1941, Heber Blankenhorn, a former newspaper reporter familiar with industrial espionage, produced an investigative report on the Ford espionage system. Broadly speaking, the Ford spy system had two components—one associated with the production departments under the control of foremen and another directed by the Service Department. The production spies, commonly called "spotters and stool pigeons," made their reports directly to the departmental foremen and occasionally to servicemen in Bennett's department. Inside the plant, a large staff of sweepers and janitors served as informants in the massive River Rouge complex. These nonproduction jobs, Blankenhorn noted, kept them "continuously moving around the plant and talking to employees." In such positions, they served as spies, gathered information on workers, and reported to the River Rouge manager and not to Bennett's organization.[18] Sometimes these production spotters and stool pigeons "graduated" to the position of regular servicemen.[19]

Harry Bennett's Service Department was a brutal and savage system of industrial espionage and personnel relations at Ford. Bennett's brawny minions came from varied discredited and disreputable backgrounds—indeed, Ford servicemen often had mob connections. They were bruisers and thugs who came from the Detroit underworld or were sometimes grateful parolees who came directly to Ford from Jackson State Prison. Others were wrestlers, boxers, or other large and intimidating athletes from Detroit's muscular and male sporting culture.

Beefed up and enhanced during the initial 1937 Ford organizational campaign, the Service Department, Blankenhorn reported, "handled most of the organized 'inside' spying." These inside spies were "muscle men or direct gangs of muscle men." They were the factory gate watchers or plant patrolmen who collected information from the various stool pigeons. Other muscle men or gangsters often controlled different subgroups within Bennett's organization. For example, Elmer Hogan was a former welterweight boxer who recruited toughs from one of the affiliates of Detroit's Purple Gang—from Tony Dana's Downriver gang. In order to maintain good relations with the mob, Bennett even allowed Dana the contract to transport Ford automobiles to Michigan automobile dealers.[20]

Besides the spies and stool pigeons, the Service Department, Blankenhorn noted, also had a system of more "organized violence" to intimidate and to bully Ford workers, to scare them away from any talk or action in favor of unions. These were the "strong arm men, some armed," and their job was "to intimidate or assault union members." Additionally, various other groups or departments were scattered through the River Rouge plant and were known as "strong arm men, muscle men, jeeps, gangsters, and cruisers." One such group was the "firehouse gang," first organized at the time of the outbreak of the Flint sit-down strike in late December 1936. Two Detroit mobsters from the Downriver gang directly supervised the firehouse gang—Joe Tocco, a beer baron, and Angelo Caruso, the mob boss who, along with other thugs, greeted Reuther and Frankensteen and savagely beat them at the River Rouge gates in 1937. Soon after its creation, the firehouse gang moved to a main gate near the Service Department offices and near a storeroom for ammunition.[21]

Another major group was known as the "A" gang, so named because their badges began with the letter A. Charles "Kid" McCoy, a former world middleweight boxing champion, hired into Ford in 1932 after his parole from a prison sentence in San Quentin for the manslaughter of his paramour. McCoy personally recruited the A gang's four hundred men and divided them among the three River Rouge work shifts. Armed with revolvers and with access to automobiles to move quickly through the large industrial complex, some men were stationed at each plant gate; a few locations were even equipped with tear gas bombs. Others worked to protect critical operations, such as the pump house, coke ovens, and testing laboratories; they even monitored toilets. "Instructions," Blankenhorn noted, "were to take care of union men with fists and heels." Other men staffed "cruiser gangs" and drove around and through the huge Ford complex, presenting an intimidating presence to Ford workers.[22]

The "jeeps" constituted still another group of Ford bruisers who came mainly from the Ford workforce. Their task, Blankenhorn wrote, was to "intimidate as well as participate in beatings [such] as the 'Battle of the Overpass'" in 1937. In one instance, a motor building boss took "75 to 100 jeeps to the foundry where they would split into groups of 4 or 5 and walk up and down the aisles glaring at employees at the same time that a group from the foundry would be glaring [at workers] in the motor building." As with many of the servicemen, many jeeps were criminals from Detroit's underworld and sporting culture. As sit-down and union fever declined, managers returned many disgruntled jeeps to their production jobs. When union organizing returned in late 1940, the jeeps were reactivated as "button snatchers" who tore off the UAW buttons union members wore to demonstrate their commitment to the auto workers union.[23]

Bennett also ruled through a corrupt Dearborn city administration and through contacts with African American religious leaders who often received generous Ford contributions. One River Rouge worker remembered that through the Machiavellian political machinations of Bennett, "Mr. Ford owned the city lock, stock and barrel. He owned the police force, the city council, the mayor . . . and they passed any ordinance that Ford wanted."[24] Working through Detroit's African American churches, the Ford personnel department selected loyal and grateful black workers in order to further divide an ethnically split workforce.

Ford workers had absolutely no privacy. The Ford service man, Maurice Sugar noted, "will go to the lunch boxes of the men coming to work to see if he can find any literature advocating organization. He will go through the lockers, he will go through the pockets of the coats of the men in the lockers as a part of his duties to prevent organization in his plant."[25] Martin Jensen recalled the early Ford union meetings—secret meetings of Ford workers who "actually went to these meetings masked."[26] One Ford worker characterized the River Rouge plant as "just a place of fear. You would get individuals to fight against it but they still had that fear in them."[27] Carl Haessler, a Rhodes scholar and labor journalist, described the Bennett regime as "the mother of everything evil in the rest of the Ford system."[28]

In 1932 the Ford Hunger March revealed just how brutal and evil the Ford resistance to any efforts at worker organization was. On a cold March afternoon, a crowd of around three thousand workers and supporters gathered just outside the Dearborn city limits, intending to march to the Ford employment office to present their demands. Although "the march began in a peaceful, good-humored manner," the situation rapidly deteriorated when the marchers refused to obey a Dearborn police order not to proceed, and they crossed into Ford-controlled territory. Thirty to forty police officers attempted stop the demonstrators and fired canisters of teargas at them. The now-angry crowd then surged toward the fleeing police, throwing rocks and stones at them.[29]

In the end, after firing several hundred shots, Ford servicemen and police killed four marchers and wounded more than two dozen demonstrators. The dead ranged in age from sixteen to thirty-two. The other injured marchers "received bullet wounds in either the head or the chest or both." Many were shot in either the side or the back, indicating an effort on their part to turn and run. The only injuries of the Dearborn police and the Ford service men came from the angry fusillade of flying rocks and stones.[30]

The funeral of the four "Bloody Monday" victims turned into a massive leftist demonstration against the outrages of the Dearborn and Ford police. Thousands viewed the open caskets in a hall decorated with red drapes and bunting. To the strains of the "International," the caskets were transported from Workers Hall to the waiting hearses as onlookers raised their fists in protest against the Ford demonstrators' deaths. Tens of thousands gathered on the street outside Workers Hall and later along Woodward Avenue. The funeral procession slowly drove to Woodmere Cemetery, located in the shadow of the huge River Rouge complex. Several thousand mourners participated in the secular services as the four caskets were lowered into a common grave.[31]

David Moore, an African American River Rouge worker, claimed that Bloody Monday awakened his political consciousness and deepened his commitment to the leftist and union cause. Years later he said: "that's when I grew up to be a man. I was in the march." In the course of the bitter struggle, he saw friends die in the shooting. The bloody event initiated his long struggle for eventual Ford unionism.[32]

In late spring 1937, after successful sit-down strikes at General Motors, Chrysler, and elsewhere, the UAW initiated a major Ford organizational campaign. In the jubilant wake of these successful campaigns, UAW leaders decided to take on Ford, the third major automobile firm. By mid-May the UAW was poised for a major confrontation at the gates of the massive River Rouge complex.

Through the spring of 1937, Bennett had built up and augmented his Service Department's internal and external industrial espionage system to thwart any possible union campaign. After the formal launch of the Ford organizational campaign, UAW president Homer Martin appointed Dodge sit-down leader Richard T. Frankensteen and others to direct and to work with the newly created "Ford Organizing Committee." At Dodge, management officials had specifically targeted Frankensteen for surveillance and had paid a close friend to spy on him. The selection of Frankensteen, a former high school football player and a large man, indicated that he would be useful in the union struggle with Bennett's servicemen. The committee's goal was organize Ford and to "make the city of Detroit a one-hundred-percent union town."[33]

After opening two union offices near the huge Ford plant, Frankensteen and Walter Reuther issued a press release and announced that they intended to pass out fifty thousand handbills, titled "Unionism, Not Fordism," to River Rouge workers. Since the Dearborn city clerk issued a license to distribute the leaflets, the union organizers anticipated an uneventful leaflet distribution and noted that UAW members from other plants and UAW Women's Auxiliary members would pass out the materials as the day shift left and the afternoon shift entered the huge plant. The successful General Motors and Chrysler campaigns and the Supreme Court's recent ruling upholding the constitutionality of the National Labor Relations Act finally inspired hopes for a successful Ford union drive.[34]

But when the approximately fifty UAW members and supporters, both men and women, arrived at the various River Rouge plant gates, all hell broke loose. Government officials, ministers, educators, and reporters witnessed what the UAW later labeled the "Battle of the Overpass" at the main gate on the Miller Road. After newspaper photographers took pictures of Frankensteen, Reuther, J. J. Kennedy, and Robert Kanter, a group of Ford service men stepped forward and ordered them to get off Ford property. As the union group started slowly to leave, the Ford bruisers jabbed Frankensteen from behind in the ribs, and the union leader struck back at them. Around forty servicemen suddenly appeared and severely beat and kicked the four UAW organizers, sending them down the overpass stairs. They also chased the photographers and either broke their cameras or removed the film from them.[35]

In this violent incident, Frankensteen, Reuther, and others were viciously and professionally beaten. Reverend Raymond Prior Sanford, a Chicago minister and witness, described how "a group of the bruiser, thug-type of individuals" approached the two UAW organizers and assaulted them. Frankensteen's beating was especially savage. As an "increasing number" of Ford servicemen "of a heavier type" surrounded Frankensteen, Sanford testified, he was held by each arm while other men kicked him in the stomach and groin," and then others joined in the beating. While Frankensteen was on his back, the Ford "sluggers" grabbed him "by either foot and spread his legs apart while others kicked him in the groin." Reuther also received the savage attention of the burly Ford servicemen. As Reuther held a stair rail, a "husky thug tore him lo[o]se and hurled him down the first flight of stairs." The kicking and beating continued all the way down the stairs.[36] After the incident, an iconic photograph of the two bloodied and beaten UAW leaders revealed the savagery of the assault on the two UAW leaders.[37]

The Ford servicemen also delivered methodical and professional beatings to other UAW organizers. According to a UAW press release, the men who savagely beat Frankensteen and Reuther "went about their business with cold deliberate science and precision." Their arms would be lifted so that blows could be delivered to the ribs or they would be turned on their sides to be kicked in the stomach.[38] The Ford thugs incapacitated Frankensteen by pulling his suit jacket over his head, pinning his arms, and obscuring his vision. One bruiser had his right hand taped around his knuckles to protect them in the manner of professional boxers. Two of the three "original assailants" of Frankensteen and Reuther were Ford foremen and another was a Ford servicemen and former wrestler. The NLRB later concluded that many of Bennett's minions who participated in the attacks on the UAW organizers at the River Rouge plant gates were professional boxers and wrestlers or Detroit mobsters.[39]

Elsewhere, Sanford noticed some of the women who were leafleting Ford workers. The UAW had hoped to moderate the use of excessive force by Bennett's thugs. Even the Dearborn police, who were in Bennett's pocket, had meekly suggested "the girls not be dealt with so violently." Yet the women suffered the pushing, shoving, and violence of the Ford servicemen as the thugs pushed them back into the streetcars; the women experienced "a general mauling." One young woman, Sanford said, "was kicked in the stomach, and vomited at my feet."[40] Overall, the union casualties totaled eighteen organizers, including eight women.[41] As leaders of the Ford campaign, Frankensteen and Reuther received the most focused attention of the Ford servicemen. But other injured UAW organizers received far more serious injuries. A couple of months later, William Merriweather appeared at the Ford NLRB hearings still in a cast with a broken back and with what doctors said might be permanent injuries. The doctor of another UAW casualty, Tony Marinovich, told the NLRB that Marinovich "sustained a fracture of the skull, a severe concussion of the brain, and . . . an inflammation of the brain, due to [his] injury." His prognosis was "headaches and dizziness for an indefinite period to come."[42] One Detroit newspaper, however, reported that only one Ford serviceman was injured and he "suffered a cut over his eye."[43]

After losing the Battle of the Overpass, the beaten but unbroken UAW Ford organizers promised that they would not lose their struggle for the unionization of Ford workers. A defiant Frankensteen told reporters, "If Mr. Ford believes that these tactics will stop us, he has another think coming. We'll go back there and give them a dose of their own medicine." In press statement, UAW president Homer Martin criticized "the use of brute force through paid thugs and mobsters." Ford workers, he asserted, would not "see their rights crushed by the 'black shirts' of Dearborn."[44] One Ford campaign leader announced an ominous and threatening call for a special meeting of the UAW flying squadrons "to discuss plans for the continuance of the drive."[45]

But the renewal of the Ford campaign would have to wait almost four years. After the overpass incident, Wayne County prosecutor Duncan C. McCrea requested that the Dearborn mayor and police chief to bring to his office "all parties involved in this riot." After they refused cooperation, a Wayne County grand jury issued subpoenas for the testimony of the Dearborn and Ford officials and for the arrest of service men who participated in the savage beatings of the UAW organizers. None of the Dearborn or Ford officials cooperated. Many of the Ford service men left town, heading for other U.S. or Canadian cities.[46]

In the first weeks of July 1937 the NLRB began its hearings in Detroit on the Battle of the Overpass, on workers fired prior to and after the overpass incident, and on Ford anti-union activities. In December 1937 the NLRB issued a ruling that concurred with the union charges and ordered the Ford Motor Company to stop intimidating workers and interfering with their self-organization.[47] For the next two years Ford officials challenged the NLRB order in the federal courts and refused to comply with any of the NLRB decisions. The overpass battle and the subsequent legal proceedings stalled the UAW organizational drive at the River Rouge plant. The campaign stumbled along through the summer and fall of 1937 and was eventually abandoned.

Additionally, internal union factionalism captured the attention of UAW leaders. Between 1938 and 1939 this internal struggle involved Homer Martin's conservative Progressive Caucus as well as Walter Reuther and Wyndham Mortimer's Unity Caucus. The internecine factional battles weakened the UAW and exhausted its organizational momentum at Ford. When Martin attempted to cut a sweetheart deal with Harry Bennett to bring Ford workers into the AFL, the UAW split into two factions—Martin's UAW-AFL and R. J. Thomas's UAW-CIO. Always stronger in the larger automobile firms, the UAW-CIO retained the loyalty of a vast majority of Ford and other UAW members. In the factional conflict, the UAW expended much energy against Martin supporters in union halls, at plant gates, and on streets. When the UAW's factional struggles finally ended, it once again turned its attention to a unionization campaign to bring Ford workers into the UAW in the fall of 1940.

This time, both the CIO and the UAW jointly launched a new Ford unionization drive. In early October, Michael F. Widman, the CIO assistant organization director, arrived in Detroit to assume direction of the new Ford campaign. Widman claimed that the UAW and CIO campaign would involve "a staff of 40 organizers, nightly radio broadcasts, a weekly Ford workers newspaper [*Ford Facts*], a concerted legal campaign to win the nullification of the Dearborn anti-handbill ordinance, and a nation-wide campaign to acquaint the public and car purchasers . . . of the circumstances under which Ford cars are made." UAW leaders announced that union "membership among Ford workers" was "at the highest point in years." Other UAW locals enthusiastically and generously supported the Ford drive with a special $1 assessment on members. The new Ford campaign, Widman announced, would "proceed in an orderly and peaceful manner" and would try to avoid "strikes or cessation of operations."[48]

From December 1940 through March 1941 the UAW and CIO leaders repeatedly appealed for an NLRB representation election to determine who would represent Ford workers through collective bargaining.[49] Finally in March, after the U.S. Supreme Court decided in favor of the NLRB in the Ford case, the UAW and CIO organizers increased their efforts at the River Rouge plant with extensive union handbill and literature distribution. Unlike in the past, formerly reluctant Ford workers often accepted the UAW leaflets and fliers. Though worker fears of Ford goons and thugs had eroded considerably, a major struggle for unionism loomed for the near future.

Throughout the organizational campaign, Ford officials continued their vigorous resistance to unionization. While Ford attorneys challenged the decisions of the NLRB in the courts, Bennett returned to his more insidious methods of union avoidance, mainly a strategy of dividing and conquering AFL and CIO supporters. He conferred with AFL president William Green about the possible organization of Ford workers into the more conservative American Federation of Labor. Finally, as the union campaign grew stronger, Bennett began to hire in large numbers of anti-union workers (including African American strikebreakers), many who were large men with questionable reputations. If until 1937 he relied mainly on Italian American goons and thugs, Bennett now depended heavily on African American ones. By March 1941, Ford foremen and service department men started to solicit membership into a Ford AFL local to divide the workforce.

For the UAW organizers the main target of their campaign was the River Rouge complex. They developed a two-pronged campaign to win over new UAW converts. On the one hand, the organization attempted to gain support in the local communities where Ford workers lived, mainly in the ethnic and African American neighborhoods in Detroit and its working-class suburbs. On the other hand, it engaged in a bitter shop-floor struggle to undermine the Ford regime of fear and intimidation that Bennett had established since the 1920s. In late February 1941, the UAW issued a thirty-day strike notice "with the state labor board and also notified President Roosevelt of its strike plans." At the same time, it petitioned the NLRB for a representation election to select the UAW as sole collective bargaining agent for Ford workers.[50]

Within the River Rouge plant the UAW conducted union button campaigns and tried with some success to establish informal grievance processes in different shops and departments. In its mid-December 1940 appeal for a union representation election, the UAW claimed that several Ford workers now wore union buttons on the River Rouge shop floor. Ford officials, the UAW asserted, "forced" them to remove their buttons and discharged "several" of them. In contrast, Harry Bennett claimed that only "about thirty men put on their union badges and began parading around the plant making a lot of noise." These men, he asserted disingenuously, "weren't fired." Instead, loyal Ford workers "finally put the union men out of the plant because they became so noisy." Similar shop-floor incidents of union aggression and Ford reaction would characterize shop relations until the strike actually broke out. By early March, so many Ford workers began to wear union buttons that the

UAW claimed its supply of buttons was "completely exhausted" and made appeals to other locals for funds to purchase more.[51]

Prior to the actual outbreak of the strike, UAW members also established informal mechanisms for worker representation and grievance resolution at the shop or departmental level. In mid-March the UAW reported that in the assembly building workers protested discriminatory transfers and discharges. They even managed to hold a "meeting with the supervision to negotiate grievances." With worker enthusiasm high for organization, shop-floor supervisors needed to make some accommodation to assure smooth production. In effect, UAW assembly workers actually managed to negotiate "a temporary seniority system and grievance machinery." A similar informal arrangement also emerged in the motor building. In the axle plant, UAW workers won the reinstatement of twelve discharged workers after a one-hour "spontaneous stoppage" resulted in negotiations and their return to work.[52]

By now, many River Rouge shops and departments seethed with worker resentment and dissatisfaction against the repressive Ford system. At the end of March, such deep discontent signaled the possibility of a spontaneous strike at the huge Ford plant. UAW leaders wired the federal Office of Production Management, stating, "it is becoming increasingly difficult to prevent a strike at the Ford Motor Co." Bennett had actively encouraged the AFL organization to counter the CIO drive. "Beginning at the end of last week," the *Daily Worker* noted, "company stooges, with dues books from the AFL, began collecting dues right in the shop and with the aid of the service department and foremen, high-pressuring workers into the AFL." Bennett continued his divide-and-conquer strategy and began to rely on the more conservative UAW-AFL as a bulwark against the more militant UAW-CIO.[53]

More ominously, Bennett's divisive strategy seemed intent upon dramatically raising racial tensions in the River Rouge foundry. After the UAW campaign began, he hired a large number of African Americans; some were simply loyalists due to the Ford tradition of progressive hiring policies, and many others were hardened strikebreakers and criminals from Detroit's underworld. "Professional provocateurs brought into the foundry last Thursday night," the Communist newspaper added, "brandished knives and threatened union committeemen in an attempt to start fights in the foundry." The River Rouge foundry employed a large number of black workers and a large contingent of Southern and Eastern European immigrant workers. Despite the provocation, the UAW leaders managed to use the union's "strong discipline" to prevent "riots from breaking out."[54]

The sudden dismissal of several UAW shop committeemen in two departments escalated tensions between the UAW and Ford management. The dismissed committeemen "had previously been recognized as spokesmen in their respective plants." On April 1 the dismissals were a crucial topic of shop-floor conversation throughout the industrial complex. The day and evening shifts had short and spontaneous work stoppages. The dismissal of several more rolling-mill committeemen resulted in a major stoppage of six thousand Ford rolling-mill workers at three that afternoon. Next, one thousand open-hearth workers stopped work. Then, fifteen thousand stopped work at the final assembly line where Ford assemblers "were standing on boxes and machines making speeches."[55]

By the time of the shift change at 11 P.M., a huge number of the River Rouge workers had engaged in a "spontaneous stoppage," possibly intended as a sit-down strike. The rolling-mill, open-hearth, pressed-steel, and, finally, assembly-line units had ceased "all operations." With its large contingent of strikebreakers, the foundry was the major holdout. Some of the men from the next shift went into the plant while others milled around the only open gate, Gate 4, the site of the initial overpass struggle. Around midnight, CIO organizational director Widman called on the workers who remained in the plant to leave. However, Bennett apparently intended to have the workers remain in the plant so that he could claim an illegal sit-down strike and have state authorities evict the strikers. Fearing public censure for a possible illegal sit-down strike, UAW leaders declared "the strike effective immediately" shortly after midnight. They also appealed for "all Rouge workers to report for picket duty" early the next morning.[56]

Inside the River Rouge plant, informed of the strike authorization, Ford workers "greeted" the news "with hysterical shouts" throughout the huge manufacturing complex. Ford workers from the pressed-steel and rolling-mill buildings marched to the tool-and-die department, where some two hundred skilled AFL men continued to work. "We marched right in the building shouting '*strike's on*,'" one striker related, "but these guys kept at work. Then we yelled '*every one out*' and most of the AFL men left—all except two fellows who kept right on working. We carried them out and everything was fine then."[57]

After the midnight strike call, UAW organizers went to Gate 4 and shouted orders to evacuate the huge industrial complex. "All UAW-CIO members," one yelled, "come out of the plant—the strike *is* on!" Small groups of Ford workers left the plant "cheering and singing the union's anthem 'Solidarity.'" Later, "several hundred workers" from the main assembly department "paraded through Gate 4, many wearing UAW-CIO overseas caps and most of them wearing UAW-CIO buttons." A few minutes later, "a singing, shouting parade of several thousand marched through the gate, after a circuit of the factory in which they shouted to various departments to 'come on out.'" Only the foundry, with its large contingent of black Ford loyalists and strikebreakers, contained a significant number of holdouts. The spontaneous strike surprised and stunned both the UAW leaders and Ford officials. Through the night, many Ford workers attended a large and hastily organized meeting at the nearby Ford organizational headquarters.[58]

The River Rouge evacuation was a massive demonstration of collective union power. "We had no trouble getting things going in our building," a UAW member in the axle department told a Detroit reporter. "We picked up axles weighing around 20 pounds and waved them like clubs," he said. "We went through the building yelling: '*Everyone stop work!*'" All stopped work and later went to join other strikers in the main part of the building. Similarly, a "husky UAW man" who worked in the rolling mill told how other UAW members dealt with the AFL supporters in his department. The strikers closed his building after "a lot of AFL men stopped work and started soliciting members on company time." He and his fellow union members protested, and "the boss ordered the AFL men out." A few minutes later the AFL men returned to renew their solicitation. The superintendent then "fired our chief steward and we all quit work and sat down." Around a dozen AFL workers ran for the doors and "[t]wo of our men tried to stop them and the men pulled out knives and slashed our guys." The AFL workers then left the building.[59]

Union supporters also savagely fought back against Ford servicemen and shop supervisors. On the first day of the strike, one Ford worker, Nick DiGaetano, described an extremely violent incident in the machine shop: "One of the Italian company guards pulled out a gun . . . and he went to the guys. He said, 'If you leave the machine shop, I'll blow your brains out.'" In response, one of the shop workers, an "Italian boy, who was a union man," emerged "from somewhere between the machines and . . . pulled out a knife and cut this company guard's belly wide open." According to DiGaetano: "His guts came out and they had to take him to the hospital right away." After this, the Ford workers left the machine shop and marched to the picket line.[60]

Through the night, the *Detroit News* reported, unionists "roamed through the dark streets on the plant [grounds], seeking departments which failed to join the walkout." In one instance, one hundred workers pushed aside plant protection police from the entrance to the motor building. "Squads roamed through the plant," the newspaper added, "urging non-strikers to leave their jobs, and soon most of them were out." At one point, two hundred union supporters surged through police lines and headed toward the foundry. This bastion of Ford loyalists and muscular street thugs remained open and contained many non-striking workers. One union committeeman yelled, "Let's clean out the foundry." Joining forces with other Ford workers, an hour later "they marched out cheering" and claimed it was "down 100 per cent."[61]

The *Detroit Free Press* stated that the Ford River Rouge strike was "the largest ever called in a single plant." In the morning, the second overpass battle occurred. In the early morning, the *Detroit News* reported, "the strikers barricaded the roads leading to the plant with automobiles and packed lines of marching men." On the major roads to the River Rouge, plant automobiles "were jammed fender to fender, 30 to 40 deep. Only a single traffic lane was left open to union cars." The arrival of buses and streetcars further blocked these roads and made them "even more impregnable." Some loyal Ford workers attempted to go through the picketers and automobiles, but they had to run "the gauntlet of shouting, angry men" who threw "bits of metal and bricks." In several instances, "drivers headed into the mass of men but after they narrowly escaped being overturned, they backed away from the menacing pickets."[62]

In contrast to earlier struggles at Ford—the 1932 Bloody Sunday massacre and the 1937 Battle of the Overpass—the relatively united Ford workers successfully resisted Bennett's efforts to contain them. The *Detroit News* recounted that the barricade of "stalled cars lined up for half a mile to a mile in all directions." And, at "Miller and Dix roads, a dense horde of men, carrying signs, had halted all traffic." According to the *Detroit Times*, "Some of the pickets carried placards attached to heavy laths, some four feet long, three inches wide and half an inch thick. Some of the others carried laths without placards." Later that day, Bennett described the giant union blockade as "an all-out communistic demonstration on the highways leading to the Rouge plant."[63]

On the same morning, hundreds of Ford and other UAW workers amassed at River Rouge plant Gate 4, where Frankensteen and Reuther suffered their savage beatings a few years earlier. Newspaper photographs reveal many, many workers standing on and around the bridge where Ford strikebreakers soon assaulted them. Shortly before 7 A.M., a "general melee" broke out when hundreds of black workers "burst suddenly from the plant gates, armed with steel rods, bolts and bits of metal." Ford and UAW loyalists engaged in pitched battles at the Miller Road gate. Once again, the Dearborn police feebly stood by. "After considerable fighting," the *Detroit News* reporter observed, "the unionists drove their opponents back into the plant."[64]

Two hours later, Bennett's minions conducted a second assault on the massed UAW picketers. They began with a barrage of missiles from the factory roof and then followed up with an attack across the overpass. "Pickets threw some of the missiles back at their opponents and fought," the newspaper reported, "but they were driven back with two- and three-foot steel bars, hammers, and wrenches." Another report described "several hundred Negroes with steel bars and knives charged out of the main gate." Many of the injured were strewn across Miller Road. "After a 15-minute battle," the newspaper added, "the union lines reformed and the other group [of Ford loyalists] was driven back to the plant." In these two battles, many UAW fighters suffered injuries, some serious. One UAW member possibly had both arms fractured, another caught a knife slash. At the Ford plant hospital, forty-one others received treatment. Still, unlike 1937, the UAW emerged the victor of the second of the overpass battles.[65]

When they formally authorized and sanctioned the spontaneous Ford work stoppage on the first day of the walkout, the UAW strike leaders publicly issued their formal list of strike demands. These included the "immediate reinstatement" of workers discharged for union activity, a ten-cent-per-hour wage increase, the establishment of a seniority system and a grievance system, the "abolition of the Ford spy system" and its infamous service department, and other "elements of a contractual agreement which will make possible operation of the River Rouge plant on a basis of equity for the workers."[66]

When the strike broke out, the UAW took advantage of its recently developed contacts with the Detroit-area African American community. It staffed a sound truck with a local black clergymen to calm tensions in the Ford foundry. Reverend John W. Crawford, pastor of the Spiritual Israel Church and also a Ford foundry worker, appealed from the truck's public address system for workers "to refrain from violence." Three days later on April 5, Crawford published an "Open Letter to Boxers" in the UAW strike newspaper and appealed to the "young fellows hired in the last four weeks in a frantic effort to pack [the Ford] factory with people who did not know the issues involved in the present fight between the union and the company." As strikebreakers, he wrote, they now bore "the names 'goon,' 'jeep,' and 'scab.'" In the boxing ring, Crawford noted, "you were cleancut, classy, and fair. You never hit a man when his back was turned and you fought according to the rules." In the current strike, he said, Ford is "asking you to forget fair play."[67]

Homer Martin, the discredited UAW leader, reappeared on the scene to roil the already treacherous racial waters of Ford labor-management relations. Bennett's AFL loyalists invited Martin to address Ford workers. Martin addressed a crowd of three thousand at the Forest Club Auditorium, a major African American entertainment venue located at Hastings Street and Forest Avenue in Paradise Valley. According to John Gillman, the head of Ford AFL union, Martin was an "AFL 'representative' assigned to seek members among Ford workers." Donald T. Marshal, the African American Ford personnel officer in charge of hiring black workers, also addressed the large crowd of mainly African American workers. In line with Bennett's earlier public pronouncements, Martin blamed CIO communists for causing the disruptive strike. "[He] cautioned his listeners not to attempt to cross the picket line individually, then added: 'But give us a few days and we'll organize 40,000.'" The two speakers intended to organize a huge back-to-work movement that would pit mainly black Ford loyalists against mainly white UAW supporters. Martin told a large audience to listen for a local radio broadcast the next evening for the time and place for workers to assemble if they wished to return to work in the Rouge plant.[68]

This dangerous Martin-Marshall plan played the race card to divide the Ford workforce and to break the strike. The normally conservative Detroit AFL leaders almost immediately distanced themselves from the provocative plan. Even as Martin spoke to the assembled Ford loyalists, Detroit Federation of Labor delegates "unanimously passed a resolution asking the national executive council of the AFL to force Martin to cease representing himself as the authorized representative of the AFL." Frank X. Martel, the Detroit and Wayne County AFL president, said, "Martin does not represent the central body of the American Federation of Labor and has no business acting as if he did." Quickly, national AFL president William Green also distanced himself from the Martin-Marshal scheme and removed Martin "from his national representative post" the next day. Instead of Martin's back-to-work broadcast, Ford AFL union head John J. Murphy made the radio speech and claimed Martin was "a friend of the Ford workers and an enemy of the CIO and Communists." He mentioned, however, no time or place for the back-to-work movement. Thus, the *Detroit News* concluded, ended Martin's "three-day comeback as a labor leader."[69]

The UAW Ford drive leaders criticized Ford's "disreputable tactics" and "the vicious practice of sowing hatred and discord between Negro and white workers." Appalled at the real prospect of possible racial conflict, the UAW continued its efforts to make closer connections to the Detroit black community. A NAACP sound truck appeared at the UAW picket lines, broadcasting appeals to black Ford workers not to become strikebreakers. The anticipated back-to-work movement never materialized, and state troopers separated around one hundred "mostly Negro foundry workers from a large UAW picket line."[70] Nonetheless, the tensions persisted on the streets and in the shops.

As the Michigan State Police and the AFL and CIO unions calmed tensions on the streets of Dearborn, the River Rouge complex devolved into a savage and violent Hobbesian world of a war of all against all. Trapped in the foundry when the strike began, Charles Harp, a white, twenty-five-year-old Ford worker, described the brutal world of male and racialized violence during the first days of the strike. Harp estimated that about twelve hundred workers remained in the foundry after the strike started. Most of those who stayed, he wrote, were new workers, "hired in the last sixty days." Even though Ford officials assigned "heavier work" to foundry workers who joined the union, the shop ran smoothly until the eve of the strike. Just before the strike broke out on April 2, Harp testified, "many men from other departments appeared in the foundry dressed in street clothes with pads of paper in their hands and wearing AFL buttons. These men were all colored." In line with Bennett's plan to use the prospect of AFL unionism to foment factional union violence in the Ford shops, these men "approached workers in the foundry and told them to join the AFL." They also threatened them, saying that "if they didn't join they would be taken care of outside or that they would be given tough jobs."[71]

The next day, only seven hundred foundry workers clocked in at a quiet plant. Harp recounted that "there was no production in the plant at all." After waiting a "restless and frightened" two hours, Sam Taylor, a Ford supervisor who figured prominently in the first Battle of the Overpass, "picked several colored men who he appointed as leaders, and told these leaders to take charge of the men." Taylor also told the foundry workers that the "CIO men on the outside were beating up all the men who left the plant and were severely cutting them up and breaking their heads." He urged the black foundry workers to patrol the plant and watch for CIO men.[72]

After spending the night in the Ford plant, Harp described the morning assault on CIO pickets. He reported that "a service man by the name of 'Tex' organized a gang of about 75 men." All wore "Ford 100%—AFL" buttons. Leading them out of the plant, Tex shouted: "Let's kick those CIO men over the railroad tracks and smash their heads." Using steel rods, crowbars, ice picks, clubs, and even three-foot tool-steel swords machined in the Ford shops, they assaulted UAW picketers on one of the forays at the plant gates. While shop supervisor Taylor watched, they beat up around fifteen CIO pickets. Subsequently, Taylor made twenty of these men leaders and organized patrols within the plant. Soon they went to the grinding department to fabricate additional weapons. Harp described the weaponry:

> Most of the steel used was tool steel which was sharpened into pretty wicked weapons. The men also got leather from the leather department which they made into belts which they swung from the shoulders and to the hips in which they carried the swords.

With supervisory complicity, the foundry rapidly degenerated into the swaggering bravado of an armed, dangerous, and masculine camp.[73]

Although many Ford foundry workers wanted to leave, Sam Taylor told his leaders that "they could control the plant on the inside and while they were doing this they would get paid and be fed." Gradually, the situation became ominous and dangerous. Food and cigarettes ran short. "The bigger men," Harp noted, " were taking money away from the smaller men. There was fighting going on all the time." Some of Taylor's men took some new Mercury cars from the line and raced them around the plant. Eventually, the auto engines froze up, since they did not have any oil in them. In the evening, the Ford workers trapped in the foundry found it impossible to sleep. As Harp noted: "It was cold. It was dangerous. The men feared each other." Someone decided to get pads and cushions from another building to sleep on. But, said Harp, "this situation caused more fighting among the men. The bigger men would take away from the smaller men the cushions or pads or mats."[74]

Fights constantly broke out over food as well. When the first major shipment of food arrived at the Rouge plant by boat on Wednesday evening, "about 200 colored men armed with their swords rushed the tug, took control of all the food and kept it to themselves. . . . This started general fighting among the men for the food." Those who controlled the food sold it to others. Despite several attempts, even the Ford "star men," or shop supervisors, could not control foundry chaos. "Fighting," Harp related, "was going all the time about the food. There was fear that the men would not be fed." Finally, at suppertime, the lunch wagons reappeared and "food was passed out. This time there was more order and most of the men got some food."[75]

Fights also broke out over gambling. Harp reported that when the strike began, many of the foundry men had just been paid. "Crap games were going around all the time." Even in the presence of supervisors, service men, and Dearborn police (who also "joined in the games") fights were common.

Unlike the collective discipline of the Flint sit-down strikes, discipline among the armed gangs of foundry workers was something Ford officials either would not or could not enforce.[76]

Almost from the beginning, the white foundry workers were extremely uneasy about the chaotic situation in the River Rouge plant. "The white men in the plant," Harp reported, "were anxious to leave because the colored men were roaming around with dangerous weapons in their hands either fighting among themselves or shooting crap." The manly and cocky swagger meant the domination of the weaker by the stronger, the smaller men by the larger ones. "There was fighting going on all of the time."[77] When federal conciliators arrived and made an unsuccessful request to vacate the River Rouge foundry, Harp managed to sneak out of the foundry as the conciliators entered. The strikebreakers remained inside and refused to leave.[78]

Despite the madly unrestrained situation, the UAW strategy to sway black Ford workers in their local communities was successful.[79] Walter Hardin, a UAW International representative and director of Negro Activities, worked to bring African American Ford workers into the UAW fold. He believed that the African American UAW loyalists far outnumbered the Ford loyalists. Though his numbers did not match some of the earlier press reports, he estimated that Ford employed fourteen thousand African Americans and that only about five thousand remained inside the plant, some intimidated and reluctant and some committed to Ford and Bennett after the strike started. Since the Ford tentacles of control reached deep into working-class communities, the struggle inside River Rouge quickly became a struggle within the African American community to gain the support of black Ford workers and their families. When he became involved in the Ford campaign, Hardin wrote, "sharp clashes were going on between two factions of Negroes"—supporters of the AFL and those of the UAW. When the strike started, he added, "violence broke out on a larger scale and extended from the plant and into the following communities: North Detroit, West Side Detroit, Ecorse, River Rouge and Inkster," the Detroit neighborhoods and suburbs where black Ford workers resided. The Ford Service Department allowed African American loyalists to leave work "to go out in the communities and carry on full time agitation for the AFL." Another Service Department activity was "organizing goon squads" with "orders to do a job on the head of every CIO man."[80]

In order to diminish these racial tensions, the UAW strike leaders brought in many black organizers to work in the shops and in the African American community. A full-time staff of ten and a volunteer staff of twenty occupied two offices, one on Detroit's East Side and one on the West Side. Others operated the union sound cars full time in the black neighborhoods and at the picket lines. Religious leaders worked the Detroit's African American churches in support of the union cause. Christopher C. Alston, an African American UAW supporter, served as editor for a special black edition of *Ford Facts* and distributed fifty thousand copies at plant gates and in the black communities. Gradually, these concerted efforts successfully brought the black community over to the union side.[81]

Near the end of the two-week strike, this success manifested itself on the picket line. Two black UAW supporters used male banter and posturing to undermine the wills of nonstrikers. Hodges Mason recalled being "devilish" and having "fun" as he and another black unionist, Shelton Tappes, staffed the union sound truck at the gates of the River Rouge plant. Mason remembered: "A very beautiful woman came down the street and she has a platter in her hand. . . . I said over the public address system, 'My, my, my! Have mercy, my, my, my! I wonder who she is going to see.'" The two unionists decided that they could have fun with one of the strikebreakers in the plant. Over the PA system, Mason said: "Lady, as beautiful as you are, why would you come out here and support a scab, bringing him something to eat? Don't you realize you are bucking the union, and the union is fighting for a living wage for your husband and that means more money for you." As the woman smiled, Mason then said: "Lady, don't take him anything to eat. Give it to one of these guys picketing out here." When she gave the nonstriking worker the food and leaned over to kiss him, he said: "Lady, don't kiss him; he's a rat, he's a scab."[82]

Mason and Tappes continued with their picket-line banter and gradually questioned the nonstriker's manhood. They asked:

> My, my, my! Fellow, you are going to let your wife go home alone? Don't you know better than that? You've been away from home two weeks. You'd better go home and see about your wife. Lady, if he doesn't come home, as lovely as you are, he thinks more of Mr. Ford that he does of you. He's making a terrific choice.

After this, the woman began to grin. To the nonstriker they said:

> Fellow, as lovely as she is, you should be there at all times. Fellow, you'd better go home and see about you wife. Someone as beautiful as that one is at home? You'd better go see about her. You've been out here for two weeks.

Gradually, the strikebreaker's commitment waned.

At the continued prodding of Tappes, Mason kept on needling the foundry worker. "If you don't go see her," he added, "someone else will." Becoming annoyed, the nonstriker responded: "Listen fellow, don't play that." Mason replied: "I'm not playing, I'm serious. Lady, if he don't come home with you, leave your telephone number with one of those guys. They'll give it to me. And I'll come." As she departed the factory gate, the woman "nearly died laughing." Mason kept up the goading until after the woman left. Then the foundry worker called Mason over to the factory gate. Pointing toward the UAW picketers, he reiterated the Bennett position on the strikers' reaction to the strikebreakers: "I want to come out, but I'm scared of those guys—they're going to kill me." After Mason promised not to hurt the nonstriker and pulled back the picket line to allow him to leave, the pickets cheered. Mason then said, "That's the kind of sports we are fellow! You don't have to worry about anything. We want you out, we're not going to bother you."

At this point, the man ran out of the gate "like a blue streak." Another foundry worker said the he also wanted to leave and Mason told him: "All you guys better go home and see about your wives. You've been away about two weeks now." For Mason, this incident represented the beginning of many nonstrikers eventually abandoning the huge Ford plant.[83]

The UAW's extensive work with the African American religious community and with its political leaders eventually bore fruit and thwarted Bennett's effort to break the union's collective strength and to divide black and white workers. Black workers either took a less oppositional and more neutral position on the strike or sided with the UAW. The masculine banter of Mason and Tappes succeeded in breaking black men from their loyalty to Ford.

In the midst of the bitter River Rouge strike, the National Labor Relations Board finally ruled on the 1937 Ford cases and called for a representation election in the Ford Detroit plants, namely the River Rouge and Lincoln plants. On April 7 the NLRB announced that the election would take place in forty-five days and that the ballot choices would be the UAW-CIO, the AFL Federal Labor Union, or neither.[84] The UAW's campaign for the representation election made the Ford Service Department a central issue. Its UAW press release noted that "plant protection" was "only an incidental function of this department. Primarily its function was espionage—spying on workers." The NLRB concluded that the Ford firm "resorted to brutal violence against union members or Ford workers suspected of union sympathies." It was "unhampered by the restrictions and responsibilities of a governmental police or detective force." Aside from union representation, a central issue was the "un-American" Ford anti-union institution. Hence, the UAW demanded the abolition of the Service Department and, most important, "all necessary members of a plant protection force be placed in uniform." Other important UAW issues included wage rates, secure employment, speed-up, and grievance machinery.[85]

Ford officials finally gave in and agreed not to fight the proposed NLRB elections. Although some black workers still supported the UAW-AFL in the May 21 election, 70 percent of all River Rouge workers voted for the UAW-CIO. (Around seventy-four thousand valid votes were cast; almost fifty-two thousand went to the CIO, slightly more than twenty thousand to the AFL, and almost two thousand for neither.)[86] With this huge majority, the UAW negotiated its first contract with Ford in July. It proved one of the most generous in the automobile industry. The UAW-Ford agreement created the first union shop in the automobile industry in all Ford plants. It offered wages as high as or higher than those of Ford competitors, provided for the check-off of union dues, established systems of departmental and job classification seniority, and created a shop-steward system with at least one steward in every department and an additional steward for every five hundred workers in large departments. Ford automobiles would carry the union label. And most important, Ford service men or plant-protection men would wear a distinctive uniform or special insignia.[87]

Although the UAW-Ford agreement ended the acrimonious strike, it did not end the bitter memories of Bennett's brutal industrial regime. Kenneth Bannon, a River Rouge worker and later head of the UAW Ford Department, described the rancorous shop-floor situation after strikers returned to the huge River Rouge complex. Upon their return to their shops and departments, the Ford strikers, he said, were "very, very bold." The bloody legacy of the spies, goons, and thugs created "a lot of bitterness." The Ford UAW leader and many of his workmates, Bannon remembered, "did some things that would not have been done if this bitterness had not been with us." Sometimes, he said, "[we] would work if we felt like working." The legacy of repression often resulted in vengeful anger, "cracked" heads, and sometimes "a get-even process." In a diminished role, many of the former Ford servicemen ended up in production and became coworkers with the UAW unionists. For those "assigned to our ranks," Bannon remembered, "we made rather certain that they received some of the treatment that they had handed out years ago. No one was injured to the extent that he was crippled in any fashion. It was just a matter of trying to even a few scores."[88]

The most serious incident occurred in early March 1943, almost two years after the Ford strike at the River Rouge plant. The caustic residues of the old Bennett regime still remained and shaped the acrimonious shop-floor relations in the River Rouge plant. Harry Shulman, who became the Ford Labor relations mediator, even characterized this incident a "bloody riot." In fact, this serious incident hastily caused UAW and Ford officials to negotiate its umpire-based arbitration system to process the final stage of grievances.

So serious was the case that federal officials with the War Manpower Commission also became involved. In his very first arbitration decision as Ford umpire, Shulman noted: "The parties have undertaken to substitute reason and justice for force in the adjustment of the day to day conflicts that attend large scale production." This grievance revealed auto worker resentment toward members of the Ford plant-protection department that replaced the service department. The Ford umpire characterized the violent event an "assault and mass disturbance." The grievance consolidated the cases of thirteen Ford workers, all but one a UAW official or shop representative. Management disciplined all of them with punishments ranging from a one-week layoff to discharge.[89]

The bloody riot began when Lawrence Yost, the union financial secretary for the Rouge Aircraft Building, attempted to enter the Ford plant around 11 P.M. Earlier, Yost had spent the evening meeting and drinking with a couple of Ford Rouge union members. At dinner, he "had several bottles of beer at a beer garden." After his union colleagues left, Yost continued drinking. At around 10 P.M., he headed for one of the gates at the River Rouge plant. When he arrived, Frank Gilder and John Donelli, two members of the plant-protection department, "noted that [Yost] was intoxicated to such a degree that he could not be admitted to the plant . . . [and] that he did not belong to this shift and did not have his badge on." The plant guards advised the union officer to return in the morning, whereupon Yost said "that he was financial secretary of the Union, that he was there to attend a meeting, and that he would call out the 12,000 Aircraft Building employees to beat hell out of [Gilder]."[90]

Only two years after the UAW organization of the Ford plant, the deep hostilities between union members and plant protection men still festered. The financial secretary, Shulman noted, "continued his abusive language, poked his fingers in [Gilder]'s back and chest and finally slapped [Gilder]'s face." Gilder then struck Yost, and the union official fell to the ground. "An unidentified worker," the umpire continued, "called upon employees entering the gate not to let [Gilder] get away with what he was doing to a good union member and take [Gilder] into the building." A crowd formed and responded to the appeal for aid to a fellow union man. They assailed Gilder and Donelli, subjecting them "to some pushing and shoving." Then the plant protection men "exchanged blows with some members of the crowd." They were marched to the union committee room. When Gilder attempted to explain his version of the event, he "was howled down by the crowd which was shouting that he be hung, beaten up, and so on."[91]

On the way to the plant-protection office, Gilder "was tripped and pushed." And while in the office, he received "many blows" and was "pushed" through the glass panel of one of the office doors. Intimidated by the raging crowd, the plant-protection supervisor wrote Gilder a quit slip, noting that his actions were "wrong." Although promised "safe conduct" from the plant, the crowd shoved and pushed Gilder out of the plant, "intermittently beating and kicking him."[92]

After Gilder managed to leave the plant, the harassment and abuse continued. At one point, some enraged Ford workers "formed a semi-circle around" Gilder. Several cried for someone to fight him. "One of the [union] men, a professional boxer," Shulman related, "was particularly called upon to fight and was pushed into the center of the semi-circle." In self-defense, the plant-protection man knocked him down and then "threw himself to the ground to avoid further punishment." The crowd's anger continued: "While he was down he was kicked again and called upon to fight others." Finally, an automobile arrived and drove Gilder off to the hospital. His injuries included "lacerations and contusions about the face, neck, and hands, a fractured jaw, and torn cartilage of the ribs."[93]

A central issue of this grievance was whether or not the Ford plant protection men wore their uniforms, something now required in the Ford union contract. Ford UAW president Paul Ste. Marie, who later arrived at the scene, stated: "I didn't know they were service men because they did not have uniforms."[94] Several others agreed. The Ford union contract called for the wearing of uniforms or badges.

For many River Rouge workers, despite the drunken and aggressive bravado of their union recording secretary, the fact that the plant protection men laid hands on a fellow unionist and that the plant guards were not uniformed seemed to hark back to the bad old Bennett days. So deep was the Ford worker anger and resentment that one item of Gilder's clothing came to represent and to symbolize the worst of the old Ford regime. The workers collectively destroyed Gilder's coat that was left behind in the factory. According to the umpire, "it was torn and cut up into shreds. It is said that the coat was hung on a conveyor and mutilated as it passed along." The dreaded conveyor line became a mechanism for a symbolic ritual of revenge against the service department's past abuses.[95]

In this complex grievance, Shulman had held the proverbial wolf by the ears and could not release it. Through their attorney, Ford-plant protection men wanted some justice for their brutally beaten and mauled colleague. Both civilian and military authorities also desired some form of either civil or military penalties. The union protested the disciplinary layoffs and dismissals of thirteen union members, including twelve important union officials or shop representatives. Only two years into union organization, Ford workers continued to vent their angry male rage at a representative of the detested plant protection department. In his ruling, Shulman noted: "Hostilities engendered before unionization, should not be permitted to mar relations after a strong union and a good grievance procedure have been established." Rather than sternly uphold punishment for what was aggressive and outrageous male behavior, the delicate restoration of industrial order in wartime was his prime objective. After careful consideration of the thirteen cases, he reduced the management's discipline of nine workers reducing the layoff time, reinstating those discharged, and maintained the layoffs of only four workers.[96] In the end, the Ford Local 600 members received what amounted to a mere slap on the wrist.

As the first Ford grievance to go to arbitration under Harry Shulman, the "bloody riot" revealed the deep and widespread workplace tensions in the mammoth River Rouge plant. The rancorous legacy of Bennett and his Service Department persisted through the war years. Other grievance cases underscored the profound discontent in the River Rouge plant. Ten days after the bloody riot, another shop-floor incident occurred and Harry Shulman later heard his second appealed grievance. A union committeeman in the aluminum foundry cursed an assistant superintendent who attempted to have a worker demonstrate a "new method for shaking out castings." The committeeman thought the suggested method was "hazardous." He and the superintendent got into an argument where the supervisor called the union man a "saboteur" for interfering with war production. The union representative replied: "I'm not afraid of you, you big ----------." He actually used a male term of severe derision, calling him a cocksucker, or as Shulman noted, "an oscular caresser of the male organ of copulation." He said that the phrase was "a general term of contempt and opprobrium, the degree of contempt connoted being rather great."

The two men certainly engaged in male posturing before an audience of fifteen to twenty witnesses. Ford officials gave the union committeeman a two-week layoff, and the UAW local appealed the decision to the umpire. For Shulman, such "abusive, ill-tempered language" by a union official destroyed "harmonious relations" between the company and the union. He added that there was "no question" that such language was "beyond the scope of tolerance even in the rough and tumble of the shop." Consequently, the arbitrator upheld the two-week layoff.[97]

Other incidents also demonstrated the deep divisions between union members and management representatives. In July 1943, Ford officials discharged three union-building committeemen and a D district committeeman for "forcibly ejecting" the D district job foreman from the aircraft building. Several days later, another worker got into a fight with his foreman in the press steel department. As the "aggressor," the press steel worker "knocked the foreman down. And while the foreman was lying on the floor pinned down on a fixture," the angry worker "kicked him in the face."[98]

The UAW campaign to organize the unorganized through the 1930s and into the early 1940s was indeed a masculine struggle for recognition and representation. For Ford River Rouge workers, their successful organization into the UAW allowed them to regain and to reclaim some of their lost manhood that resulted from years of humiliation. This bitter struggle eventually transformed postwar labor-management relations on the shop floor. Dave Moore, the black UAW activist radicalized in the Ford Hunger March, noted "a big change in attitude." The Ford workers "were more defiant to the supervisors. They had their say so." If someone argued or disagreed with a foreman or supervisor, he added, "everybody in that department could stop and come to his defense." After the UAW success, Walter Dorosh, a Slavic worker and UAW leader, remembered that the supervisors now "were afraid. They were hiding. We had real power." For the Italian UAW activist Archie Acciacca, UAW membership provided the secure path to the family wage. Acciacca recalled: "We started getting security, we started living like human beings. . . . we got more and more and more; and we got a lot of nice things today."[99]

When the UAW institutionalized itself on the shop floor, it created and established a densely masculine environment. Despite the struggles to win over African Americans, it was nevertheless a white and male domain. Through the war years, other shop-floor issues moved to the foreground, namely issues of race and gender. As more and more men left for distant European and Pacific battlefields, a severe labor shortage developed, and automobile manufacturers had to dip into its reserves of men and women not normally hired for machine and assembly positions. White women and African American men and women broke into white male industrial terrain and presented serious challenges to traditional white male workplace attitude and values.

5

Fashioning Dense Masculine Space

*Industrial Unionism and Altered
Shop-Floor Relations, 1935–1960s*

The bitter struggles to build industrial unions embedded the rough masculine culture in the shop-floor traditions of mass-production workers. Though workers strove for the responsibility and respectability of the family breadwinners, auto workers fought hard for recognition of their worth and dignity. In their struggles, however, the rough dimension of manhood prevailed and their new unions, such as the UAW, mirrored many of its elements. At the workplace, the male culture of aggression flourished; fighting, cursing, drinking and all manner of manly misbehavior prevailed. Numerous union grievances captured the dense male culture that revealed the details of the male character of the shop floor, and many such grievances often typified workers' manly quest for dignity and worth.

Through the 1930s, flying squadrons were the main actors in the union creation process. A response to managerial repression and violence, these CIO institutions rested on membership participation and involvement in the struggles to build meaningful worker representation. The UAW flying squadrons were both masculine and tough, and they established the style and tone for the deeply male shop culture after unionization. Often composed of large, brawny, and combative young men, these union squadrons were the first line of defense against management's thugs and goons who attempted to menace and intimidate union supporters. Usually union activists, rank-and-file shop leaders, and dedicated unionists, their members served as models of fighting manhood for fellow auto workers. A Toledo Auto Lite striker remembered his union's early flying squadron: its members were "people fighting for their bread and butter, American men, good honest men, fighting for their liberty, fighting for justice, fighting for just recognition." He added "we was all ready to die, if necessary. We didn't care; we was ready to give everything we had to win that strike." Another observer recalled the various UAW flying squadrons who aided the Flint sit-down strikers: "Every local had a flying squadron of tough, muscular members of the local. They were there to protect the union's interest, and any other local's interest that happened to be in danger."[1] These committed union supporters were a militant minority who formed the solid core of activists, who shaped labor-management relations, and who established the deeply male shop culture after the formation of unions.

The UAW flying squadron members were indeed strapping men, chosen for their size and fighting abilities, to battle their corporate and, after the Homer Martin split, AFL foes in the plant and on the streets. They defended organizational picket lines and in solidarity assisted other unions with picket duty. They sold tickets for and policed union dances, visited sick or injured union members, engaged in union sports leagues, and participated in educational activities. The Briggs flying squadron detailed the requirements for these union activists: "Anybody desiring to belong to this body must be paid up union member, aggressive and militant, and have an understanding of the Labor movement."[2]

As an almost paramilitary organization, flying squadron members often dressed in a uniform manner with similar jackets, shirts, and hats. Proud of their collective identity and reputation, the Briggs flying squadron members "wore leather jackets with the UAW local name on the back, a symbol and means of identification in a fight." Some CIO critics disparaged the UAW flying squadrons. One Mechanics Educational Society of America (MESA) member labeled them "storm troops" using "the language of fascism Americanized." Their uniform appearance reminded him of Germany's National Socialists. "These storm troopers or flying squadrons," he observed, "collect dues outside factories, . . . they will picket department stores, cafes, and places of amusement and insist that all customers and patrons have paid their party or union dues." The combative militants, he believed, were much too intolerant, overbearing, and dictatorial.[3]

A few UAW local leaders even tried to temper this fearsome and aggressive reputation. The captain of the Murray Body flying squadron wrote to his local's newsletter to announce his intent "to stifle forever rumors and insinuation that we are the nucleus of a band of desperadoes." The flying squadron's slogan, he reminded his fellow unionists, was "Preserve Order." He added: "Every member is pledged to prevent riots and its attendant violence in case of strikes in our own local and the International Union." He personally did not believe in violence and concluded: "No member of Local 2 or any person for that matter, need have any fear of it ever."[4]

Another Hudson flying squadron member decried the overly masculine character of his group of UAW militants. He noted that the UAW represented many women who worked in small auto-parts plants. "Why is it," he asked, "that a certain member of the Flying Squadron is always proposing stag parties? This fellow has a wife. Why aren't the wives at all the affairs given by the Flying Squadron?"[5] This male custom of stag parties certainly did not establish a welcoming climate for union sisters.

Through the late 1930s and into the 1940s, such men brought culture of confrontation and aggression onto the shop floor and into the unions they formed. The union structures and cultures mirrored the cultures of the men who engaged in the process of union formation. Through the years, one of the central demands of auto workers was for a mechanism to redress the balance of power on the shop floor. Since the late 1910s the earliest automobile unions consistently called for a network of workplace representatives, or shop stewards, and a grievance process to resolve workplace disputes. By the late 1930s such institutional forms of worker defense emerged in various configurations in the larger and smaller automobile firms. In the mid-1960s Walter Reuther described the early UAW goal: "One of our prime objectives is a grievance process to protect the worker against petty tyranny at the plant level."[6] Chrysler had a steward and committeeman system with a dense representation of stewards on the shop floor, a troublesome system that consistently challenged management rights. More cautious and more concerned about ceding workplace control, General Motors conceded only to a more limited committeeman system with a much thinner representation of workers. Although Ford recognized shop stewards, it was closer to GM in terms of the density of shop-floor worker representation. Reuther claimed that the 1940 establishment of an "impartial umpire" as the final step of the grievance process at GM was an important UAW achievement. By the early 1940s all three auto makers had adopted an impartial arbitrator or referee as the final stage in the grievance procedure.[7]

Typically, these grievance procedures had several steps for workers to resolve their complaints with management about their work situations. The process began with the worker raising the issue with his or her foreman with the assistance of a shop steward or shop committeeman. The next step often involved a union representative raising the problem with the plant superintendent. After this, a committee of labor and management sometimes met and attempted to discuss and to resolve the disputes. If still unresolved, the union or management could appeal the grievance case to an impartial arbitrator, also known as a referee or umpire. Since the grievance process brought rules and order to management-labor relations, labor historian David Brody labeled this formal and legalistic process the "workplace rule of law" or "industrial jurisprudence."[8] Under an umpire or referee system, the decisions of the arbitrator became precedents for future grievance cases.

Most important, these grievances served as windows into the workplace. Often well documented, the grievance files included the original written complaint to the foreman, notes or transcripts of plant committee discussions, and the sometimes-published decisions of the referees or arbitrators decisions. They offered glimpses into the day-to-day interactions among workers and between workers and shop-floor supervisors and revealed just how densely masculine the culture of industrial unionism was on the automotive shop floor.

Worker resistance to the rigors of the mass-production regime often took two forms—one boyishly playful and one angrily bitter. The playful resistance attempted to transform the workplace into a space of leisure, of hijinks and of fun and games, often at the expense of supervisors or workers lacking acculturation to unionism. The bitter resistance reflected the abuse and exploitation suffered in the non-union era and the sometimes violent struggles for unionism. Auto workers displayed their impish playfulness when they sang, joked, played pranks on each other, gambled in lavatories, or collectively vexed their supervisors and managers. Sometimes they were angry and bitter men annoyed at the rigors of the mass-production regime and involved in cursing, drinking, fighting each other or their supervisors.

Though leisure at work is often considered within the context of pre-industrial settings, auto workers attempted to turn the most advanced industrial space into a boy-like arena for leisure and play. The gradual creation and evolution of a distinct masculine culture for mass-production workers forces us to rethink our classic notions of time and work discipline in the transition from pre-capitalist to capitalist forms of work, discipline, and culture.[9] These notions have emphasized the loose and informal structures and patterns of pre-industrial work and the tight and disciplined ones of industrial work. Although in the pre-industrial world people worked hard for long hours, typically from sunrise to sunset, their working lives involved a loosely structured mix of work and leisure, of production and play, in their daily, weekly, and seasonal activities. With the progressive advance of industrial capitalism, the argument goes, these activities took on a new management-imposed and clock-controlled regularity, which eventually separated the realms of work and leisure. As Edward P. Thompson noted, the new industrial man required "new disciplines, new incentives, and a new human nature upon which these incentives could bite effectively."[10]

But sometimes the disciplines, incentives, and this new human nature failed to take root in the modern workplace. Although the general thrust of this argument captured the essential elements of the transition to an industrial capitalist work culture, it failed to apprehend human agency and its abilities and capacities to remake their working lives and workplace cultures. Despite efforts to impose new disciplines through the ever-increasing elaboration of factory work rules and managerial work regimes, industrial workers often continued to behave in their pre-industrial and inefficient ways. Despite the Taylorist and Fordist production strategies, workers continued to act as though their world of work was also their world of play and leisure.

Frequently, auto workers used the new forms of masculine culture to resist the routinization, degradation, and monotony of disciplined work routines. In his study of the British automobile industry, Paul Thompson discovered that auto workers had three possible responses to disciplined and regimented work—avoiding it, changing it, or accepting it and "putting one's heart elsewhere" while at work. In essence, the last strategy meant the redefining and reshaping male work culture and the transformation of the shop floor and workplace into a site of leisure or play.[11] In his investigation of early-twentieth-century German factory workers, Alf Leudtke distinguished between the "legal" breaks, the officially sanctioned rest periods for "physical replenishment," and the "illegal" breaks, the workers' expropriation of "bits of time formally designated as working time." Once industrial capitalism separated company time from personal time-that is, work time from leisure time—managers and workers struggled over the appropriate use of company time. During the illegal breaks, Leudtke observed, factory workers "broke with the demands and constraints of the factory system as well with the toil of labor and reproduction." Activities such as shop-floor horseplay were "a mixture of claims against supervisors' demands maintaining customary rights and of striving for the humanity of the individual and his comrades."[12] This struggle for independent space connected to working-class masculine culture. This illicit behavior also connected with male oppositional and confrontational rituals and displays of power to challenge the newly established Taylorist and Fordist industrial order.

Moreover, this illicit behavior suggests that the distinction between work and leisure never fully broke down. Masculine play sometimes meant simply not working dutifully and consistently at one's routinized job. In their individual and collective forms of illegal or illicit behavior, some workers ate, read, drank alcohol, read books or newspapers, fought, or gambled while at work. Others took overly long breaks, aggressively challenged their supervisors, engaged in incessant play, or conducted work slowdowns or stoppages simply to obtain a break from the factory regimen. Many of these illicit activities and oppositional gestures derived from the rough masculine culture often characterized by drinking, contestation, and violence.

For many auto workers, the restroom, the most private of human spaces, often served as a sanctuary from the inhuman rhythms of factory production. Within automobile plants, a most frequent complaint was the contested issue of relief to perform natural bodily functions, an issue that sharply delineated the natural human world and the artificial mechanical one. For recently unionized workers, the position of relief man, along with scheduled breaks, helped to humanize the tightly regimented and controlled workplace.

The shop lavatory remained a private and individual respite and escape from the pressures of mechanized line production. In 1947 the UAW's Board of Review, a three-man committee that approved grievances sent to the General Motors umpire, denied a worker's appeal of discipline for spending thirty minutes in the toilet. It noted a recent umpire's decision that "a twenty-two minute unobserved absence in the toilet" justified disciplinary action for "loitering." In 1950 the Board of Review considered a case where a supervisor charged an auto worker with "reading a newspaper while sitting on the stool with his pants up." Somehow, the worker secured two witnesses who affirmed his denial of the supervisor's charge. Nonetheless, the UAW board refused to send the case to the umpire because testimony of worker witnesses contained discrepancies.[13]

The shop toilet was also the social space for more collective expressions of relief from work pressures. In 1943, two Bendix Products workers protested William Hornyak's discharge for his alleged participation in a crap game in the Strut Division toilet. According to a manager, it was "the worst [toilet] in the plant for crap shooting." Apparently, a plant security guard walked into a circle of eight or nine workers engaged in a crap game with $50 to $100 lying on the restroom floor. Although one worker admitted to loitering (he "was standing near a post watching the game and smoking"), Hornyak did not participate in the illicit game. When the guard asked for badge numbers, most of the group, the union representative said, "walked right by the cop. He asked them for their badges and they said, 'No.'" Hornyak claimed: "I was sitting down and all at once something happened and I got up and was ready to go . . . when the cops came in and stopped me." When the security officer asked for his badge number, Hornyak willingly complied, though he emphasized: "I was not in the game." After a union representative argued that he was not "a habitual hanger arounder of that toilet," management officials eventually rescinded the Bendix worker's discharge.[14]

Although the men's lavatory was a common site for worker gambling, this male activity occurred elsewhere throughout automobile plants. In 1965 Thomas Anderson, a millwright in the Baltimore Chevrolet plant, protested his two-day layoff for participating in a crap game during his lunch period. After hearing "the sound of money being thrown on the table and the clicking of dice," two foremen and a plant-protection sergeant caught four men—the millwright, two carpenters, and a welder—gambling at a maintenance shop workbench. As the general foreman confiscated a pair of dice, Anderson protested: "This is the first time we shot dice since we were caught the last time [almost three months ago]." Although the union disingenuously claimed that the men were simply "standing or sitting around," that the money was for "coffee, buns, and hot dogs" from the "wagon outside the main gate," and that "no Plant rule" forbade "carrying a pair of dice on your person," Chevrolet management upheld Anderson's suspension.[15]

In a multitude of grievances, auto workers demonstrated how they used their masculine culture to confront and to oppose the relations of authority and power at the regimented workplace. For example, they frequently and publicly postured against their shop foremen, supervisors, and superintendents. In one instance a Briggs worker insisted on his right to yodel on the job despite a threatened two-day layoff. With an almost boyish testing of the limits, union officials noted the absence of a specific Briggs rule against yodeling. In this particular shop, Briggs workers, they maintained, had a common practice of singing "at the top of their voices" to relieve their monotony at work. "You should be thankful," they counseled Briggs managers, "that you have a department where they are happy." Managers thought quite differently, asserting: "This is a place of business and we don't subscribe to yodeling or whistling in our departments at any time." They added: "If the men think they can go out there and yodel, . . . they are badly mistaken."[16]

While such male horseplay often redefined the work environment and made it a looser, more friendly, and more human space, it sometimes created safety hazards for other workers. In 1937 two Briggs trimmers "were heckling" a third worker and "throwing chalk" at him. According to the union representative at the grievance hearing, the worker "had his head shaved off and the boys were peppering him with chalk." Angered, the victim "lost control" and "threw a hammer at the man that was throwing chalk at him, missed this man and hit somebody else," who suffered a split lip. Briggs officials fired the two offenders; a few months later, the men were rehired but lost their seniority.[17]

But—men were men (perhaps "boys" is the better word), and they persistently insisted on their male right of such social interaction on the shop floor. Since horseplay sometimes endangered the personal safety of other union members, union leaders often cooperated with management and tried to contain this illicit behavior. Nonetheless, auto workers still asserted their right to unsanctioned breaks from the rhythms of mass production. In 1942 twenty-four Briggs workers signed a petition that "demand[ed] a special meeting for setting our chief steward right or electing a new one in his place." The union steward's offense: he did not "live up to relief regulations" and also reported "horseplay of [union] members to [the] foreman jeopardizing their jobs." In 1944 the Executive Board members of the Seaman Body UAW local issued a recommendation to discourage horseplay. They complained about the "many cases of horseplay . . . which have caused bodily injury" and the large amount of "lost time for Local Union Officers" on grievances that did not benefit "any great number" of union members. Recognizing management's right to discipline workers, the UAW Executive Board refused to defend members who "insist on indulging in the practice of horseplay."[18]

Another traditional masculine vice was the use and abuse of alcohol at the automotive workplace. For mass-production workers in the automobile plants, alcohol—and later in the 1960s, drugs—numbed the body's senses and reduced the tedium, fatigue, and monotony of work. Especially when they worked in isolated work areas, men sometimes drank on the job. They also drank in taverns near their plants before and after work. When allowed to leave the workplace for lunch, they drank then too, in parking lots or nearby taverns. Again, another common male leisure activity persisted in the disciplined modern workplace. Drinking alcohol also complicated workplace personal and social relations. Lubricated by a bit too much drink, an inebriated worker might act overly aggressively toward a co-worker, engage in excessively rough horseplay, express more overtly deep ethnic or racial antagonisms, or even verbally deride a shop supervisor.

Consider, for example, the case of Carl "Tex" Leonard, a UAW Local 1250 shop committeeman in the Cleveland Ford Engine Plant, recently transferred from the night to the day shift. Shortly after his transfer, on a Monday morning, Leonard apparently went on a tear through the assembly room and directly challenged several foremen. Coming from the night shift, his personal experience with shop behavior and discipline was often much looser.

After the event, D. W. Starner, the labor-relations supervisor, asserted: "A committeeman that goes on a rampage can destroy quite a bit of harmony."

From the moment he arrived on Monday morning at 8 A.M., Leonard began bouncing into and arguing with Ford shop foremen. When foreman Jay O. Reynolds joked with Leonard and another worker, inquiring whether they "pulled him off midnights," Leonard replied: "Yeah, I'm on days now and I'd better not catch you working, or I'll pull every f----g man out of your department." He then moved on to another foreman. "I was standing there," Ray F. Hart reported, "instructing [an] employee . . . on a better method of securing the damper onto the crankshaft." Leonard walked up to him with "a strong odor of alcohol on his breath," with an "unshaven face" and "a general haggard appearance," Hart wrote, and said: "I'm the committeeman—goddamn it, lay off these men. You're nothing but a fuckin' production pusher."

After this, Ted Reitz, the shop's general foreman, reported how Leonard threatened to have him fired:

> I was talking to a Pipefitter . . . when Leonard waved and said, "Hey, you, come over here." I walked a distance of some six or seven feet toward him; and as he approached he said, "You haven't had any trouble with a committeeman lately, but I'm warning you that if you get out of line the same thing will happen to you that happened to Sprouel." I asked what was that. He said "I got his job, and I'll get yours if you get out of line—and if you tell anybody this, I'll deny it."

Earlier, Sprouel had been dismissed for his overbearing and abusive behavior toward workers. The general foreman, too, thought that he smelled liquor on the union shop committeeman's breath.

To still another foreman, William Fort, who was teaching two repairmen how to use a tap extractor, reported that he heard "in a loud and obnoxious manner" Leonard shouting, "You son-of-a bitch, you keep your hands off the f----g tools or I'll have your job."

By this time, the plant superintendent and several foremen reported the incidents to Guy Baker, an industrial-relations representative, who initiated a general search for Leonard. Eventually, management found the aggressive committeeman and sent him to the labor-relations office. When Leonard arrived at the office at 12:20, he had his union representative with him. Starner requested that they go to "the Plant First Aid office to be examined by the doctor." In his report on the incident, the labor relations supervisor noted: "I had reasons to believe that he was suffering from the lingering effects of some type of stimulant." After conferring with his union committeeman,

Leonard told Starner: "The company doctor would be biased and . . . if he could have his own doctor here to be jointly examined, he would comply with the request." After Leonard again refused, the Ford labor official suspended him and escorted him from the plant.

The union committeeman apparently had imbibed a bit too much, but the Leonard incident was much more dense and complicated than the surface facts revealed. First, in the mid-1950s, the Ford Cleveland Plant witnessed the genesis of industrial automation and seethed with worker discontent. Automated production technologies wreaked havoc on traditional work processes and skills and resulted in numerous grievances over job classifications. Moreover, in order to protect workers' jobs, UAW contracts often banned foremen from directly engaging in production or actually performing a workman's job. All of Leonard's confrontations involved foremen who either touched a piece of work or instructed workers how to perform their tasks. As a committeeman, Leonard aggressively, perhaps overly so, guarded his co-workers' right to perform their work without supervisory intervention or interference.

Second, within the context of widespread technical change, UAW Local 1250 officials vigorously defended the committeeman against several charges:

> Obscene, Disrespectful and Abusive Language to Supervision; Disobedience to Proper Authority; Out of Assigned Representative Area; Reporting to Work Under the Influence of Alcohol or the Lingering Effects Thereof.

Despite this seemingly outrageous behavior, union leaders contended that Leonard never refused to see a doctor and "merely requested" the presence of his family physician. Though shop foremen claimed that Leonard was under the influence of alcohol, the more qualified Baker, they argued, did not "detect the odor of alcohol" in his "small and closed Labor Relations Office." As for being "out of his assigned representative area," the union officials maintained that he was new to the daytime shift. They also defended the committeeman's choice of words as the typical masculine talk on the factory floor: "the language of the shop is not the language of the parlor." This "premise," they believed, was "universally accepted."

Generally, in Leonard's defense, the Local 1250 leaders asserted: "In spite of the multiplicity of charges against that aggrieved, none of them are warranted nor can be proven." In the highly charged discourse, they contended that the Ford Motor Company "is trying to render our committeemen impotent to do the work of which he and others were elected and are dedicated to. The Union would not be worth the powder to blow it to hell if the company had the right to penalize a committeeman who is willing to fight for the employ-ees he represents."[19]

Often, the confrontational games men played slid into even more direct challenges to managerial power and authority. For sociologist Michael Bura-woy, "making out" was "a series of games in which operators attempt to achieve levels of production that earn incentive pay, in other words, anything over 100 percent."[20] Shop managers encouraged such individualistic play or games because it drew workers into the managerial goal of increased pro-duction. "The very activity of playing a game," Burawoy observed, "generates consent with respect to its rules," since "one cannot both play the game and at the same time question the rules." Consent to the industrial order and its power relations, he asserted, "rests upon—is constructed through—playing the game."[21]

Still, the human agency and human will of automobile workers, especially in unionized UAW work settings, often resulted in the creation of different rules for different interests. On the shop floor, soldiering and output restric-tion, that is, the individual and the collective establishment of shop activities, behavior, and rules, often rested on masculine bonds and understandings developed in the locker room, barroom, union hall, or shop floor. Whether an individual or collective form of "manly bearing," such behavior often took on an oppositional or confrontational posture toward plant management.

In the South Bend Bendix Products plant, department 5B was "infamous for its slowdown tactics in protest of first one thing and then another." The union men in this brake shop turned "making out" into a different game and created their own shop-floor rules. In May 1946 the Bendix workers in 5B engaged in "a concerted slowdown in protest" against new piece rates on the brake shoes that they produced. The workers claimed that the "rates were too tight" and that they could not "make out" on the new piece rates. In fact, during arbitration before Harry E. Shulman, the Bendix workers and their UAW Local 9 union leaders even denied that they were conducting a slow-down strike and "contended that the employees were giving us a full day's work and that they were unable to earn any greater efficiency simply because the rates were too tight." The union officials asserted that "it was impossible for these men to run 100%." In the midst of "confused" testimony, however, several union witnesses said that "they could run from 105% to 112% if they worked at top speed." Shulman declared: "This was not individual action; it was action in concert." Hence, it was impermissible.

The Bendix workers quickly abandoned their work slowdown and over three weeks their "earned efficiency" immediately rose to 157 percent, 161 percent, and then 164 percent. During one month in early 1947 the Bendix brake workers averaged 156 percent. Bendix managers finally recognized that workers discovered a way "to 'beat' the system." In one instance, brake-shoe grinders figured out how to best the counters on the machines that recorded their production. The machine operators, one report noted,

> found that they could place two shoes on the fixture and [have] the 1st machine run indefinitely with the counter recording two pieces each time that the fixture made a complete revolution. This could be done without removing the shoes from the fixture. Thus, the count increased with each revolution and no parts were produced.

In another, the machine operators also discovered "that it was possible to 'fan' the counter manually to increase the count." At the end of the shift, a "weighbill man" took the total off the machine counters and reset it for the next shift. Concerned that worker "cheating" meant that Bendix Products "paid for 34,285 more shoes than were produced," managers installed a scale to "weigh count" the brake shoes produced. This action resulted in another round of slowdowns, with the earned efficiency falling from 156 percent to as low as 88 percent. In accordance with state legislation on minimum wages, the Bendix workers then demanded that they be paid the minimum earned rate.[22]

Such male group camaraderie and solidarity also existed in other parts of the same Bendix Products plant. In May 1948, when the department 5B brake-shoe grinders conducted an "unauthorized" wildcat strike that resulted in layoffs in other departments, the brake-shoe assemblers began their own slowdown. Two days after the grinders struck, the brake assemblers of department 9A were "evidently displeased about something, so that they were running about 80% efficiency." By the afternoon, their efficiency had "fallen to about 25%"; the next day, "they averaged about 10% efficiency for eight hours." Then, the Bendix assemblers demanded the state minimum wage for the day where they only produced 10 percent.[23]

In both cases the fraternal bonds of manhood remade and refashioned the rules of the game of making out. As elsewhere, one can almost hear the smug, shop-floor laughter as union leaders and members recounted their disingenuous testimony at the formal grievance hearings. Nurtured in the tavern, the union hall, or the workplace, these bonds of masculine culture facilitated the collective airing of shop-floor grievances and the collective rebalancing of power on the factory floor. To be sure, Harry Shulman certainly did not condone such behavior, but the Bendix workers surely communicated their oppositional perspective to Bendix management.

Masculine banter and horseplay sometimes verged on homoerotic activities and behaviors in the all-male space of the automotive shop floor. Reflecting on his Fisher Body experience in the 1970s, John Lippert reported "much time working with men in almost complete isolation from women." Although "none of what happens between men in the plant is considered 'sexuality,'" he discerned in the intensely competitive male environment "a pretty basic need for physical intimacy or reassurance." The Fisher Body workers expressed these needs "very simply, through putting arms around shoulders or squeezing knees, but it can become much more intense and explicit, through stabbing between the ass cheeks or pulling at nipples." Although such behavior "seem[ed] as absurd as possible," Lippert asserted, "many men enjoy[ed] this physical interaction."[24]

Within this context, arbitrator Edward L. Cushman ruled on a REO Motors shop-floor incident of male horseplay that displayed the interconnected themes of work, play, and power. In his ruling on an incident of male horseplay, Cushman wrote:

> On Wednesday, December 9, 1953, . . . Joe Brzak was walking west, down an aisle, when a lift truck driver, Arthur Trescott, passed him going in the same direction. M. D. Murray, Chief Inspector, . . . claims the he saw Brzak goose Trescott. Foreman Garth Barrett also claims that he saw Brzak move his arm with the apparent intent of goosing Trescott and that . . . he assumed from the startled reaction that Brzak had in fact goosed Trescott.

Additionally, two supervisors asserted that Trescott "stopped his truck, stepped off, and chased Brzak a few steps, making an upward motion of his arm as if to goose Brzak." Possibly smiling privately as he drafted his legalistic description of the shop-floor incident, Cushman added: "Both the alleged gooser and the alleged goosee denied the alleged goosing."

For violating three shop rules, "disregard of safety, horseplay, and distraction of attention," the foreman discharged Brzak. On the surface, the goosing grievance appeared a simple case of a reasonable management effort to control possibly dangerous play in the REO plant. Beneath the surface, however, it represented a more basic conflict over the relative power of labor and management on the shop floor.

In their brief, REO managers emphasized the incident's dangerous nature. The lift truck was "a stand-up type," and the location was "a busy area traversed by a long main aisle" with "many entrances, stairway areas, and intersecting aisles." The location, they maintained, clearly possessed "a high potential of injury, damage or death."

From the REO management perspective, the factual details were quite simple. Brzak engaged in dangerous horseplay. Brzak, they maintained, "stepped forward toward the driver and 'goosed' him. Brzak's hand touched Trescott's body. There was some reaction on the part of the driver. Trescott then stopped the truck, stepped off, and chased Brzak for two or three steps." Although a foreman witnessed the incident from twelve feet away, he could not confirm that Brzak's hand touched Trescott's body. Nonetheless, he was "certain [that] it did because of the position and movement of Brzak's body and arms, and the 'start' by Trescott, followed by a retaliatory chase by Trescott." When the foreman questioned the offender, "Brzak denied that he goosed Trescott, but admitted [that] they were *fooling around.*"

In the REO brief, the most important "real" issue was "management's right to control dangerous conduct by disciplinary action." Other issues included the right to have "an adequately flexible pattern of penalties," the "credibility of responsible" management officials versus the "self-serving denial" of workers, the "freedom of supervisors to discipline workers," and the union's "responsibility . . . to cooperate with Management in legitimate discipline cases." In management's eyes, "Brzak was guilty of conduct that was most dangerous. Control of unsafe practices is a grave supervisory responsibility." In order to exercise its appropriate managerial authority and power, management required the right to impose severe disciplinary sanctions, "measures . . . sufficiently effective to prevent repetition." Consequently, they held that the arbitrator should deny the union appeal of Brzak's grievance.

Despite management's claim for the power to control illicit behavior, UAW Local 650's brief portrayed an entirely different and more complicated situation. For union officials, the fundamental issue was REO management's discriminatory actions toward an aggressive union member. Due to the "discriminatory nature" of Brzak's discharge, the union officials demanded that the referee "reinstate Employee Brzak with full seniority rights and compensate him for lost time."

First, the UAW Local 650 union officials denied that any violation of plant rule occurred. Since Chief Inspector Murray was sixty feet, not the estimated thirty or forty feet, from the incident, he could not have seen the alleged incident. Though only twelve feet away, Foreman Barrett "saw no actual goosing, but assumed there had been from the action he observed." Even Trescott, the alleged goosee, presented a notarized statement: "*At no time did Joe Brzak['s] hand come in contact with my body as the company claims.*"

Second, the union officials claimed that management had an established pattern of intimidating aggressive union members who used the grievance process. In 1953 Brzak successfully grieved a three-day disciplinary layoff. In one instance, Foreman Barrett attempted "to influence the election of a Union Steward." In another, someone in the personnel office suggested that the departmental supervisor "was out to get" Brzak's union committeeman. Additionally, the union officials also noted three separate instances where management disciplined workers who questioned or grieved managerial authority on the shop floor.

Local 650 officials offered the example of a previous goosing grievance to prove management discrimination against Brzak. This involved Herman Langus, a worker on the truck assembly line, who upon being goosed "turned around and pushed" his assailant, "causing him to fall on a sharp edge of a fixture." The other worker even had to go to the hospital. Despite this serious injury, shop officials gave both workers disciplinary warning slips only. Moreover, after six months, management removed the warning from Langus's personnel record.

In his decision, Edward L. Cushman was "convinced that Brzak was guilty of initiating horseplay with Trescott in disregard for safety." Whether or not an actual goosing took place was "immaterial." Horseplay, the umpire continued, could have "serious adverse results." The two workers had "an obligation to each other and to their families to refrain from horseplay." Although REO officials had "the right to take steps to prevent" such activities, Cushman believed that discharge was "an excessive penalty" for the Brzak case. In the absence of evidence that Brzak had "undesirable record," and since a prior goosing penalty was rescinded, he reduced the penalty to a one-week layoff as a "sufficiently powerful inducement for him to refrain from horseplay in the future." Then Cushman ordered Brzak's reinstatement with full seniority and compensation for lost time since the discharge.[25] In this case, a simple incident of horseplay, an illicit break from the regimented routine of industrial work, was transmuted into a question of power, management versus union power in the REO factory.

Sometimes auto workers playfully challenged the symbols of shop-floor authority. For example, neckties were important signs of managerial authority, power, and control on the shop floor. Often referred to as "the man in the middle," the foreman frequently stood with one foot in the blue-collar and one in the white-collar world. He knew the dirty world of men, metal, and machines, but he lived in relative affluence and security compared with the blue-collar workers he supervised. With the rise of militant auto-worker unionism and the related threat of foremen unionism, some automobile firms attempted to distinguish and separate foreman from the men and women on the shop floor and required them to dress in white shirts and ties. By the early 1940s an aggressive UAW class identity conflicted with the new management vision of shop-floor social relations. Hence, neckties became bold emblems of labor-management conflict.

In 1941, one auto worker directly and aggressively challenged the new symbol of managerial authority in the Fleetwood plant—the necktie of the foreman. At the time, General Motors and other auto manufacturers began to require their foremen to wear white shirts and ties to emphasize the social divide on the shop floor. A Fisher Body worker, G. B., apparently resented the new symbol of shop-floor authority. According to the GM grievance umpire, he walked up to his foreman and "cut off" his "necktie without any provocation." Although the grievance does not indicate where this bold act occurred, given its symbolic nature, it must have been a public one in front of other workers. We have no account of the possible laughing, raucous hilarity, or goading and cheering of other workers on the shop floor. We have only the indignant reactions of the GM officials and the GM umpire.

For this audacious act, the shop supervisor sent the Fleetwood worker home with a one-and-a-half day layoff. When the worker returned to his job, the plant manager decided that he merited harsher punishment for the "highly improper act." The GM official indignantly proclaimed, "It is not a question of a cut necktie. The act itself was a deliberate attempt to cast reflection on the supervision, so instead of giving you a suspension, I am discharging you this morning."

Even the appalled GM umpire commented that under "any standard of decency," the worker's conduct was "repulsive." He was further dismayed at the Fleetwood worker's "refusal to *be man enough* to admit responsibility for his act."

Still, the necktie grievance case turned on the issue of double jeopardy—management first imposed the layoff and then subsequently added another penalty—the discharge. The GM umpire rescinded the auto worker's discharge but emphasized that "the present decision cannot be construed as any vindication of him." Despite the Fisher Body worker's reinstatement, his actions were "repulsive and irresponsible."[26]

Four years later a foreman's necktie again became the despised target of three Flint Fisher Body workers. This time a bit of New Year's Eve "horseplay" and hijinks slid into a violent confrontation between several workers and their foreman on the shop floor. The workplace incident began, the GM Umpire observed, when three workers "attempted to cut off Foreman C's necktie." In this instance, "the Foreman resisted [and] . . . in the ensuing struggle . . .

[he] was struck and beaten so severely that he required medical treatment for his cuts and bruises." In defense of the three workers, the UAW local officials contended "that the tie-cutting started merely as a bit of New Year's 'horse play'" and that the foreman "brought his beating on himself by growing angry and striking Employee G." Clearly, the shop supervisor vigorously struggled to retain his necktie and to avoid public and demeaning humiliation from the three workmen. Though the necktie incident began "in a spirit of fun," the umpire ruled that it was "no excuse for the violent attack that followed the Foreman's resistance." He emphatically stated that he did not "expect Management to tolerate physical assaults upon members of Supervision." The maintenance of the shop-floor status and authority of management certainly required the GM umpire's strengthening and reinforcement. He upheld the three workers' discharges.[27]

For *Business Week*, incidents such as cutting foremen's neckties were part of a "general breakdown" of industrial discipline in America's war-production plants. In late 1944 on Christmas Eve and New Year's Eve, auto workers recognized that the "disciplinary reins on them were becoming slack." The business news magazine reported: "It is now freely admitted that numbers of big Detroit plants were scenes of disorder . . . [and] liquor was brought openly into some shops by workers." As telling testimony to the new worker indiscipline, the magazine described the inflammatory situation in one Detroit aircraft plant. It "was the scene of a free-for-all necktie cutting party. Gangs of men armed with shears roamed the plant snipping off ties of fellow workers, supervisors, and management. Several workers were treated for cuts caused by the scissors wielding; one man was seriously hurt."[28] The festive shop environment of holidays often meant a complete breakdown of discipline.

Sometimes male workers collectively mocked and challenged managerial and supervisory claims for respect and authority from their subordinates. In the Dodge Main plant, a majority of a group of three hundred men supposedly booed their supervisor. According to the union president, the shop supervisor "was unable to handle the situation that arose when the booing started, and deliberately set out to make employee Kanisto the 'goat' for the whole affair." When he singled out the disobedient worker, the supervisor asked: "Why are you booing me?" The worker replied, "It makes me feel good!" The supervisor "warned him to cut out that horse play [and] if he were caught again he will get three days off." When Kanisto returned with his shop steward, the union representative said that the supervisor could not "send him home for booing." The supervisor reiterated that Kanisto had been warned.[29]

Later, when the supervisor returned to the insurgent department, "Kanisto did the same thing." After calling him over, the supervisor said, "You just won't behave. You are still booing!" Kanisto replied, "Yes, and I will keep on booing." The supervisor then gave the Dodge worker a three-day layoff. Ten minutes later, after the supervisor returned to his office, Kanisto, the steward, and about twelve other workers marched in and insisted that they all go home with Kanisto. Eventually, the plant committeemen got the others to return to work. Although the union initially supported Kanisto, it eventually withdrew the grievance.[30]

In an incident labeled the "Shirt-Tail Parade," the General Motors umpire combined three grievances that involved 145 Chevrolet Transmission Division workers. The worker protest began after the safety supervisor reproached a Chevrolet worker "who had his sport shirt hanging outside of his trousers and discussed with him the safety hazard of this form of dress." Though the night-shift worker complied with the supervisor's request to put his shirt inside his trousers, he "filed a grievance protesting being singled out for violating safety practices." The next day, Friday, two union committeemen and another worker wore their shirts outside their trousers. When they refused to obey an order to dress properly, management sent them home, and they subsequently filed a grievance. On Saturday morning the local union president, the chairman of the Shop Committee, committeeman, and another worker "were sent home for the remainder of the day for refusing to obey orders of supervision to conform with Safety Rule No. 13, while wearing their shirts outside of their trousers." They too filed a grievance.[31]

Three days later, Chevrolet managers noticed that "all employes were wearing their shirts inside of their trousers during the first hour of their shift." But later they reported:

> At approximately 8:20 A.M., a large number of employes began to pull their shirts out of their trousers and continued to wear them in that manner. When these employes were approached by supervision and instructed to place their shirts inside of their trousers many of them complied. However, 138 employes refused to do so and Management assessed a two-day disciplinary layoff against each of them for refusing to obey an order of Management that was designed to prevent a safety hazard.

When these 138 workers filed their grievances, a total of 145 workers protested the management policy against them wearing their shirts outside of their trousers.[32]

According to the dismayed umpire, both union and management officials lightheartedly referred to the series of disciplinary layoffs as the "Shirt-Tail Parade." Management officials complained "that the entire situation 'was deliberately executed with the full support and knowledge of the local

[Plant] Committee.'" For the disciplined workers, their layoff took on the air of a "holiday." Union officials reported that "a majority of them held a party at the local union hall for most of the time that they were not in the plant."[33]

The workers' mischievous behavior deeply offended the General Motors umpire's middle-class sense of propriety. It was "unfortunate," he observed, that the shirttail episode "should be dignified with so much as a single-line decision." He castigated the local union president, the shop chairman, and the shop committee members who "aided in directing the entirely improper mass demonstration." The protesting Chevrolet workers, he added, followed an "irresponsible leadership." He even censured the union leaders for their "thoughtless action." And he asked: "Is their any credit to those who activated a mass demonstration to gain the insignificant right of employes to wear their shirt tails outside of their trousers at the cost of a real impairment to the war effort?"[34]

Sometimes, automobile workers used plant rules to mobilize workers, to organize their plants, or to reshape the shop rules. In two General Motors factories, the Fisher Grand Blanc Tank plant and the Grand Rapids Stamping plant, workers conducted multiple mass protests over factory rules on smoking. In 1942 nineteen hull welders in the Fisher plant "left their jobs, without permission, to smoke at the plant entrance." Two weeks later, "approximately one hundred employes left their jobs with the express statement that they wanted to smoke when warned that Management would enforce disciplinary action if they insisted on leaving their jobs to smoke." After being warned of three-day disciplinary layoff, forty-one workers "stayed out of the plant, formed a picket line, and an eight-day work stoppage resulted." After labor-management negotiations, an NLRB election was conducted and the UAW-CIO became the exclusive representative of the Fisher workers.[35]

Over the next several months, although the union representatives repeatedly attempted "to obtain extensions of the smoking privileges," the issue initially caused "little trouble" in the Grand Blanc Tank plant. Then, eight months after the original incidents, a worker was caught smoking during working hours and disciplined. The next day, "fifty-nine employes of the day shift in the Hull Welding Department smoked and were reprimanded." General Motors officials then warned the union committee "that severe disciplinary action would be taken if there was a repetition of the mass smoking demonstration." Despite the warning, nineteen additional workers insisted on smoking the next day, and management initiated steps to suspend them. After this, another fifty-seven workers joined in a mass smoking demonstration.

GM officials suspended all the workers pending a review of their records. In the end, they gave most of the employees a three-day disciplinary layoff.[36]

However, General Motors discharged all those who participated in the July organizational demonstrations. The GM umpire agreed with the union that the July protests were "an integral part of this organizational drive" and that discharge was too severe a punishment. With the exception of one worker "with a record replete with in fractions of shop rules," the umpire rescinded the discharges of the other eight workers and imposed five- to eight-week disciplinary layoffs.[37]

At the Fisher Body Stamping plant, 240 production workers conducted "five mass smoking demonstrations." In this case, ten workers grieved their disciplinary penalties. Another 196 workers without prior records received three-day layoffs and the remaining forty-four workers with poorer records got "more severe disciplinary action," ranging from four-day layoff to discharge. For the vast majority of workers, the umpire upheld their punishments.[38]

In the deeply masculine world of American automobile plants, shop-floor fights often revolved around the defense of manly pride and honor in the public presence of one's workmates. Fighting, another prototypical form of masculine behavior, was a common and frequent means for the aggressive settlement of shop-floor disputes between workers. Numerous grievances concerned testosterone-filled workers aggressively displaying their "manly bearing." Sometimes violent behavior involved fists, sometimes boards and two-by-fours, sometimes knives and even guns. In 1938 Nelson Saunders, a Briggs worker, protested his layoff and loss of seniority for his involvement in a knife fight. According to the grievance, the other worker was the aggressor who "pulled a knife on Saunders, and Saunders fought back in self defense." Furthermore, it added: "A complete investigation . . . found that the man that attacked Saunders, had on three previous occasions been involved in knife incidents." Saunders had his seniority restored. The rough Briggs plant and numerous other auto plants had many similar incidents.[39]

In another instance, W. F., a Pontiac Motor plant worker, could not stomach a shop bully's needling and harassing of another worker. S., the bully, had left his work station and "provoked a fight" and "jumped upon" A. Then, W. F. went to his foreman and told him "that S. had better be taken out of the side gear line or he would be in trouble and 'someone would get hurt.'" Within the context of respectable manhood, the stronger man should help and defend the weaker one. When W. F. returned to his machine, he became involved in an altercation with the workplace bully; S. evidently attempted to hit W. F.

and missed. W. F. hit S. and "clinched, holding him until the foreman came upon the scene." Both W. F. and S. received a two-week disciplinary layoff for fighting. Since union and management officials could not agree on who initiated the fight, the General Motors grievance umpire denied W. F.'s appeal and upheld his layoff. Nonetheless, the umpire acknowledged the aggressive and combative nature of the shop floor: "Although it would unquestionably be inequitable to penalize a 'participant' who was defending himself," an "unprovoked attack" was "a rarity" among factory workers. In the absence of "obvious evidence" that one worker was the aggressor, the GM umpire reverted to "the old saying that 'it takes two to make a fight.'"[40]

In another case a Chevrolet Flint worker also encountered a shop bully and allowed his swelling anger to overflow into a physical confrontation. According to the GM umpire, P. was a thirteen-year employee who "has shown no other evidences of temper, and on the whole appears to be a steady and up-right man." P. and B. got into an argument about how B. pushed a piece of work onto the table where P. was working. Chevrolet officials reported "that a general exchange of profanity occurred," that the heated argument ceased for half an hour, and that it resumed a few minutes before the lunch break. At this time, B. threatened "that he would 'beat up' P., if P. again accused him of pushing cab tops down on P."

In their defense of the smaller man, union officials noted the size and the demeanor of the two men. They noted that the bully "weighs at least sixty pounds more than P., has experienced many arguments with other men with whom he worked, and has 'bullied' many of the men in his immediate vicinity." When P. asked him "not to push cab tops on the table quite so hard," B. left his workplace, and stepped rapidly toward P. shouting 'You are a G-- D--- liar.'" B. appeared to have an object in his hand and "P. then struck out at B. with a dinging hammer in self defense." B. "suffered a fractured skull accompanied by a concussion."

The Flint police arrested P., charging him with "felonious assault." He later faced a civil suit for striking his belligerent workmate. Although Chevrolet officials had no alternative but to discharge P. for causing "severe injury" to another worker, the GM umpire concluded that P.'s "excellent" record had been ruined by "his single thoughtless act." Moreover, his "punishments which pyramided so rapidly" revealed to him "the severity of his act." Consequently, he felt that P. would be "a model workman in the future" and should be re-employed when a suitable job became available.[41]

Sometimes, practical jokes and horseplay resulted in angry altercations between men on the factory floor. These boy-like pranks often helped to alleviate the tedium and monotony of assembly-line work, but occasionally they got out of hand and turned uncontrollably violent. In a California General Motors plant, R. J. I. supposedly initiated the "horseplay in throwing some small cotton wadding at B," who evidently had the "disgusting habit of spitting at other employes in retaliation for any of their actions he resented." After B., who had previously been warned about his crude habit, spat in his face, the GM worker waited for the foreman who saw the spitting to discipline B. But when nothing happened, male pride required that R. J. I. "had to do something about the matter so he jumped over the conveyor and the two men engaged in a fight." According to union officials, R. J. I. "had to take action to preserve his self-respect." The issue, they maintained, was simple: "It is asking too much for a man to stand and let another man spit in his face." Nonetheless, since the GM worker initiated the horseplay and started the fight, the umpire upheld his discipline.[42]

In the early UAW years, disputes between union and non-union workers and between UAW-CIO and UAW-AFL members often resulted in physical encounters between and among auto workers.[43] In the early phases of UAW organization, union members frequently pestered and hounded non-union workers into signing membership cards. Sometimes, an altercation resulted. In the Chevrolet Baltimore plant, H. F. K. protested his disciplinary layoff for a fight with a non-union worker. Initially, the general foreman discussed the matter with the two fighters and advised them that they would receive a two-week layoff. After further consideration, Chevrolet officials gave H. F. K., the union member, a five-day layoff and B., the non-union worker, a two-day layoff. They felt that H. F. K.'s "part in the trouble was greater because he coerced B. . . . and because he struck the first blow." They reasoned that "while both employes engaged in a fight, one was the aggressor and the other only a participant." Union officials felt quite differently: "The 'key' to the case is that B. is a non-union man whereas K. is an active Union member and committeeman." The GM umpire agreed with union officials: the "results [of an investigation] . . . do not provide convincing evidence for designating K. as the aggressor." He believed that the "inequality of treatment" was indeed a consequence of H. F. K.'s union activism and urged that Chevrolet officials somehow equalize the two penalties.[44]

At times, the manly aggression of auto workers moved onto the nastier terrain of ethnic or racial hostility. In a Chevrolet plant two workers engaged in a workplace altercation over "the surrender of Italy" near the end of World War II. According to the General Motors umpire, "Employe C. (of Scotch descent) admitted to participating in the altercation after having made a joking remark to Employe R. (an Italian) which had been heard by Employe Y. (also of Italian descent)." The second Italian worker clearly took deep offense at C.'s comment. "When Y. overheard the remark," the umpire noted, "he called C. several profane names." The skilled Scottish worker admitted that he struck Y. three times with his fist and twice butted him with his head, but "contended extreme provocation." Both received a two-day disciplinary layoff. Y. appealed his layoff: "I never lifted my hand as my back was turned." However, since he provoked C. with "extremely profane language," his grievance appeal was unsuccessful. Within the rough male culture, such language entailed "fighting words," which often justified a belligerent assault from another.[45]

In the Ford Pressed Steel plant, a racial insult resulted in a black worker attacking a white worker. The foreman had assigned X., an African American, to replace an absent worker and work across from Y., who was white, on a flanging operation. The two men, who did not know each other, performed similar work tasks and shared tools. The Ford umpire offered the black worker's account:

> On the bench were two [T-]squares used in the operation. One was in good shape; the other was not. X used the good one. After about twenty minutes, Y told him not to use that square but to use the poor one because the first was Y's.

The black worker responded that it was impossible to do a proper job with the broken and unusable T-square and "that they both should use the good one alternately." The white worker refused even to share the tool with X. He walked over to him and said: "'You black son-of-a-bitch, I don't like you anyway,' poked him with a file, and reached for an iron bar on the bench." The black worker then struck the white worker on the head with a hammer. Though the white worker denied the provocation, other witnesses confirmed some details of the black worker's account. Since "the physical make-up of the two men" differed (the black worker was "older and more portly" and the white one was "younger and tougher"), the Ford arbiter reckoned that the black worker had to strike "a surprise blow" and hence bore responsibility for starting the altercation. Moreover, he thoughtlessly observed: "No verbal provocation justifies such an assault under the law of the land or the law of the shop." And so he upheld the African American worker's discharge.[46]

For management officials and industrial arbitrators, male aggression toward foremen and supervisors was far more serious than such behavior toward fellow workers. Fights among workers simply created workplace disruptions and threatened the general safety and good order of the shop or department. Confrontations with foremen and supervisors directly challenged managerial authority over workers. Unlike clashes between workers, which often resulted in disciplinary layoffs, these cases involving superiors frequently merited the ultimate sanction of discharge. Moreover, the residual memories of past indignities and humiliations spawned less impulsive and more deep-seated angers and resentments toward these low-level managers. In the recently unionized automobile factories of the early 1940s, production workers often tested and probed the boundaries of shop-floor authority with a vigorous and renewed assertiveness.

When auto workers questioned the sometimes-vague margins of managerial authority, they acted much like mischievous boys who challenged a teacher's authority in the schoolroom. A shop-floor wise guy might see how far he could go and how outrageously he could behave. One such General Motors worker was a probationary employee who the union claimed was "sick" and who needed a restroom break for the second time. According to union officials, he "waited until he started to ---- in his pants and was forced to use a barrel." Although only a probationary worker, he was a union member. The union contended that management dismissed the man to challenge the union's right to represent a probationary worker. The umpire, however, ruled that his shop-floor behavior was "highly objectionable and irresponsible" and "tended to create unsanitary conditions in the plant." The auto worker's foul conduct, he argued, "was essentially a 'smart Alec' exposition that was apparently undertaken at the suggestion of other employes who simply should have had better sense."[47]

More often, workers and union committeemen verbally abused or threatened their foremen and supervisors. In one instance, a Flint Chevrolet worker appealed his discharge for "[i]mmoral conduct or indecency." After receiving several warnings, Y. was "sent home and disciplined for not turning out the required production." Using "profane and abusive language," he immediately got into an argument with his shop foreman. As the foreman left, the angry worker followed him down the aisle, "shouting further indecent and abusive remarks . . . accompanied by motions too indecent to be described herein, to emphasize the remarks." The Chevrolet officials discharged the incensed worker because his words and actions were "morally offensive, impure, obscene, and unfit to be seen" and did not display "reasonable respect for supervision." This scandalous behavior necessitated "a penalty of firmness" necessary to prevent a recurrence of similar insubordinate behavior. And that penalty was the worker's discharge. The shop grievance turned on the question of what was immoral or indecent in the masculine culture of the factory floor. The union officials even admitted that Y. made certain statements to his foreman, they but asserted that the words were merely rough shop talk and denied that the statements were immoral or indecent. The General Motors umpire agreed but still found the worker guilty of "abusive remarks." So he rescinded the discharge and ordered instead a one-month layoff.[48]

In another instance, S., a union committeeman in the General Motors Linden assembly plant, verbally threatened C. G., the general foreman. When the foreman grabbed a grievance from his hands, the UAW committeeman recounted: "I asked for it back. He gave me dirty looks. As he had been doing when I present[ed] the grievance[.] I told him if he met me outside I would change the expression on his face." For this indiscrete remark the union representative received a one-week disciplinary layoff. Union officials contended, however, that over time a deep "personal animosity" had developed between the UAW shop committeeman and the GM foreman. Recently, S., who had received no reprimands or disciplinary actions, suddenly received a rash of formal reprimands from the general foreman. Moreover, "considerable friction" had developed between the shop supervisor and the department's workers. A "large number of men in his department" had filed a collective grievance against him. S.'s grievance turned on the exact nature of his remarks and on whether or not a union committeeman was "permitted more latitude . . . to argue and disagree with Management." Union officials maintained that a combination of the "strained personal feelings" between the committeeman and foreman and the accepted use of "'men's language' which 'has been commonplace in this plant'" should mitigate S.'s punishment. The GM umpire partially agreed and reduced the layoff to only two days.[49]

In still another instance, a Flint Chevrolet worker angrily responded to a shop-floor accident. As M. walked through a department, "he was struck by a table which another employee was moving to the aisle." Evidently, the table hit M. "with great force in the groin." In his extreme pain, the infuriated worker angrily "shoved the table a few feet and then overturned it in the main aisle, close to where several other employees were standing." When two foremen told him to "control himself," he quickly "became abusive and used obscene and profane language to both of them." When they reported him to his foreman, M. "came up to them belligerently and again addressed them in abusive, obscene, and profane language." Although union officials argued that M.'s "great agony made his reaction to the foreman's reproofs only natural" and that his language was "strong, but not personal, shop talk," the General Motors umpire upheld his discharge.[50]

Sometimes, as more and more black workers moved into production jobs, worker confrontations with foremen mirrored the seething racial tensions in wartime automobile factories. C. was an African American worker in the Ford Highland Park plant who had previously been disciplined for striking a foreman. A year later he again reacted angrily when Superintendent H. "addressed him as 'Lightning.'" (Lightning was the name of a character in the then popular radio show *Amos and Andy*. In the show, Lightning was depicted as slow-witted and lazy, a demeaning caricature of a black man.) In response, the black worker informed the superintendent that "he did not like the name and did not wish to be called by it." Moreover, he threatened that "'someone would need first aid' if H. called him that again." A while later, S., a foreman, approached the black worker and called him "Lightning." C. informed S. about the recent incident with H. and "warned S not to call him by that name again." The foreman attempted "to persuade C that he should not take offense." S. again addressed him as Lightning, and the black worker "struck him twice and knocked him down." After his discharge at his grievance hearing, he said that he "resented it because he deemed it a reflection upon his color." In his mind, the aggressive act was a defense of his black manhood.[51]

The Ford umpire's reaction to the black worker's grievance reflected wartime racial sensibilities and was far more astonishing than the insensitive shop-floor incident. "In no court in the land," he reasoned, "would C's assault be altogether excused by the alleged provocation. The law of the land does not sanction physical violence to avenge this kind of name-calling." The Ford umpire simply characterized the incident as "verbal horseplay." Although he believed that "an individual's dignity must be respected in the shop as it is outside," the insensitive umpire added that "shop language and relations are not the language and relations of the State Department." The disciplined worker, he indicated, "was entitled to his own pet aversions." If words were to mitigate the penalty for assault, the Ford arbitrator noted, they were "of the kind generally recognized in the community as so insulting or repugnant as to incite violence in a person of normal insensitivity." The insensitive arbiter reasoned: "The appellation 'Lightning' does not generally carry such connotations of reproach, contumely or insult." Rejecting the grievance appeal, the umpire advised the African American auto worker: "One's personal or racial sensitivities should not be carried like a chip on the shoulder, asking to be knocked off."[52]

In several instances, auto workers assaulted their supervisors in public space beyond the plant's boundaries. Some even attempted to mitigate their disciplinary punishment with the argument that their fights with or assaults on foremen occurred away from the realm of management authority. When a Pontiac worker received a reprimand for poor work, he then "directed profane language at the foreman." After being sent home, the disciplined worker waited outside the plant for the foreman and "in a belligerent manner insulted the foreman . . . and made every effort to provoke a fight." One-and-a-half hours after the initial confrontation, he again accosted the foreman and an assistant superintendent "on the public sidewalk outside the plant." The GM umpire reported: "After again displaying a belligerent attitude and refusing the advise [sic] of the assistant superintendent to calm down, L. struck the foreman several blows." He lost his grievance appeal.[53]

A similar assault took place at the Ford Hamilton Plant. After his transfer to another department, the Ford worker, X., evidently "waited outside of the plant gate for a foreman and beat up the foreman because of 'an incident that occurred in the shop.'" Apparently, he had a strong "personal dislike" for the foreman that dated back to the pre-union years. He even refused to speak with the Ford foreman for four or five years. After the union came, he then decided to try to make amends with his shop supervisor. "He asked the foreman at that time," the umpire related, "to 'forget that old trouble' and try to get along in a friendly way." Then the foreman "started riding" him in ways that posed direct threats to his manhood. Once, "in the presence of several girls," the foreman mentioned "his advancing baldness." Another time, he snidely remarked about "the fit" of X.'s clothes. Finally, when the foreman heard that X.'s wife was to have a child, he commented that he "did not think that X was man enough to get one." At the time of his transfer, the Ford worker believed that the foreman was no longer his "boss." So, the umpire noted, he "waited until the day he was transferred and resorted to his fists." He, too, lost his grievance appeal.[54]

In this grievance decision, the Ford umpire generally discussed shop-floor fistfights and management's authority to discipline workers. "Unfortunately or otherwise," he observed, "some men still believe in fisticuffs as a method of settling grudges. A grudge fight after working hours outside of the plant having no purpose other than that of satisfying the mutual instinct for a fight can hardly be outlawed by shop rules." However, if "mutual instinct for a fight" were allowed to settle shop-floor differences, both management and labor would face the "fear of reprisal through violence outside the plant." Alluding to Ford's recent tumultuous labor relations, the Ford umpire added: "Such a degradation of labor relations would be a reversion to what has been called 'jungle warfare.'"[55] The workplace rule of law, under the authority of the umpire and embedded in the contract and the grievance process, tamed and civilized the savage auto workers.

In 1944 the Ford umpire decided a grievance appeal that involved a shop worker's "discipline for assault on [a] foreman." A Kansas City Ford worker, X., quarreled with his foreman. In the course of the argument he "hit the foreman, knocked him down, and was restrained from hitting him further by other employees who grabbed his arms." Ford officials discharged him. Although X. admitted that he struck the foreman, he claimed that "he was provoked into this action and deserves no punishment." According to the umpire, the Ford worker cited provocation because the foreman had "constantly nagged" him. In the course of their "verbal quarrel," the foreman "poked X in the chest with his fingers, and called him a 'son-of-a-bitch.'" The union defense did not consider the nagging, quarreling, and poking as "sufficient acts of provocation" but rather as the "surrounding circumstances emphasizing the seriousness and hostility . . . of the offensive words." The words "son-of-a-bitch" were "claimed to be the provocation."[56]

In effect, X.'s defense rested on deep cultural notions of masculine pride when confronted with "fighting" words. In his testimony before the umpire, the Ford worker claimed that "he was brought up from childhood to regard that name, when uttered without a smile, as an extreme insult constituting an invitation to fight to which no *he-man* could decline." With such provocation, a real man, a proud man, a he-man could only respond with his fists. The discharged worker added that he "was bringing up his son in the same belief, and . . . he would be ashamed to face his father if he did not respond to the insult." He justified his belligerent behavior in the patriarchal defense of an unconscionable affront to a woman—his mother.[57]

The middle-class arbitrator who operated in the world of words and ideas seemed a bit troubled that so many others in the Kansas City region shared the Ford worker's "adherence to the rugged manners of the frontier." In the presence of fighting words, the manly form of behavior was not turning the other cheek but rather an immediate and aggressive physical response. Even the Ford worker's foreman "testified that anyone indulging in such language in this area should be prepared to run or fight."[58]

Despite the rough "community customs and beliefs," the Ford umpire believed that "civilized law and order can hardly accept the principle that an individual in society may undertake by physical force to avenge insulting word." He concluded that "X was justly subject to discipline; and the only question is whether the penalty of discharge was too severe." Since Ford officials did not normally discharge workers for "an ordinary fight," since the assault was not especially "vicious," and since X. had "no prior record of misconduct," he "deserve[d] the opportunity of corrective discipline." The Ford arbitrator ordered reinstatement without loss of seniority but with loss of back pay, "his lost time . . . regarded as a disciplinary lay-off." In this instance, despite the loss of pay, the "he-man" defense worked. Rarely did a worker avoid discharge when he assaulted a foreman.[59]

In conclusion, American workers created and maintained a dense masculine culture at the workplace. Though a variety of masculine cultures existed, age, ethnicity, and race determined their construction. Most important, the dominant culture was white and male. Workers constructed and reconstructed their public postures of manhood in their relations with each other, with their employers, and with women. During World War II this dense male and white shop culture confronted new challenges as more women and more African Americans entered their domain.

6

The Female "Invasion"

Women and the Male Workplace, 1940–1945

The densely masculine auto manufacturing workplace was essentially the creation of men and mirrored many of the rough elements in male culture. Though native-born and immigrant women worked in the automobile industry almost from its origins, their numbers were never large until World War II, typically from 5 percent to 10 percent of the workforce. Frequently, women were relegated to their separate spaces in the automobile factories, away from men in the cut-and-sew operations and to the light-assembly and machining operations in manufacturing small automobile parts. The outbreak of World War II, with its huge increase in the volume of defense production and with the eventual departure of male workers to European and Asian battlefields, caused severe labor shortages in American plants and factories. As the war progressed, the auto and (later) aircraft industries brought more women into positions formerly reserved for men. These new female workers challenged the privileged position and dominance of men on the shop floor and tested the premises of the densely male shop culture. They rearranged and reconfigured the social contours of the automotive workplace.

Although white American and immigrant women worked limited gender-stereotyped positions, black women were notably absent from automotive workplaces, except as janitors for women's restrooms. The wartime labor shortages brought large numbers of women into defense plants that produced the autos, trucks, tanks, and aircraft for war. Their presence raised management fears and concerns about the potential for the disruption of smooth workplace and industrial relations. For many managers and male workers, the solidly masculine shop floor was definitely not considered a place for women.

The war years changed all that. Women challenged and threatened the male domination of the workplace.[1] The War Manpower Commission labeled the massive influx of women "Industry's Petticoat Army." In the automobile industry, for example, women constituted a small proportion of the total workforce as of April 1941. The 31,600 women employed in automobile plants and factories constituted only 5.4 percent of the total workforce. In contrast, the 199,400 women employed in October 1943 represented more than one-fourth (25.7 percent) of the entire automobile workforce. The aircraft industry also had few women at the outbreak of World War II. "But," Gregory W. Chester noted, "by the end of November 1943, a significant change had taken place: the government contracting aircraft engine and propeller plants employed 486,073 women, representing 37 percent of the entire industry's working force." By this time, aircraft plants, "which had employed either no women or only 1 percent in 1941, were employing from 25 to 52 percent female labor and some plants making small parts employed as much as 60 to 70 percent."[2] In the peak years of war production, women workers became a formidable presence on the auto and aircraft shop floor.

The increased presence of women meant the managers, union leaders, and workers needed to make their social and cultural accommodations with the new workplace conditions. Some managers recognized the fundamentally male character of the many shops and factories of wartime industries. Though one General Motors manager claimed to accept women workers, he conveyed the typical male attitude: "The factory had been a man's domain—and we liked it that way." Another factory manager suggested that women actually enjoyed their work in this masculine domain: "The woman in overalls" was "'thrilled over the heretofore purely masculine world of machinery.'"[3]

More typically, managers held gender-stereotyped reactions to women doing men's work. An industrial journalist for *Iron Age* maintained that women needed "conditioning to factory work." They were "often frightened by the huge power-driven machines that chew up steel and shred it at high speed. They must be 'conditioned' first by light work—filing and other bench work, or work at sensitive drill presses." After working close to machines and becoming "accustomed to them," women learn to work to closer tolerances than men and "pride of accomplishment is born." He concluded: "Then their housekeeping instinct asserts itself. They keep their machines clean and in good order. Steady production results."[4]

As already noted, men socially and culturally created the factory shop floor as their space, as their densely masculine environment. For working-class men, the aggressive and rough elements of male shop culture alleviated and challenged the rigors of managerial discipline and the monotonous regimen of factory work. This rough male culture spawned an inhospitable environment for many women workers. In their separate and segregated work groups, women auto workers sought to create more comfortable and more hospitable spaces and places for themselves in the rough male world. In the process, especially in their self-contained and all-female work groups, women created, maintained, and nurtured their own distinctive work cultures that differed dramatically from those of their male counterparts.

In her study of women workers in Canada, Pamela Sugiman described and outlined the complex shop cultures of women in automobile plants. On the one hand, they "conformed to social prescriptions of proper feminine behaviour and complied with their employers' demands for high productivity." Though they conformed to gender roles, they also questioned them. For these women, Sugiman added, "their strategies were formulated as they lived in a context of unequal relations between men and women, as well as workers and employers."[5]

In the all-female departments of Canadian automobile plants, these women created a strong "highly conventional" women's shop culture. This conventional female work culture, Sugiman observed, "was more difficult to sustain in work groups that were situated in or near men's departments."[6] This female shop culture centered on a feminine sense of fashion, an interest in courtship, marriage, and domesticity, and the solid social bonds of woman-to-woman relationships. These women workers, Sugiman noted, "not only accepted sexual divisions and inequalities, they celebrated conventional roles and images of womanhood." Separate jobs and separate work cultures, she suggested, "offered women and men the security and comfort of the familiar and the social validation of 'womanhood' and 'manhood' through involvement in 'women's work' and 'men's work.'" Through their "conventional feminine culture," women auto workers "expressed their womanhood in a male-dominated society."[7]

Compared with their male shop mates, female automobile workers also had quite different uses and expectations for their work spaces. If men reveled in a rough and competitive environment—in fact, a degrading and inhumane one—while women attempted to re-create and to refashion their shop space into a more social, more humane, and more congenial one. Leaving their homes, they saw the workplace as a space for social interaction with other women.

In the United States, one female Guide Lamp worker recalled the "real cohesion" among the women who worked with her on the assembly line. In the Indiana small parts plant, she remembered:

> We'd celebrate everybody's [birthday] just one day a month. . . . And we'd bake cakes and bring them in, you know, bologna and cheese and crackers, things like that. . . . We'd take a big cardboard and put everybody's name on it that had a birthday that month. So, we—you know—we broke the monotony of things. And if anybody had trouble, you know, like maybe a wreck or something like that, or an operation, we'd all send get well cards to him [sic]—we had a nice friendship down there.[8]

In such a work setting, a female congenial cooperativeness countered a male attitude of aggressive competitiveness.

Women also refashioned the rough male work space into a more congenial venue. Elizabeth Pichotte, an AC Spark Plug worker, was appalled at the indignities and the humiliations of the women's restroom. Without doors on the stalls, privacy was non-existent. She told an interviewer, "If I tell you this, you're not going to believe it. We had a restroom that had no doors, none whatever . . . a ladies restroom. There was no paper to wipe . . . no way. You couldn't even wash your hands." Well before the coming of unionism to the AC Spark Plug plant, these women reconstructed their space and made their own little improvements. If men were content to urinate in troughs along the wall or even on the floor, the women wanted to create a more humane and dignified workplace. Pichotte remembered: "The girls would buy, would take cretonne from home and take nails and put it on the different stalls to cover them."[9] If men relished crude and undignified work spaces, women attempted to refashion them and to soften the rough edges of their dismal surroundings.

Sometimes the softening reflected elements of the female work culture. In the Ford Willow Run bomber plant, Dorothy Haener recalled how female auto workers adapted to the serious shortage of free time while employed in World War II factories. Without the needed time for proper grooming, she noted, "many women would put their hair up the night before and then wear a babushka to work or wear it tied up. They would come into work and someone would help them comb it."[10] If men stole moments and minutes of time for drinking or gambling, women did it to accommodate their sense of self-image and fashion.

In another instance, the lure of fashion was much more complicated. A Packard worker went so far as to establish a "beauty shop in the ladies room, and [give] hair-do's to other women employees." Some of her work mates even "cover[ed] up for her, and she spends long periods of time as a hairdresser while her machine is idling or being operated sporadically," according to George Romney, then head of the Automotive Council, in a report to Congress. Apparently, her supervisor discovered that she "left her machine running for long periods of time and was often unaccountably absent." A subsequent investigation revealed "that she was spending the time in the ladies room and while there she was operating a beauty salon." According to Packard officials: "Her customers were made up of other female employees within the division." Her workmates desired her services so much that they even "operated her machine sporadically in an attempt to cover up" her illicit activities. When management attempted to discharge the shop-floor hairstylist, the union appealed the case to the plant committee.[11]

Managers also recognized the potential moral problems in the auto, aircraft, and other industrial plants in wartime. Often, the blame for such moral problems fell on women. "Women workers," historian Karen Anderson observed, "were assumed to pose special social and moral difficulties while male workers were thought to have problems that were more directly work-related." An industrial editor observed that "morals" represented "a vital problem in wartime industrial production" in defense plants. The massive influx of women workers, he proclaimed, "has put sex into the industrial plant." This "morals problem" took two specific forms on the shop floor—in the relations of male and female workers and those of supervisors and female employees. Whether supervisor or ordinary worker, the principal problem was the "wolf—the lone male employee with roving hands, a predatory eye, a steady 'line.'" As young men departed into military service, another plant manager feared that "older men thrown with younger girls to some extent" with possible moral consequences. Among these "outstanding conditions" that would become "foremost personnel problems" in war production plants, the editor listed: "Looser talk by the girls." "Male encouragement of girls not conducive to past concepts of morality." "Increased spending in saloons, cabarets, public dance halls, gambling places." "Reading of cheaper matter, including sensational (often lewd) pictorials." "Lack of feminine modesty, much open flirting." "More surreptitious love-making; petting."[12]

To some extent the sociologist Lowell Juilliard Carr agreed that such fears had a real basis. In a diary from his study of the wartime Ford Willow Run bomber plant, he recounted a conversation with one of the plant guards as he exited at around 9:30 in the evening. The guard said that he had to check out the folks leaving the plant and indicate the time that they exited on their pass. When Carr asked why, the Willow Run guard answered, "Sex pass-outs. We've got to watch so these guys slip out one door and some girl friend slip out another and meet 'em in the parking lot."[13]

The concern for loosened morals led many industrial and personnel managers to pay attention to how women should look or dress on the shop floor. As one management journal related, "Many personnel men claim that the wearing of slacks or cover-alls reduces sex problems within the plant. . . . [C]lothing that de-emphasizes sex can help."[14] But in the dense male environment, the interlaced notions of male sexuality, pants, and fashion were difficult to separate and sort out.

Two Ford wartime grievances illustrated just how complicated such a process was and how even slacks became problematic. In one grievance about red slacks, William H. Oliver, a former UAW Local 400 union leader and head of the UAW's Fair Practices Committee, reflected on the case about "the lady in the red slacks" at the Ford Highland Park plant. Similarly, Mildred Jeffrey, a former director of the UAW Women's Bureau, expressed surprise that her interviewer did not know about "the famous case of the woman in the red slacks."[15] In this incident, Carolyn Miller arrived at work wearing a pair of bright red slacks. Her shop foreman sent her to the labor-relations office, where she was sent home with a short disciplinary layoff. Soon thereafter, UAW Local 400 members, most of them men, set up an informational picket line to protest Miller's unfair discharge. The incident of the woman in red slacks attracted the attention of the Associated Press and other wire services and newspapers.[16] Miller's grievance case, Oliver recalled, was "one of the celebrated umpire decisions of the early Ford bargaining days." The case of the woman in red slacks revealed the deep social and sexual tensions that surfaced with large numbers of women coming into a work setting dominated by male workers and their male work cultures.

When Caroline Miller decided to don her red slacks and report to work, she asserted both her personal identity through fashion and her intent to violate an unreasonable shop rule. All of the men involved in this case sexualized her actions. In their role as moral guardians, managers disciplined her for wearing sexually charged "red" slacks. In a classic example of the harassing "male gaze," management, her union colleagues, and even the umpire viewed Miller exclusively as a sexual being.

Even decades later, William Oliver, Miller's workmate and union brother, remembered her as the "lady in red slacks," with vivid impressions saturated with sexual content. The grievance case, he recalled, "was about a redhead who was very shapely and who had decided to wear a pair of red slacks to work that morning"; she "had on an exciting pair of red slacks on which fit very neatly and closely." When she arrived at her work station, "the foreman protested vigorously, saying that such a display of curves on the human body would certainly upset the whole male work force." Clearly, Miller was neither a naive nor an innocent woman, for she had been told not to wear the red slacks on two prior occasions. Mildred Jeffrey also recalled the sexually charged resonance the red slacks: "There was lots of controversy about slacks, lots of controversy about what women were doing to the morals of the man and that sort of thing."[17]

When Ford umpire Harry Shulman eventually heard the case of the woman in red slacks, he too sexualized Miller and her behavior: "[She] was reprimanded and docked one half hour because she wore slacks described as bright red in color. The objection was to the color, not to the slacks." In their argument, Ford officials again expressed their concern for "safety and production hazards" due to "the tendency of the bright color to distract the attention of the employees, particularly that of the male sex." Although Shulman conceded that "certain forms of attire tended to distract the attention of employees in a 'co-ed' plant" and might result in "safety hazards and interference with production," management had not "promulgated or published any rules as to the color of employees clothing." They merely asserted "a general understanding that bright colors were taboo." And Shulman reasoned:

> Apparently bright green slacks were tolerated. And there was no effort at specification of other articles of clothing, or the fit thereof, which might be equally seductive of employees attention. Yet it is common knowledge that wolves, unlike bulls, might be attracted to colors other than red and by various other enticements in the art and fit of female attire.

Since management made "no effort to survey the field and to prescribe knowable and enforceable rules," the umpire ordered Ford officials to expunge Miller's reprimand from her record and to reimburse her for time lost. In a report touting the advantage of the new Ford arbitration system, the UAW local simply noted that the grievance of the "lady in red slacks" meant that "women employees may wear any color slacks they so desire."[18]

The second Ford grievance concerned the length of rolled-up slacks. In addition to the case of the "woman in red slacks," Harry Shulman also heard a case about women with "rolled-up slacks." In the Hamilton, Ohio, Ford plant, two women workers, identified as A. and B., "were given a disciplinary lay-off of three days for violating a safety rule by rolling up their slacks above their ankle." In this instance, management masked their concern both about female fashion and female morality in the rhetoric of women's safety. The questionable behavior of these two workers, Ford officials maintained, presented the "risk of injury to their legs." Although no specific written rule existed on the length of slacks, each new hire was told "not to wear open-toed shoes and . . . not to roll her slacks above the ankle." In his sexualized deliberation, Harry Shulman, the Ford umpire, specifically pondered whether management's core concern was one of either "safety" or "aesthetics." Or, as he phrased it, "whether the rule was intended to protect the girls' legs or to subdue the novelty of feminine charm."[19]

For the Ford umpire, the basic issue was the ambiguous nature of the shop rule on the length of slacks and how shop supervisors and workers interpreted the imprecise regulation. Clearly, women's own sense of style or fashion, indeed their sense of social identity, informed how they appeared in the Ford plant. The desexualized nature of their work wear led them to make minor modifications to accommodate their personal sense of style and identity. The Ford women engaged in shop-floor guerrilla warfare over the length of their slacks. "Apparently," Shulman noted, "supervision had difficulty enforcing compliance with this rule. The girls rolled their slacks up and were told by supervision to roll them down. . . . But violation of the rule apparently continued." Despite the persistent requests to roll down their slacks, the Ford women repeatedly attempted to dress as they pleased.[20]

Even the shop supervisors did not understand the ambiguous shop rule on the length of women's slacks. "One," said Shulman, "thought that the rule required the girls to button the flap on the legs of their slacks around the ankle. Another thought that this was not necessary so long as the slacks were rolled down sufficiently. They differed also as to the height to which the slacks could permissibly be rolled, and differed in their judgments on sample demonstrations."

One of the suspended women did not even have her slacks rolled up on the day she received her discipline. The Umpire noted that "her slacks simply did not reach far enough down her leg."[21]

The shop-floor war over length of slacks was so strong that the two disciplined women were "not the worst offenders." Said one foreman, many others "rolled their slacks higher." He added: "It was not feasible to discipline all the girls. Management simply decided to instill a new regimen of discipline and to make an example of the two disciplined women. . . . [A] beginning in discipline had to be made somewhere and these two girls happened to be the beginning."[22]

But this did not satisfy the umpire who sided with the union and the women. The imposed discipline was "inappropriate." If management wanted to regulate the length of slacks, the rule should be published and "its enforcement should be regular rather than sporadic or whimsical." Furthermore, Shulman ruled, the discipline should be converted to a reprimand, and the women should be compensated for their lost time.[23]

Management fears of female sexual immorality and male predatory aggression created and fostered concerns about women's interest in how they looked or dressed at the workplace. For Sugiman, a women's sense of fashion and style was an important component of female work culture. She observed, "Physical appearance, make-up, clothes, and hair styles—all defined by contemporary standards—were central to this culture."[24] One management journal emphasized the significant effect that "looks play in [the] morale" of women workers. A recent survey, it reported, "showed that women would rather sacrifice any luxury than their beauty aids." Moreover, the appearance of work clothes was important to these women, "Evidently any uniform which adds bulges in the wrong places is not conducive to employee contentment."[25] Management fears of female morality and of male aggression conflicted with women's legitimate concerns about appearance and fashion. An attractive woman who wore bright red slacks or who revealed too much leg touched on major concerns about the sexuality and morality, and ultimately the efficiency, of the female workforce. And the women struggled and fought, even engaged in shop-floor guerilla warfare, to assert their right to choose their style and fashion with regard to how they looked on the shop floor.

Nonetheless, a morals problem did exist in the workplace. Mostly it involved the shop-floor power of male supervisors or sometimes even male workers over women workers; it predated the women's invasion of the wartime workplace. As revealed in oral histories, the labor press, and public testimony, it was the predatory sexual behavior of supervisors toward women on the shop floor and outside the plant before World Was II. Union activist John W. Anderson remembered a hidden history of the abuse of female auto workers, some of the "other things that were not generally known" about a woman's situation in the 1930s. A woman, he said, "had to do not only the bidding of the foreman on the job, but she had to go out with the foreman and do his bidding off the job." Moreover, he recalled "common talk around the shop" about the position of the man who wanted to keep his job involved how "he often had to respond with his wife or his daughter to the wishes of the foreman." The shop supervisor "would visit the home or he would take them out." These things, Anderson believed, were "common knowledge in talk around the industry during those years."[26]

Women often got softer jobs or kept favored jobs if they accepted the advances of or dated their supervisors. A Studebaker worker described the sexual advances of shop foremen and supervisors. "Doubtless," he observed, women "have to allow the assistant foremen considerable liberty in order to keep their jobs, as I saw him run his hand through a girl's hair as he passed her machine." Along with the "miserable wages" at the Flint Fisher Body, one worker noted that "the women have to take a lot from their boss. If they accept his caresses without complaining, maybe he won't ride them so hard." Women, too, told about their vulnerability to abusive supervisors. A Milwaukee auto parts worker told the Automobile Labor Board: "The discrimination is terrible. The pets are shown all the preference, seniority or no seniority." The spouse of an auto worker told an interviewer that she worked her "whole married life." But when jobs were scarce, "if the boss liked you or you went out with him, which I know a few of the girls that went out with the boss. They had a job!"[27]

One angry Muskegon worker testified to the Automobile Labor Board about the work in his wife's shop that "employed a good many women." The women "that do the work will sell their bodies to hold their jobs with the foremanship." If the women did not consent to such "appointments with these foremen or bosses in their departments, in going out with them, they were out of a job." He feared for his wife and other women who could not "protect" themselves from the "likes of a slink of a boss." Furiously, he proclaimed it "a damn poor policy."[28]

The union activist, Frank Marquart, recited a long list of pre-union employer abuses of workers and then mentioned the sexual harassment of women: "foremen in the Dodge plant used to invite second-shift women to accompany them to the roof at night and made it miserable for those who refused the invitation."[29] After the arrival of unions in the mid 1930s, Marquart asked female Midland Steel striker "why she joined the union." Expecting "better wages as her main reason," he confessed, "I was wrong. She said: 'When you belong to a union the foreman can't screw you. Last month my foreman asked me to go out with him. I told him "to hell with you, Charlie, I know what you want." He got mad, but he did not try to spite me. He knew damn well the union would be on his neck if he did.'"[30]

Dan Gallagher, the leader of a Hudson Motors UAW local, told of a supervisor's extreme abuse of male and managerial authority over women in his shop. Discussing the need to "pay homage" to shop supervisors, Gallagher described the rape of a woman by a Hudson superintendent and also the indifferent reaction of the victim's male shop mates. The plant predator "took a girl into a room where they stored seat cushions. He took a guy off the line to watch the door so nobody would disturb them and he was there with her for two hours. She came out crying and disheveled, but there was nothing that anybody could do." After the sexual assault, the superintendent "went around bragging about copping a cherry." Then, Gallagher remembered: "He pointed to another girl and said, 'You're next.'" Much worse was the reaction of the women's fellow workers, "laughing it off and saying, 'The babe got took, that is all.'"[31]

Such predatory traditions continued into the war years. Bette Murphy recalled the low-level supervisors who conducted the on-the-job training of women workers. Some were "4F fellows, the younger fellows [excluded from the military draft], and they took advantage of the fact [of their positions]. In other words, 'So, if I'm going to help you, if I am going to help you get that angle in just right, what are you going to do for me baby?'" UAW leader Caroline Davis recalled a shop-floor fight with her foreman. After she complained, her superintendent said: "Uh, well, Caroline, why don't you try being a little nice to him?" In the course of the heated conversation, Davis proclaimed that the foreman was "a louse. . . . he's a skunk, he's no good!" The foreman had a problem, the superintendent told her: "Ah, he wants to have a date with you." Angrily, Davis retorted: "A date with him? What do you think? I wouldn't date anybody to make better working conditions, or a job." She added:

> Roy, any time that I have to protect a job by going out with somebody, I'm not going to start at the bottom and go out with a foreman, and then the superintendent, and then somebody else, to hold my job. I'd start at the top, the president of the company. So, forget it. I am never going with the president of the company. And I'm not working my way up for a job anyway.

These strong and forceful women could protect themselves and other women.[32]

Nonetheless, supervisors sexually harassed and abused women through the war years. One of the most notorious examples occurred in a small parts plant in Redman, Michigan. A union organizer described the nasty and horrid situation of women in this small plant that manufactured small motors for windshield wipers. The UAW organizer described the factory as "nothin' but a whorehouse with a whistle on, that Redman plant." Under oath, the women who worked in this plant testified "that they either get fired or entertain outside salesmen sellin' steel and equipment and so forth." The UAW organizer added, "they were picked strictly for sex objects." Furthermore, "they testified that they went on parties with strangers they never saw before and had spent nights in motels on the boss's orders."[33] So outraged were these women auto workers that the union organizer led a strike and successfully organized the rural parts plant into the UAW.

In the Chrysler "Tank Arsenal" plant, management dismissed a female probationary employee for providing the union with information on "some shady things that are going on during the 2nd shift of Dept. 25." With less close supervision, one industrial reporter noted that "the night shifts are somewhat gayer than personnel men will admit."[34] In this case, a factory "janitress" encountered two department supervisors and two women workers who were sisters on a Saturday night while she was cleaning in the basement of the administration building. "I went to this room," she recalled, "and when I got to the water fountain, I met H. and May's sister and we said 'Hello' to each other. I went to open this door to get into this room and [the other supervisor] was up against it, and when I pushed on the door, it was right up close to me. He was fully dressed but his pants were open and it was out." Although a friend suggested that she report the incident, the probationary worker decided against it.

Several times during the next week, the supervisor whom she surprised questioned her about whether or not she reported what she saw to management officials. Gradually, rumors of the incident spread through the department. And when the woman heard that the supervisor had just fired someone, she responded to a workmate that "he should fire people for having intercourse in the basement." Soon after this, she met the supervisor again. She said, "[He suggested] that I either quit my job [as janitress] or go into the plant. . . . So I told him that I didn't have to change my job because I had seen too much. So I told him that I'd stay at home when he asked me what I was going to do." He took her badge and she left the plant.

While departing, she met another supervisor; he questioned her about what happened and then took her to the labor-relations office, where, she said, "I told the whole story and it was taken down in shorthand there." For a few days, the woman worked the day shift while management investigated he allegation. Then she was informed that she "was to be laid off for giving out the wrong story." In her mind, she "was laid off Thursday night, because 'I talked too much.'" The union filed a grievance over her dismissal, requesting her reinstatement with back pay and the punishment of the offending supervisors. Ultimately, an umpire hearing the case reaffirmed management's dismissal of the woman, ruling on a technicality that she was a probationary employee and that the union could not represent her.[35]

Through the war years most women suffered mainly from their shop supervisors. For the most part, male auto workers enjoyed the presence of female shop mates, sometimes teased them, and sometimes protected them. They were in the factories for the duration of the war, contributed to the war effort, and were not competitors for hard-to-find jobs. Since women workers may have been the wives, sisters, or daughters of the men or their workmates, a patriarchal instinct prevailed. Often the interaction involved playful good humor; Clayton Fountain, a UAW activist, remembered his interaction with a group of Polish women. He and his workmates, he related, "found time to fuss around with these gals, asking them for dates or reaching down the line to give one of them a pinch or a pat. Most of the gals were buxom Polish lasses—they had to have muscle to stand the gaff—who endured our sportiveness with tolerant good nature. They cracked back at us with steady wits, belittling our boasted amatory powers and advising us to take our passions to the Hamtramck brothels."[36] But some male workers were not so considerate, and they harassed or abused their supposed union sisters.

At the instigation of male colleagues and in the context of male shop culture, some men treated women differently from their protective brothers. In two instances, a bet or dare among men resulted in sexual harassment or assault. In the first, a young female Mexican American aircraft riveter recalled an incident with a fellow worker in the Douglas Aircraft plant. He and her leadman were the only men who worked in her area of the plant. The leadman, she said, apparently "made a bet with him that he would not kiss me. I think it was Christmas, or something like that, some holiday." He "came over and kissed me[.] I was so shocked, I didn't have a chance to do anything about it. It just happened; that was it." The main problem, she recalled, was "my mouth [was] full of sandwich." For the woman, the incident "was no big deal, and he won his bet. I mean it's things like that went on. Just a lot of fun in a way."[37]

In the second incident, a workman's aggressive behavior was clearly much, much more offensive. So too was the union's and the umpire's reaction to the incident. Once again, the precipitating event was a male bet or dare. A Ford River Rouge worker and four or five other men were "eating lunch around a table on the production floor. A female employee was working near them. The men joked and laughed while they were eating." One of the men "tore a piece of cardboard from a shoe box in which he carried his lunch and wrote on it in pencil without signature, 'Please give me a little pussy.'" The Ford worker then delivered the note to the woman. Although he immediately apologized, the woman complained, and management dismissed both the worker and the man who wrote the note. The UAW local then filed a grievance for a reconsideration of the offending worker's case and asked for the restoration of his seniority, claiming "a doubt that he knew the contents of the note."

While Ford management took a firm and forceful position on this instance of sexual harassment, the UAW Local 600 leaders and Harry Shulman, the umpire, sympathized with the man who lost his job and seniority. Though the River Rouge worker "denie[d] that he knew the contents of the note," the Ford labor relations official claimed that he "had knowledge of its contents" and that he gave "evasive" answers when questioned. Moreover, when the worker "proceeded toward the girl[,] he laughed, looked back to his fellows, and said, 'I'm going to give it to her! I'm going to give it to her!'" Shulman agreed with these basic facts, namely, that such a note was "obviously undesirable and dangerous conduct in the plant which cannot be condoned," he nonetheless added, "It is clear that the note was passed as a sort of boyish prank without any serious import." Given his nine years seniority, his "spotless record," and "immediate and voluntary apology, to the girl, as well as the prankish nature of the incident," Shulman ruled that the Rouge worker be reinstated without loss of seniority. In other words, both the union leaders and the umpire felt that boys will be boys.[38]

An almost pathetic case involving a lovelorn Ford worker revealed the social complications of older men and younger women mixing on the shop floor. In this grievance, a forty-six-year-old Ford Willow Run worker apparently fell in love with a twenty-two-year-old female co-worker. She complained to management, and he was dismissed. Her complaint was simple and direct: "[He] has been molesting me in regards to love and I do not care to be molested under any circumstances." In many war plants, especially aircraft plants such as Willow Run, older men with military deferments often worked with younger women. According to the older man in this case, he first met the young woman when she arrived in his department, and they "worked together a substantial period of time," during which he "developed a strong affection for her and thought that she liked him. She accepted some favors from him, [but] they never went out together." She then transferred to another department. Subsequently, the Willow Run worker sent flowers and a letter to the woman's home and two other letters about her to a third party, another woman who was a mutual friend. His first note with the flowers said: "If you will give me a break and go out with me it may save me getting flowers when I cannot smell them. Please try and find time to say yes." In other words, he implicitly threatened suicide. Similarly, the two other letters "expressed his loneliness and his need for her friendship, if not her love." They, too, suggested that his "unrequited love" might drive him to suicide.

Once again, Shulman's grievance ruling favored the perspective of the male worker. "No evidence," he indicated, "has been introduced of any reverberations in the plant resulting from his love for the girl." The correspondence, he added, reflected "an idyllic love" and the suicide suggestion "evoke[d] pity or sympathy rather than fear." This man's "emotional make-up," the umpire declared, was beyond "what is commonly called normal." Moreover, his love was "platonic, or . . . romantic, but it certainly was not vulgar or wolfish." Because the Willow Run worker had a satisfactory work record and had not bothered other women, and because no shop rule prohibited "an employee from falling in love with another employee," the umpire decided that his actions did not warrant dismissal. Shulman reasoned: "So long as the wooing is carried on away from the plant on the employee's own time and makes no threats or promises with respect to the beloved's job in the plant, it cannot properly become the employer's concern." He then ordered the Ford worker's reinstatement with compensation for time lost.[39]

Though not wielding the same power and authority that male supervisors possessed, some women may well have wanted the flirtatious attention or the illicit liaison with male auto workers. Wherever men and women socialized and interacted, they created and cultivated an environment filled with social, psychological, and sexual expectations and tensions. In the war years, the respectable women workers generally labeled the young women who sought the attentions of men—especially supervisors—"party girls." One female Douglas Aircraft worker described the younger workers:

> We had our party girls and they weren't fooling any of the rest of us. We knew what was going on when they had their Saturday night parties. They would say, "Well the Saturday night party held over to Sunday morning" and some of them would take off and go to Mass and come back and keep partying the rest of the day. . . . [T]he men, there were so few of them, they could be very picky, very choosy on who they went with and what they wanted.

In her plant, she noticed a divide between the younger and the older women: "Some of them were the party type and they were always inviting the bosses out, which the older ones didn't appreciate. 'Stop by the apartment for a drink after work,' or something like that." When asked about "sexual advances" in her shop, she replied: "Not unless you asked for it. You can always make yourself open to those. . . . But if you weren't so inclined, they didn't force themselves on you." Most of the men, she contended, "were friendly. They acted like your big brother; they'd come around and put their arm around your shoulder; they let you know that they liked you, you could be friends, you could talk. You didn't have to put up with any sexual abuse or anything like that."[40]

Other women felt similarly. Asked about men who made passes, one expressed a general attitude and when she replied: "Usually, if they did, the women asked for it. It was their own behavior." Another remembered a young inspector: "She'd walk around there with her mirror and her tight pants, tight tops." Still another recalled a young woman in her department: "Her attitude was that she would hold her job on her back." Throughout the department, rumors maintained, "it wasn't what she knew, it was who she knew."[41]

Despite, or perhaps because of, the hardships of war, some of the young women who worked in the auto and aircraft plants still wanted to enjoy themselves. They wanted to date, to go to dances, to have a good time. At a Detroit Chrysler plant, a number of young women workers conducted a wildcat strike over the closing time of local taverns and beer halls. UAW leader Sam Sage recalled that they worked the night shift: "They were getting off at 1:30 in the morning and the beer gardens closed at 2:30. They did not get a chance to get to the beer gardens. These were women! They wanted to strike because they did not get a chance to get to the beer gardens." Apparently, it took the women half an hour to change and leave the plant, so they only had half an hour to drink before the tavern closed. Eventually, Sage remembered, "We worked out with the police department at that time a way so that we could have swing-shift dances. All we had to do was prove that this was a third-shift party and it was strictly local union."[42]

The activities of two "party girls" and their male supervisors attracted the attention of management officials and union leaders. In 1944, G. Allan Dash and Ralph T. Seward, both umpires for the General Motors UAW cases, ruled on a grievance that concerned two female workers, B. S. and J. S., who "were with their supervisors at various beer taverns during the early morning hours between 2:30 A.M. and 6:30 A.M. . . ." The initial incident occurred earlier in January at the AC Spark Plug Division in Flint. According to Seward, "the affair was not prearranged. The girls had stopped at a tavern on their way home from work and were drinking beer with some friends. Around Midnight Foreman B. came in for a beer and seeing them at the table, came over and sat down. Later Assistant Superintendent H. came in with a friend and also joined the group." After the tavern closed they went to a friend's home for liquor and to another for wine. In the early morning they stopped at a hotdog stand for food. After eating, one woman and a supervisor drove to Saganaw to pick up a car and eventually returned home.[43]

According to management officials, the January incident produced "considerable comment," suffused with moral condemnation, throughout the plant. The supervisors were the general foreman and an assistant superintendent. One was "a married man with a family." The two women workers "were separated from their husbands."[44]

Since the Flint factory "employed women in substantial numbers," AC Spark Plug officials had a policy of discharging "both parties if Supervision insisted on 'running around' with girl employes." So they dismissed the two shop supervisors and the two women workers. Such conduct, they maintained, "was certain to cause favoritism, jealousies, irritation, criticism, gossip, a general undermining of confidence and lowering of morale among employes."[45]

In an astonishing paternalistic rationale reminiscent of the "moral police" of the Lowell textile mills in the 1840s, AC Spark Plug officials forcefully asserted their right to police the morality of their workforce.[46] Their strict policy on the behavior of women workers, management argued, "was necessary to keep the working conditions of its women above criticism or moral reproach." Moreover, "such associations between Supervision and female employes," management insisted, "[led] inevitably to friction and jealousy among the other women, to charges of favoritism and discrimination, and to a general lowering of employe morale." And, the AC Spark Plug officials voiced their deep concerns over the effect of community perceptions on the recruitment of women workers. "If such associations were allowed to continue," they argued, "the Plant inevitably would receive a bad name in the local community and families might be unwilling to allow their daughters to work there."[47]

On behalf of the two women, the union appealed their unwarranted discharge, denying "any misconduct" and contending simply participation in a "'drinking party' that included the two women, two supervisors, two other employes, and a seventh person." From the union perspective, the case constituted, "management's invasion of the privacy of the two female complainants." The incident "had no injurious effect on the work" of the two women or on "the morale of the department." Furthermore, the union argued: "The private lives of employes have no connections whatsoever with the collective bargaining relationships between Management and the employes at this Plant."[48]

In Dash's analysis of this grievance case, he observed that both sides focused their briefs on "the rights of management to concern itself with the outside activities of employes." Neither side provided adequate information on details of the incident. Nonetheless, he speculated, "the male sex of supervisors" followed their "usual role" of seeking female companionship. However, on the one hand he recognized that their "positions of authority" might coerce women "to join the supervisors in an innocent incident because of their fear of antagonizing their superiors." Or, on the other hand, the supervisors might have been "enticed by the female employes into the incident, and that the incident itself may have extended beyond the realm of innocence." Interestingly, Dash considered supervisory authority rather benign and feminine charms more malignant. Nonetheless, his main point was that "the mere potential of favoritism arising out of a single outside relationship that concerns but a single innocent incident between a female employe and a male supervisor is certainly not sufficient reason to summarily discharge the female employe."[49] In the absence of more details, Dash returned the grievance case to the union and management for their additional reconsideration. He suggested that they determine whether or not "the incident extended beyond the realm of an innocent relationship" and also that "they consider in detail its demonstrable impact upon the internal employer-employe relationships at the A. C. spark Plug Division." Unless the determination of these two considerations evidenced a case for dismissal, he concluded, "there is little reason to support the need for the discharge of the female complainants in this case."[50]

Several months later the arbitrator reheard the AC Spark Plug case. Although union and management officials never provided additional evidence, his ruling did offer more detailed information about the incident. Based on the "only evidence" of brief statements of the two discharged employees and other participants, he concluded that "there was no evidence in any misconduct other than drinking with members of Plant Supervision." Moreover, the young women came to work "on time, and there had been no complaint about their condition or the manner in which they performed their work."[51]

Since the grievance case turned on its impact on attitudes inside the factory, Dash took the unusual step of personally investigating the reactions of the AC Spark Plug workers to the incident. When management invited him to interview several selected witnesses, he instead chose to speak with about one-fourth of the people who worked on the same shift as the two women. Although these workers "varied widely in their moral judgments" about the conduct of the young women, they substantially agreed on two important issues. First, the plant gossip did not start until after management began to investigate the incident and increased after the dismissal of the two women. This gossip was equally concerned with the "fairness" of the management action. Second, the AC Spark Plug workers "had never been clearly informed that any association with members of Supervision outside the plant was prohibited." In the past, supervisors and women workers sometimes mingled at company parties and later went off to less formal gatherings in bars and taverns. Indeed, he noted, "for a considerable period prior to the discharges, social contacts between Supervisors and female employes had been frequent, open, and unpenalized."[52]

Subsequently, given the vagueness of the policy against social interaction and the absence of any documented immoral behavior on the part of the women, Dash ordered that AC Spark Plug officials rescind the discharges and reinstate the two young women with full back pay.[53]

Women who entered the male terrain of the factory confronted the world of men, sometimes angrily hostile or sometimes mischievously playful. Often needing the work to support their families or to supplement the income of an absent man who went to war, they attempted to adapt or to adjust to the all-male world. Speaking about catcalls and whistling at women in the shop, a male Boeing machinist said, "You'd think those fellows down there had never seen a girl. Every time a skirt would whip by up there, you could hear the whistles above the riveting, and I'll bet the girls could feel the focus of every eye in the place." One female aircraft worker lightheartedly accepted the male attention. "Of course," she recalled, "there was a lot of [whistle sound] for the pretty girls that went by, you know. [*Laughs*] When men stop looking, they're dead. [*Laughs*]" A Lockheed assembler recollected the reactions of her male co-workers consisted of "a few cat calls," but generally she remembered "a lot of fun." "We worked. We had breaks, free time. . . . We'd go outside to eat. Then we'd socialize. We'd [also] socialize in line at the tool crib."[54]

With the sharp difference of male and female cultural styles, some misogynist men deeply resented the women's wartime invasion and presence in defense plants. Even local union leaders begrudged women on the shop floor. One recalled: "You had women getting jobs on intricate machines that never did anything but carry a baby around and a bucket of soup." In another instance, a female milling machine operator recalled the woman-hating anger of her foreman "Pappy" Dills:

> Oh, he was a good looking man and he had a horrible dislike of women. He
> loved them to love them, but working, he wanted no part of women in the

plant. And he told Florence and I in no uncertain terms. . . ."Women were not worth a God damn except in bed and don't forget it. You're not going to get anywhere in this department."[55]

As with some other male workers, he deeply resented the female presence on the shop floor and made women's lives difficult.

Sometimes men expressed a softer manifestation of their resentment. One woman recalled a subtler and more playful form of male rancor as being "sort of like these sly remarks, corny jokes." But for many men the mere presence of women created a more congenial work setting. Another woman suggested: "You know a bunch of women, it kind of lightened up their day."[56]

Whether hostile or playful, women often made their individual accommodations to male attitudes toward them. One Douglas Aircraft worker simply kept her distance and "never had any romantic feelings" toward the men in her shop. She remembered: "I talked to 'em, laughed with 'em, listened to their jokes." But she never became involved with them. Other times, women workers banded together and collectively defended themselves against their abusers. One aircraft worker remembered how a group of women in her shop dealt with an offensive leadman. The women "bodily took him up—well, the office was on the poop-deck, which is a half level overlooking the department—and insisted that he be fired on the spot. And he was."[57]

Women had to accommodate themselves to the perpetual cursing and swearing or even raunchy language on the shop floor. Though obviously a problem for many women, sometimes it was even too much for men. Flint auto worker Irving King remembered a man only known as "Dirty Joe." He was "a hard nosed union man" and "his language was so filthy." Genora Johnson recalled the behavior of men when she worked for the Budd Wheel Corporation and Briggs Manufacturing Company. At Budd the men were "really cruel" at first: "they razzed us and made sordid remarks to us," Johnson said. At Budd, the foremen "talked dirty to them, saying things like 'Get the rag out of your ass' and 'It's time to stop your screaming and bleeding.' Dirty sick awful stuff."[58]

Some women attempted to adjust to routine cursing and swearing. A Willow Run aircraft assembler said, "When I went to work there, I swore very little." Through her father, she "had been exposed to all the cuss words in the book." Whenever she hurt herself, she said to her workmate, who was "sixty and [a] white haired, beautiful, old lady, 'Marie, swear for me.' And, man could she swear." It took her years, she said, "before I got down to holding my own." One aircraft riveter recalled her own individual accommodation as using a combination of personal pride and feminine guile. "But in the beginning," she remembered, "it was a bit rough. You had to hold your head high and bat your eyes at 'em. And you learned to swear like they did. However, I made myself stop it because I don't think it's too lady-like."[59] For some women who accepted such swearing, the shop world indeed coarsened and roughened their personalities at work.

One important element of male work culture was the control of production, sometimes through the conscious and concerted restriction of output. Often, like all new workers, women came onto the shop floor wanting to prove their individual abilities and capacities in their new factory jobs. So they went against the workers' predetermined production norms or quotas and inspired the wrath of their male workmates. An assembler at North American Aviation recalled her personal inability to restrict her output and to maintain her shop's leisurely work pace. "Just your ordinary working," she said, "you didn't have to kill yourself just as long as you did a good day's job. . . . They told me I was too conscientious; they told me I should slow down. . . . They said it hurt others, 'cause others couldn't keep up with me or something and they wanted me to slow down. I couldn't. I had to keep on working."[60] As with many shop novices, she did not understand deep-seated shop traditions of restricting effort and production. For her, the pace simply seemed much too slow.

On rare occasions women endured the angry physical assaults of some men. Such men went beyond the bounds of paternalistic propriety when they targeted women workers. In the Chevrolet Gear and Axle plant, G. assaulted F., a female tractor driver. The ill-tempered and unpleasant G. had received "numerous reprimands, warnings, and lost-time penalties because of his temper and his belligerent attitude toward members of the Supervision and toward his fellow employees." Apparently, when the woman drove into the plant, she turned on two large over-head heaters. The man, the General Motors umpire observed, "was inconvenienced by the heat which thus blew down on him and [he] attempted to turn off one of the heaters." A foreman heard the subsequent fracas and "found the two facing each other ready to exchange blows." On the rough shop floor, women sometimes were forced also to display their defensive "womanly" bearing against such masculine aggression. She, the umpire reported, "said to G. 'If you hit me again, I will hit you.'" At the grievance investigation, the man claimed that the woman struck him in the face and denied that he hit the woman. She "admitted striking G. but stated that this had only been done [because] he had struck her a blow on the breast." An examination by the plant doctor revealed "a bruise on her left breast." Since some management officials vigorously policed any-thing that even had the appearance of sexual assault during the war years, they discharged G., and the umpire upheld the discharge.[61]

Other women workers were frequently the victims of male work culture, of mischievous teasing, horseplay, and pranks. Using the age-old tactics for shop newcomers, they teased and taunted their female workmates. Sometimes this meant that they accepted women into the male culture. One aircraft assembler and riveter said, "There were a lot of pranks pulled in the plant." She recalled sitting with her legs dangling through the ribs of an aircraft frame when, she said, "one of my leadmen crawled under the ship and tickled my feet and he knew I was so terribly tickli[sh], I don't know, but anyhow, it was too bad. [*Laughs*] I didn't get to the rest room in time." In her unexpected shock, she wet her pants. She said: "I had to wear a sweater tied around me for the rest of the night." She also recalled other workers who stole stuff and put it in their workmate's lunch boxes. A fellow male worker, she remembered, "went to open his lunch box and it was welded shut. He couldn't open his lunch box. Oh, it was just stuff like that all the time." But in her mind it was mostly good-natured fun. "The gang," she concluded, "was more or less jolly. There wasn't any fighting or bickering or stuff like that. Not that I saw."[62]

Other women workers recalled similar instances of impish shop harass-ment. For another woman, the tool crib was the place where men had their laughs on her. "Oh," she recalled, "they sent me after my left-handed monkey wrenches and all sort of things, you know. [*Laughs*] The new ones they'd do all that to." Her male workmates, she remembered, "thought that was hilari-ous." In another instance an electrical assembler remembered that several men "cut a lot of little black wires that wasn't too long and . . . made like little worms and they put them under my stool and showed everybody. . . . [T]hey told me I had worms." She laughed: "Yeah, they was always teasing me."[63]

A group of women were the victims of a male prankster with a rivet gun. "Oh," one said, "we had one man there . . . shot these little rivets out of a rivet gun and every once in a while when you'd be stooped over, you'd get a bing on your backside. Then [the women] got mad." She recalled one woman who "would get mad . . . she got more shots than anybody else." The women found their own way to deal with the shop prankster: "Once you spotted him and laughed at him, that was it; [he] never bothered you anymore." The male ego could tolerate female anger but not disdain or mockery. In the end, she believed that such behavior would happen anywhere "because everybody likes to have a little fun—of course, as long as it didn't hurt anybody."[64]

In a 1942 study on "The Social Dynamics of Detroit" for the Office of War Information, Rensis Likert and colleagues interviewed a number of Detroit citizens and workers. Some of the respondents revealed that men had various reactions to the appearance of large numbers of women on the shop floor. Some recognized that war work transformed the attitudes and behaviors of working women. One middle-aged Ford worker who produced jeeps for the war, observed, "Women workers are changing. They don't carry themselves the way they used to." The reason he suggested: "They are wearing pants." Although they seemed less ladylike to him, he did not feel "that they weren't ladies." The wartime Rosies were "getting mannish," but they were not real "roughnecks." Yet they were different, "smoking" and "feeling freer." Before war work, they were "more shy and backwards. Now they mingle more and get along with the men better."[65]

Like many men, another Ford worker accepted women in defense plants for the duration of the war. After the war ended, he believed, these women should leave the plant and return to their prewar pursuits to "give the boys who were coming back a chance to get back to the factories. It's all right for an emergency." As a result of her war work, the "average housewife" gained an "independence complex." Having earned her own money, she expressed her economic independence and felt, "Well this is my money and I'm trying to spend it the way I want to." Subsequently, the Ford worker believed, "after this is over, women should be forced to get out of the factories."[66]

Others, sometimes women too, felt similarly. Defense work occasionally clearly upset and undermined traditional gender relations. A married female Hudson worker cited Willow Run as a place that precipitated many divorces. Many women, she believed, "leave their homes [and] are just looking for a man." Voicing her traditionalist and racial biases, she added: if women worked, they "shouldn't mix them in with the men just like they shouldn't mix" the blacks with the whites. Such women "are just trying to wear the pants that's all." A young, single, and male Graham Paige worker feared that if women stayed in the factories after the war, then "serious things" would happen. He posited that returning young veterans might earn $30 a week and their wives $70. After war's end, he said, "I don't think they should be allowed to work and keep other men out of it." He anticipated the emergence of "a race of Amazon's" if women were "economically self-sufficient." Similarly, an older Detroit machinist feared "more divorces and broken homes" if young girls were "not raised to housework," which he felt was "degradation" of young women.[67]

As men and women occupied the gendered terrain of men, metals, and machines, some cooperated and some contested their newly shared spaces. To be sure, each group possessed its own workplace culture. And where men and women coexisted, issues of sex and sexuality often shaped their social experiences. Though men and women shared space for the duration of World War II, men continued to believe that the automotive shop floor was their masculine terrain.

Consequently, as Ruth Milkman noted, during postwar reconversion to peacetime production, management—with the acquiescence of the women's union brothers—purged female workers from automobile plants. Soon after VJ Day, the proportion of women in American automobile factories declined from a high of 25 percent to less than 10 percent. Moreover, the purge of women from the shop floor was a mean and nasty affair. One woman auto worker recalled: "There were an awful lot of men that resented women working in the factories. We were good enough during the war to fill in but after it was over, we had no business there as far as they were concerned."[68]

Clifford Macmillan, the Studebaker industrial-relations officer, remembered the rough treatment of one woman by her male co-workers. Speaking on the displacement rights of women, he said, "Toward the end boy, we had some fantastic situations." The UAW contract allowed women with seniority to "take any junior [man] out if you can do the work." And one woman's male coworkers did not react kindly to her right to displace a man. He concluded, "I saw one woman that was bucking a casting, it must have weighed 50 pounds, up onto a table, and then doing a machining operation on it. They didn't want her to do it, they kept telling her. But, by god, she was going to do it and she did it, too. So one lunch time she was sitting down eating her lunch and they tied her to one of the uprights (ceiling supports)."[69] Despite her insistent capacity to perform men's work, her male shop mates resented her performing men's work. After the war ended, things got far worse for women.

In addition to women, another "invasion" of the white and male workplace occurred. Through the war years, African American men and women entered automobile factories in large numbers and challenged deep-seated white male privileges to the best jobs. Moreover, the severe job discrimination against black women prompted black men to defend them.

7

The Challenge to White Manhood

Black Men and Women Move
to White Male Jobs, 1940–1945

In 1941 Franklin D. Roosevelt responded to A. Phillip Randolph's threatened March on Washington movement to protest discriminatory practices in the defense industry. President Roosevelt issued Executive Order 8802, creating the Fair Employment Practices Committee (FEPC), which promised black men the opportunity to escape their traditional degrading and man-killing occupations in Detroit automobile plants. One federal official later described the committee as, effectively, "an NLRB on Negro Discrimination."[1] It offered the opportunity for black men and women to achieve greater dignity and respectability in more prestigious work on the automotive shop floor. The next year, dissatisfied with the FEPC's slow progress to improve their work situations, some segments of the African American community called for a second March on Washington movement in 1942. As Detroit geared up for increased wartime production, working-class black men enthusiastically endorsed the appeal to aggressive action. In addition the slogan of "Double V for Victory," that is, victory over racism both abroad and at home, an Office of War Information report noted that this second movement had the slogan "Mobilize Now! Manhood, Courage, Guts, Determination."[2] Both slogans appealed to forceful resistance to the racial status quo in American society and at the workplace. The second slogan emphasized an almost militarized and manly resistance to the inequitable situation in the wartime auto plants.

The increase in numbers of African American men at the workplace brought differing and contentious visions of manhood to the automotive factory. White men, who had long dominated the better jobs, divided into two groups: those who strove for the respectability of high-paid union jobs and those who resented others, fearing the loss of their exclusive white privileges. The former included the men who chose the good life of the family and living wage and who thought others should enjoy the same social and economic advantages. These were the men who shared the UAW's belief that union solidarity and equity allowed all to rise and prosper together. The latter comprised those who were more self-centered and exclusionary and who chose to preserve and protect their privileges from the threatened invasions of others. Sometimes they were skilled workers who feared the dilution of their crafts, sometimes white southerners who took pride in the privileges and entitlements of their whiteness; others were labor conservatives who feared any change to the status quo. The arrival of African American men, with their sense of their pride, dignity, and assertion of rights, threatened the second group of more exclusionary whites. When black men fought for workplace equity, the more conservative whites conducted racial hate strikes to protect traditionally "white" jobs. In reaction, African American workers conducted what might best be labeled "pride strikes" to gain access to better jobs and later to improve the inequitable situation of black women in the automobile factories. These workplace struggles involved robust clashes over differing visions of manhood.

The African American manly resistance arose as a result of decades of social and especially workplace discrimination. In the early years, Southern and Eastern European and African American auto workers shared working, residential, and social space. Until the late 1920s the two groups lived in a work world where the racial and the ethnic divisions of labor sometimes overlapped. At work they shared the worst occupations on automobile factories—in the foundry, paint shop, and wet sanding occupations. They also often share neighborhoods separated from native- and North European–born Americans. Over time, African Americans and Southern Europeans separated into different neighborhood and work spaces.

For the first half of the twentieth century, white men ruled the automotive shop floor. In the early years, some Southern and Eastern Europeans were not considered white or were considered only partially white. The black southerners of the first Great Migration sought any work and accepted high auto wages in the hardest and dirtiest jobs, commonly known as the man-killing positions in the foundry, paint shop, or wet sanding departments. The so-called "hillbilly" migration from the upper South paralleled and grew with the black migration as auto firms recruited more and more unskilled white workers for the rapidly expanding automobile industry.[3] Unlike their African

American workmates, the mere whiteness of these migrants qualified them for work on assembly lines or at machines.

At the beginning of World War II, Joe Brown, a union press-service reporter, captured the enormous social and political diversity of Detroit's industrial population. "Auto workers," he observed, "are not merely auto workers. They are natives, foreigners, hill-billies, and city-born persons, Catholics and Protestants, Germans and Britishers, whites and Negroes, skilled and unskilled, educated and ignorant, Communists and 100 per centers, those with no seniority-little seniority-longtime seniority, efficient and inefficient—the list could be continued indefinitely."[4] Auto workers were indeed a complex agglomeration of many different groups of people with competing attitudes, values, and behaviors.

A conservative craft-union political outlook often separated AFL supporters from their more radical and inclusive CIO shop mates. Many socially and politically conservative workers supported right-wing associations such as Father Charles Coughlin's National Union for Social Justice. The more intolerant ones even supported racist, anti-immigrant, and anti-union organizations such as the Black Legion and the Ku Klux Klan. Their more radical workmates often favored socialist, communist, or other leftist groups. All of these divisions complicated the social revolution of industrial unionism in the 1930s and the conversion of automobile factories to wartime production in the early 1940s. The wartime labor shortages demanded the inclusion and upgrading of African Americans into the more skilled and prestigious occupations in the automobile factories. When federal officials insisted on workplace equity, their policies resulted in hate strikes against the movement of African American workers to more skilled jobs, especially at the Packard Motor Company in 1943.

In the 1910s and early 1920s, new European immigrants and African American migrants often shared social and residential space in the northern auto cities and towns. According to the recollection of some African Americans, the earlier racial boundaries of the 1920s were much looser and more fluid than in the 1930s and the 1940s. For example, Coleman Young, the future Detroit mayor, and his parents moved to Detroit in 1920. At the time, the Black Bottom, one of the few neighborhoods open to black migrants, was an integrated community of African Americans and Southern and Eastern Europeans, mainly Poles. Young did "not recall an unusual amount of racial tension." The auto worker Joseph Panzner similarly recalled Detroit's integrated ethnic communities in the early years. "Us young people on Antoine Street," he remembered, "were mostly sons and daughters of immigrants. Most of the people were Irish,

German, and Bohemian, with a sprinkling of native-born colored people. I don't remember any race prejudice. We all went to school together and played together."⁵ And others had similar recollections.

The Alabama-born and leftist union activist Charles Denby remembered relations between Detroit blacks and whites in the mid-1920s. Despite some frictions and fights between youthful blacks and whites, he observed: "Relations between Negroes and whites were close then." Fights often ended in handshakes. Black and white workers frequently lived and ate in the same boarding houses. No one bothered to notice the two groups being and socializing together. "Every Sunday," he observed, "you could see mixed couples and Negro couples and white couples on motorcycles." The adolescent street gangs, he added, "were often mixed."⁶

The black UAW organizer Christopher Alston also remembered his early years living in the Detroit ethnic enclave of Hamtramck, known as "Poletown." His parents moved there when he was one year old. At the time, he told an interviewer, "the neighborhood was all Polish, for one thing the Blacks hadn't moved up in this area." His father had worked for Michigan Central Railroad and later worked for the Briggs body plant. In order to survive in this Polish neighborhood, the young Alston even had to learn Polish. When they first arrived in Poletown, Alston, said, "[My parents told me] that when they brought me here, there were 500 people gathered around the house, Poles. Not to chase us away, but to see what a Black boy looked like. They had never seen one. They had never seen Blacks period. They were just interested." In these early years the young Alston never faced discrimination from his white ethnic neighbors: "They were never hostile in this whole area of Poletown."⁷

Over time, however, this accommodative social attitude changed. An "adversarial attitude," Coleman Young recalled, gathered "ominously around the city as the new migrant groups staked their competing claims for social status, housing, and jobs." By the mid-1920s, auto manufacturers increased their recruitment of the white southern migrants, the urban Ku Klux Klan grew, and the Americanized and newly race-conscious Southern and Eastern Europeans, earlier often considered less than white, asserted their claim to "whiteness."⁸ In the mid-1920s, after Young's family moved to Detroit, he recalled "a KKK initiation ceremony in which thousands became members in a single goddamn swoop." The Klan appealed to southern white migrants "who found themselves threatened by blacks in a way that they had never been before" and also to Polish migrants who jostled "with blacks at the bottom of the social order for jobs and housing."⁹

Two black auto workers recalled a similar process of "whitening" in Flint. Henry Clark, a Buick worker, recalled that blacks, Mexicans, and Poles worked together in the Buick foundry as late as 1927. Sharing the same residential neighborhood, Clark recalled, "the Polish used to rent Blacks rooms up above them. They lived *right together* and they did fine for a long time." He characterized the residential arrangement as "White Polish downstairs and Black up. Or Black down and Polish up. They even *shacked* together." In time, young African American and Polish American men came into conflict over young Polish women. Noting the cultural whitening of the previously not-so-white Poles, Clark observed, "the Polish begin to move out from among the Blacks." Such competition across the boundary of race caused the Poles to "become as prejudiced against the Blacks as the other whites." When the interviewers asked Clark if he thought that southern whites taught their prejudices to the Poles, Clark responded: "Yes. That's the time . . . that the Polish and the Hungarians began to get away from us." In Flint, Clark recalled, the situation became bad around 1928 or 1929. Roger Townsend also remembered sharing his Flint neighborhood with "foreign elements." The Italians and Hungarians especially "would rent upstairs to blacks." By this time, Townsend also considered the Poles as less tolerant of blacks: "The Polish were not too liberal as far as blacks were concerned."[10] By the end of the 1920s, under the influence of white southern migrants, these European immigrants adopted their racial attitudes and in the process opted for separation and whiteness.

While they may have shared residential space, blacks and whites did not often share work space. Hodges Mason, who hired into Packard in the late 1920s, said with emphasis, "Quite a number [of Negroes] in the foundry—in the foundry." When he later worked at Ford, Mason also remembered: "We had segregated *jobs* within departments." He recalled times when "the foreman would tell a Negro, 'I would like to put you on that job, but this is a white man's job.'"[11]

During the early World War II years, Robert C. Weaver, the chief of Negro Employment and Training for the War Production Board, described "a caste system" for black workers. It "perpetuated the concept of white men's jobs and black men's jobs" and "was used to secure the support of the white worker for such a system."[12] A War Production Board report observed that during the war, when upgrades for black workers were a pressing issue, some white workers argued, "This is a white man's department and we'll keep it that." White workers were deeply divided over the treatment of black workers in Detroit plants. Two "substantial elements" of workers, the report noted, assumed "an aggressive position;" one group included "those who want to 'keep the nigger in his place'" and the other "those . . . who are pressing immediate complete social integration."[13] Flint auto worker Roger Townsend described the main features of white jobs. Discussing a sit-down strike of black up-graders who wanted to work at drilling operations in the Flint Buick plant, he observed that the drilling job involved a few simple operations: "You put in this thing in, pull the thing down and let it go back up. It ran by motor. They assumed that since it ran by a motor it was clean, it was a white man's job."[14] And until the ramping up of defense production, many auto workers defined such machine work and also assembly work as white men's work.

In Townsend's eyes, other "imaginary lines" also separated blacks and whites and added to the indignities of job segregation. Black workers, he related, "were limited to the foundries part [of the plant], they were not permitted to go beyond an imaginary line even to use the bathroom." Some restrooms were "off limits" to black workers. "Whites," he said, "could naturally go there." But black workers could not cross the line and use the white restroom. Townsend added that until a black grievance over the use of restrooms was initiated, "they had piles of sand for them to urinate in."[15]

The migration of southern whites and the "whitening" of Southern and Eastern European immigrants complicated and exacerbated the racial situation in automobile plants. In the post–World War I labor shortage, the same economic forces that impelled the "great" African American migration also facilitated the appearance of a pool of Southern white production workers with marginal industrial skills. Especially from the mid-1920s on, this so-called "hillbilly" migration included the movement of poor whites from the arc of states stretching from the Appalachians of West Virginia to the Ozarks of Arkansas and Missouri. Through the same process used for African American migrants, northern labor agents and contractors recruited this flexible industrial reserve of laborers who migrated from the small towns and the rural areas in their home states in the lower North and upper South. Some large auto firms, such as General Motors, valued the flexibility of these unskilled workers who staffed unskilled mass-production jobs in the busy season and who returned to their homes when production slowed or stalled. Unlike African Americans who escaped the Deep South for northern factories and cities and who sought more permanent lives away from their oppressive conditions, the "hillbilly" migrants had a looser and more fluid relationship with the urban auto towns and their native communities. Classic rural migrants—they had one foot on the farm and one in the factory. Even transient and temporary auto work substantially improved their economic lives back home in their non-industrial and cash-strapped rural communities.[16]

Sociologists characterized these southern migrants, often disparaged as hillbillies, Okies, ridge runners, or simply white trash, as "a distinct, cohesive, ethnic group." They were "young fellows," the journalist Louis Adamic noted. "They have no close contact with modern industry or with labor unionism." The latter "is their best qualification." By the mid-1930s the recently Americanized and recently union-conscious Southern and Eastern immigrants were no longer safe bets for a docile workforce. Adamic identified the white southern migrants as, "[for] the most part impoverished whites, 'white trash' or a little better, from the rural regions"[17] For automobile manufacturers, these were safe and individualistic workers untainted with favorable ideas toward unions.

For Frank Marquart, these workers formed a "suitcase brigade," something of a reserve workforce pulled into and pushed out of the automobile industry to suit the needs of the yearly production cycle. In the late summer during the "model-change layoff," they returned home and endured a "starvation vacation." When the auto firms "were rushing like mad to get out production, they advertised for help in Tennessee, Kentucky, and Indiana." With their families back home in the countryside, they lived in "cheap rooming houses" and ate in "cheap restaurants." Marquart added, "They managed to accumulate a stake by the time the model-change layoff season arrived; then they returned to their farms." They were so favored by employers, Adamic observed, that some northern job seekers would often feign a "Southern dialect and drawl" and would "look and act stupid" to obtain a job.[18]

As with other immigrants and migrants, the southern whites carried the cultural baggage of the white South with them to the industrial centers where they settled. They especially bore their southern attitudes on racial relations. They amounted to a conservative force in automobile factories and towns; if not anti-union, they often favored the exclusionary unionism of Homer Martin's UAW-AFL, sometimes becoming supporters of the Black Legion or the Ku Klux Klan, and exacerbating shop-floor racial tensions in the Packard, Hudson, Chrysler, Briggs, and other auto plants. They surely taught some of the Southern and Eastern European ethnics the social and economic advantages and "wages of whiteness." In the late 1930s through the war years, the volatile mix of southern racial ideas, ethnic aspirations toward white Americanism, and aggressive African American demands for workplace equity all contributed to the disruptive social chaos of the automotive shop floor through the war years. These racial and ethnic attitudes exploded in the Sojourner Truth housing riots, the Detroit race riot, the hate strikes against black men and women who upgraded to white jobs, and black pride strikes against job discrimination and social and economic inequity at the workplace.

Consistent with hiring tradition, African American men went to the dirtiest, most dangerous, and most laborious jobs, often labeled the "man-killing" positions. They performed the hot and dangerous work in the foundries and later in the spray painting and wet sanding shops. Until unions raised the wages for softer nonproduction positions, black men performed the demeaning janitorial work. The union activist Frank Marquart recalled, "Negroes were confined to the foundry and janitorial work mainly." At the Briggs plant, he added, "they were sanders on the bodies." Such occupations were dangerous to health: the spray painters inhaled poisonous paint particles; the sanders the metallic dust, often containing lead. Shelton Tappes, a black union activist, remembered: "Most of the Negroes in the automobile plants, like Briggs, Murray Body, or Fisher Body, worked in the wet-sanding departments. This was the kind of work that other workers would prefer not to do, if they didn't have to. It was extremely wet; you were vulnerable to colds, pneumonia, and all that sort of things."[19]

The Packard Motor Car Company best illustrated the explosive racial tensions on the shop floor in wartime. It revealed the difficult work problems that African Americans faced in the American automobile factories. In 1943 the movement of black workers to "white" production jobs resulted in a huge hate strike, disrupting war production. Though the Packard hate strike was the largest, other plants of the Chrysler, Hudson, Briggs, and other firms confronted similar problems. Until the mid-1930s the Packard plant produced mainly luxury vehicles with its highly skilled workforce of craftsmen. In the mid-1930s, it developed a less expensive model for a wider market, introduced modern production techniques, and employed more and more mass-production workers. It thus had a bifurcated workforce of highly skilled craftsmen and newer mass-production workers—two groups with quite different social and union outlooks. The former tended to be much more conservative socially and in their AFL union orientation. The less-skilled production workers favored the more progressive CIO. James Lindahl, a former Packard UAW official, described this bifurcated production system and social composition of the workforce.[20]

The Packard campaign toward unionization was essentially a white male project and revealed potential future problems for African American workers. Unionism at Packard began with the creation of a works council, an employer scheme to weaken the drive for independent worker unions, after the passage of the National Industrial Recovery Act in 1933. The new production system caused "agitation amongst workers particularly older workers who felt that there was a need for a union." Two years after the formation of the works council, Chrysler workers created the Automotive Industrial Workers Association, a labor organization endorsed by the right-wing Detroit radio priest Charles Coughlin. Packard workers soon followed and formed their own AWIA local. Catholic supporters of Coughlin formed a conservative group within the Packard union. At the founding UAW convention at South Bend in 1936, the Packard and other AIWA locals affiliated with the new UAW-CIO. In its 1937 National Labor Relations Board election, 80 percent of the Packard workers voted formally to join the UAW.[21]

During the Martin factional struggles within the UAW, the new UAW Local 190 was fairly united and did not initially take sides. With its large complement of conservative skilled craftsmen, the UAW local divided sharply after Martin suspended his opponents on the UAW Executive Board. With the trials and suspension of the Martin opponents, UAW Local 190 officers provided financial support to the anti-Martin board members. For a time, two unions existed at Packard—the Unity Caucus's UAW-CIO and the Progressive Caucus's UAW-AFL. The two factions often collided on the shop floor, at the plant gates, and in the union hall. In another fall 1939 NLRB representation election, Packard unionists voted overwhelmingly for the UAW-CIO.[22]

On the eve of World War II, the UAW Packard local possessed several sources of potential division and tension. Age, skill levels, ethnicity and race, AFL or CIO orientation, social radicalism or conservatism, and Northern or Southern birth all figured into this explosive social mixture. For James Lindahl the Packard plant contained three distinct groups—the Poles, Italians, and African-Americans—just before World War II. As the first generation of foreign-born Poles and Italians "grew inactive or retired," he observed, the second generation "became more Americanized." As the predominant group with a "tendency to 'stay put' after being hired," the Polish workers were the most active and involved in union politics and participated along national lines. The Italians were also "numerous, nationalistic in voting behavior, but did not seem to be so prominent in the politics of the local union." Much less numerous, African American workers "played small part in the internal affairs of the local."[23]

Although in Packard's early days the Poles and Italians worked in "the hardest, least desirable jobs," the situation for black workers, Lindahl remembered, was far worse, since they were "clustered in the foundry" or were "scattered about the plant in low-status jobs such as janitor." In the first months of union activity, they suffered "a number of discouraging episodes" of blatant racism. In the "private hall the union rented for its meetings," the bartender "openly broke the glasses which Negroes had used." Obviously, African American workers were unenthusiastic about the UAW local and the foundry workers lagged in their union membership. With the national defense program, Lindahl related, "came a sudden influx of young urban Negroes." After the prodding of the union's "self-conscious Negro bloc," the UAW Local 190 leaders "conducted an energetic two-pronged attack: (a) for up-grading and integration on jobs everywhere in the plant, and (b) for adequate representation in the union hierarchy of offices."[24]

In addition to the ethnic and racial divide, issues of ideology and skill complicated the racial dimension of Packard labor politics. The union had a leftist faction of communists, socialists, and other "left-wingers," and a rightist faction of devotees of Father Coughlin and the Ku Klux Klan. The two factions contributed to the CIO Unity and the AFL Progressive caucus split within the Packard UAW local in 1938–39. In their shop-floor activities and propaganda, the Coughlinites and Ku Klux Klansmen seriously encouraged the more racist and anti-Semitic elements of the Packard workforce. Additionally, the more skilled workers "feared the dilution of their trades if production people were upgraded." Finally, a localist allegiance to a particular shop, department, or occupation—a loyalty nurtured in white ethnic and male bonding to a specific work group—further complicated an already entangled work setting.[25]

In 1940 a Rolls Royce contract to produce aircraft engines for the British and the U.S. governments again reconfigured the Packard plant. Ford had "declined" to produce engines for the British in American plants, and the contract went to Packard. The contract for nine thousand engines resulted in a $30 million expansion of the plant and in the addition of fourteen thousand men to more than double the Packard workforce for a Rolls Royce contract. It took ten months to build the new addition when the first engines were produced.[26] Although Packard officials departed from British production methods and used American mass-production protocols, the manufacture of aircraft engines favored the hiring of more skilled production workers. As war production rapidly expanded at Packard, so too did the numbers of both white and black southern migrants who added to an already unsettled social mixture.

In the late 1930s and early 1940s the Ku Klux Klan reemerged as a disruptive force in Detroit, especially in the fundamentalist churches where the white southerners prayed and in the automobile plants where they worked. In early March 1943 Claude C. Williams, a radical social gospeler familiar with rural America as a former SFTU organizer, issued a report that connected Detroit's racial strike troubles to "numbers of preachers working in plants of Detroit and vicinity." Some twenty-five hundred such preachers, he alleged, aroused "Detroit's increasing thousands of ex-rural, ex-southern population which is predominantly anti-Negro, anti-Yankee, and anti-union." The world of their small churches was "a sort of No Man's Land" and "headache for unions, liberal churchmen, [and] social workers." These fundamentalist congregations, Williams maintained, provided opportunities for more prominent demagogues like J. Frank Norris and Gerald L. K. Smith, and for the Ku Klux Klan. The churches, he maintained, served to recruit Detroit Klansmen, and "the largest Baptist and the largest Methodist church in Detroit were hotbeds of Kukluxism."[27]

The Ku Klux Klan further entangled the situation, since it made appeals for the white southern migrants to enlist in the Klan cause and targeted the black ones who sought to improve their work prospects in Detroit auto plants. From 1939 through 1941, the newly invigorated Klan began an intensive campaign to organize in automobile plants and to take over some Detroit auto worker union locals. After the Flint sit-down strikes, it focused on the CIO and other leftist labor organizations. In 1939 James A. Colescott replaced Hiram Wesley Evans as the KKK's Imperial Wizard. As part of the Klan's Midwestern organizational campaign, he planned on "mopping up the cesspools of Communism in the United States" and apparently intended to organize in urban industrial centers with significant numbers of white Southern migrants.[28]

Detroit auto unions fit this aim perfectly. In 1939 the Packard Edition of the *United Auto Worker* noted initial Klan recruitment efforts among auto workers: "The night-shirt boys are on the loose again," noting that "our good union brothers" received "innocent" luncheon invitations as "a cover-up to get union men to a meeting of the Ku Klux Klan. Only the native born, and those of Protestant belief are being invited."[29] Gradually, the anti-Semitic, anti-black, anti-foreign, anti-Catholic, and anti-labor organization made serious inroads into the Packard UAW local and increased its numbers to become a genuine threat to the Packard and other smaller UAW locals.

Between 1940 and 1941 the reports of a CIO Klan informant and a series of circular letters to Ku Klux Klan members revealed the Klan's considerable organizational activities in the Detroit area.[30] The CIO Klan spy was an older and possibly retired worker who identified himself simply as "Oldster." In addition to public Klan meetings, he attended several "closed" and "invitational" secret meetings. As part of the KKK's "inner circle," he was most likely an initiated, or "naturalized," Klan member. In Detroit, he reported, the closed meetings numbered four each week on different days and at different locations. Eight open invitational meetings occurred on Saturday or Sunday, one in Detroit and others scattered around southeastern Michigan. Occasionally, since he was "not a shop worker," he also mentioned, but did not attend, special Klan auto worker shop meetings. Attendance at the public meetings ranged from only a few on a day of inclement weather to two thousand at a large summer open-air rally in Norton's Grove in Macomb County, thirty-five miles outside of Detroit. At this meeting, Imperial Wizard Colescott, the Indiana Grand Dragon, and Michigan Grand Dragon "all gave a rotten-hell-fire bombardment speeches" with Communism as "their special issue."[31]

The principal Michigan KKK leaders were Charles Spare, the Michigan Grand Dragon, and Harvey Hanson, the Michigan Klan organizer. Since Harvey Hanson was most active in the organization of auto workers, the CIO informant wrote mainly about his activities in Detroit and around the state in such auto towns as Flint and Pontiac. Apparently, organizer Hanson had previously worked with the UAW-AFL leader Homer Martin since the CIO spy referred to him as "a former Homer stoogie" and "Homer's chief goon." At different times, Hanson worked in the Chevrolet and Packard plants. Some of the Klan union members, he reported, had "not much trust in Hanson, many of them know of his past record" as a staunch AFL supporter. Hanson chaired the KKK committee for the "Promotion of Americanisms within the UAW-CIO." He intended "to capture and Americanize the U.A.W.-C.I.O. and so block Romanism and Communism and all other isms in the union in all the shops."[32] The criticism of Romanism would not inspire the large contingent of Catholic Poles working at Packard.

In late November 1940 the Detroit KKK called a special meeting at its Forest Avenue headquarters and announced plans to "control" the Detroit UAW and CIO. Klan officials urged all members to pay their union dues and "get in good standing" with their unions. Soon, KKK members were in the Packard, Ford, Briggs, Chrysler, Dodge, and Continental Motors factories. At another meeting, "the main subject was—how to get control of the unions, especially the UAW-CIO." They also suggested that members follow the practices of their reviled foe—Association of Catholic Trade Unionists. It recommended that members learn parliamentary procedure so "that they may later gain full and complete control of the local unions." As with Catholic union activists, the Klan leaders urged members to "take an active role in the union and do everything possible to get control by electing" its members "to key positions."[33]

The Klan also brought its vision of manhood to the later shop-floor struggles against African American workers. In its effort to organize the Packard plant, especially its contingent of skilled American workers who might favor a conservative AFL unionism and to the fundamentalist white southern migrants, the KKK also appealed to a white, respectable, and Christian variant of manhood. A Klan leaflet circulated in the Packard plant detailed these principles. It emphasized the Christian religion, white supremacy, pure womanhood and Americanism, a closer relationship between capital and labor, stopping strikes by foreign labor agitators, and restricting foreign immigration.[34]

By early 1942 the Klan gained strength and posed a real threat inside the Packard UAW local. In early January, International Secretary Treasurer George Addes for the UAW warned Curt Murdock, the Packard local president, about the KKK's "disruptive campaign" within the union local. Citing the Grand Dragon's threat to "clean out the union," Addes noted that the UAW was "utterly opposed" to organizations such as the Klan and urged the local officers "to guard against disruption from these sources." He noted "the leadership of the K.K.K. in Packard in the hands of Frank Buehrle." Addes added that Harvey Hanson, "Homer Martin's chief goon," recently moved near the Packard plant "to direct organization at close range."[35]

The KKK unionists attempted to assert control in the upcoming union elections for officers and engaged in the factionalized union politics of UAW Local 190. The Ku Klux Klan had chosen Packard as target for organization because it had some strength among the local's shop-floor leadership. "Out in the Packard Plant," the CIO spy reported, "there is quite some activity by Klan members there." He identified Frank Burley (actually, Buehrle) as the Packard Ku Klux Klan leader. In early 1942, just before the local's spring elections for officers, Buehrle attempted to "dictate" a Klan slate of candidates to Curt Murdock, the local union president. When Murdock refused to accept the slate, Buehrle threatened that the Klan would get him. At the time, UAW Local 190 leaders instituted an "all-out attack" on the Klan at a February 1 membership meeting and noted the "Colescott's attack on the on the leadership of the CIO as 'Communists.'" Union financial secretary Adam Poplawski told Packard local members: "Time after time, I have seen Frank Buehrle march newly recruited members of the Klan into the local office, in an attempt to impress and intimidate your local officers." He added: "Only recently he had the audacity to corner your president and try to tell him who should be elected to local office." The Klan faction had joined with Coughlin, Martin, and, amazingly, the Association of Catholic Trade Unionist supporters. It joined with other shop-floor dissidents against UAW officers to run an anti-administration slate in the Local 190 union elections. Angry at the public exposure, Buehrle's faction began to circulate a leaflet that claimed Murdock was a Klan member, including a false personal letter to Curt Murdock from the Michigan Grand Dragon. They also circulated a reproduction of a fake KKK membership card in Murdock's name. Apparently, Buehrle desired to become the Packard UAW local's president, since he was actually listed on the ballot for union elections as a candidate for Packard Local 190 president.[36] Despite the Klan efforts to take over the Packard local, Murdock and his slate handily won the election.

Subsequently, the Detroit Klan shifted its attention to community organization in a neighborhood on the northern edge of the heavily Polish suburb of Hamtramck and later to departmental strikes over the upgrading of African American workers. In alliance with local real estate agents, it actively protested federal proposals to move African Americans into a new Sojourner Truth housing project for defense workers. After months of white protests and indecisive governmental actions, federal officials finally decided to move black families into the new housing project. The night before the planned move on February 28, 1942, around 150 white pickets patrolled the area and burned "a fiery cross" on the site. When the police arrived the next day, they found "nearly 1,200 persons armed with knives, clubs, rifles, and shotguns." An all-day riot ensued. Three times, the police attempted to disperse the crowd with tear gas. But the crowd fought back. Shots were fired. Several participants were "slashed." Some black protesters resisted white intimidation. Three policemen and about fifteen others, white and black alike, were taken to local hospitals. The incident resulted in 104 arrests: six for felonious assault, twenty-three for concealed weapons, seventy-five for inciting to riot.[37]

The next day, a "police-enforced peace prevailed," although a "picket line of white objectors" appeared. Despite the white picket line, only "a few minor skirmishes involving three or four persons" and "only four arrests" occurred. Detroit mayor Edward J. Jeffries subsequently announced that the effort to move in the new black tenants would be "postponed indefinitely." The "night after the riot," a leftist anti-Nazi newsletter reported, "they burned a second cross in triumph."[38] For almost two months, despite the desperate need for wartime Detroit housing, the new project remained vacant.

At the end of April, eight hundred soldiers protected the twelve black families who moved into the unoccupied Sojourner Truth housing project. Since a "cordon of soldiers with fixed bayonets, augmented by city and state police" protected the new tenants, no new rioting occurred. The "only hostility" involved "a picket line by about 250 persons, mostly women," who stood and protested "across the street" from the African American families desiring to relocate. When the police broke up their line, the "women booed and heckled" them. When a group of African Americans attempted to establish another picket line, the police arrested nine for "loitering." Other new residents planned to move in at the end of the week. On the Sojourner Truth riot, a wartime-tension areas report noted that it was the "first major racial conflict since the 'defense' era." It concluded: "A highly organized opposition, led by Polish-Catholic elements in the community and apparently encouraged by subversive organizations," agitated for several months through 1941 and 1942.[39]

After the housing riots, Murdock and Packard Local 190 officers decided to conduct a trial of Frank Buehrle based on the accusation that union president Murdock was a Klan member and on the Klan's effort to take over the Packard local. Buehrle's trial lasted four days, from March 31 to April 3, and it revealed that the Ku Klux Klan had chosen the Packard plant as target for organization because they had strength among the local's shop floor leadership, mainly among union shop stewards.[40] Adam Poplawski, the UAW local's treasurer, later noted that with such strength, the Klan leadership "were in a good strategic position to sort of spread out and gain new recruits, and as a result of that they became quite bold." Union president Curt Murdock alleged that the Klan, ACTU, and the Coughlin group formed "a marriage to defeat the administration and to seize control of the local union." At the time, James Lindahl estimated that more than six hundred Klan members worked in the Packard plant.[41] Although only a small proportion of the Packard workforce, KKK members constituted an important conservative militant minority that allied with other more conservative union factions and racist elements among union members.

Although the main charge against Buehrle was the effort to smear Murdock as a Klan member in the union election, the trial also elicited information on the racist attitudes and actions of the Packard Klan leader and his allies in the plant, including recent strikes against upgrading black workers. James Lindahl alleged: "Brother Buehrle was the organizer of all the anti-negro sentiment in the plant." He organized "the threatened riot in the polishing room," which ended in two black polishers being forced back to their original department. He and other Packard Klan members were "among the most vocal and the most vicious in attacking the notion that negro workers should have the right to go on better jobs, [to] transfer onto defense [positions]." At a union trial, Poplawski criticized Buehrle for his statement about "the inability of colored men to master the technique of operation of the various machines in the plant."[42]

The seven-person Local 190 trial board met for four days and heard the testimony of sixteen witnesses, including Buehrle and others who had fabricated and circulated the false KKK membership "passport." It unanimously concluded that Murdock was not a Klan member, that Buehrle "on the basis of *unchallenged testimony*" was "actively building the Ku Klux Klan in Packard," that the effort to "incriminate" Murdock was an act of "revenge for an attack" on the Klan at a union membership meeting and in the union local paper, and that Buehrle was responsible for "the fabrication and circulation of the false documents." Since Buehrle violated the Local 190 bylaws, the union trial board also concluded that he was "liable" to union discipline. It suspended the Klan leader from "active participation, of any kind, in the affairs of the union" for ten years, required him to pay all membership dues and assessments, and noted that his suspension would in no way affect "his right to earn a livelihood" at Packard.[43]

On the last day of Buehrle's trial, Packard local officers believed they had beaten back the Klan. Lindahl reported that the two black polishers threatened by Buehrle and others "were quietly transferred onto defense [work] last Tuesday." The transfer, he added, occurred with "no disturbance, no undue commotion." The two black workers were "working in perfect harmony, in perfect peace, side by side with white workers." The union, Lindahl observed, had "attacked the Klan and driven it underground."[44] Though driven underground in the spring of 1942, the Klan organization and its members certainly remained active on the shop floor until a huge Packard hate strike erupted the next year.

Frustrated by the housing riots, the Klan actions at Packard and other auto plants, and the slow progress of the Fair Employee Practice Commission to upgrade black men and women into better war-production jobs, the angry Detroit black community attempted to correct the inequitable situation. This was the context of the proposed call for a second march on Washington and for "manly" resistance to abuses at the workplace. In the early summer of 1942, the black minister Lester Walton investigated and exposed the horrific conditions of black men and women in the automobile industry. He conducted a tour of several Midwestern industrial cities to assess the situation of African American workers in defense plants and then sent a confidential report to Washington. Walton wanted to make "a first hand study of the Negro in relation to the war effort." He spoke with editors, physicians, lawyers, businessmen, ministers, and defense workers. In his interviews, African American women most vigorously protested the unfair hiring practices in defense plants. Their views were virtually unanimous, "the only difference" being that some "were more vehement in giving vent to their feelings than others." If asked to characterize the African American attitude toward the war effort, Walton emphasized: "*No one is disloyal, all are either disgruntled or bitter over discriminatory practices.*" Their profound resentment, he reported, constituted "the wave of 'righteous' indignation" that arose from "drawing the color line in the defense plants and in Federal housing projects."[45]

In his report on his Detroit visit, Walton estimated that there were about fifteen hundred defense plants in the area. "More skilled mechanics," he claimed, "are employed in Detroit and environs than elsewhere in the United States." But, he added, the "absorption of the Negro by production is slow." Three firms—Ford, Dodge, and Packard—were named for "their liberal attitude toward hiring Negroes," but they only hired blacks into racially segregated departments and occupations. Black men and women were not hired on machine or assembly work. In the near future, Walton felt, these plants would have serious racial problems. The Detroit African American community especially commended the efforts of the CIO in its commitment to racial equality. Despite some discontent among the more socially conservative members, the UAW took a firm stand against workplace discrimination. "Nothing but praise," he reported, "is heard among Negroes to the fair-minded attitude of the C.I.O. toward the race." At the Hudson Naval Arsenal in 1942, UAW president Thomas took a firm stand against a hate strike and threatened the dismissal of those who struck against the upgrading of black workers.[46]

Richard Frankensteen personally intervened in the Hudson strike to encourage the acceptance of the African American up-graders. "The Hudson plant," he said, "had been for many years the scene of 'Black Legion' activity." The Black Legion supporters from the early 1930s formed the basis of Klan organization in the Hudson in the late 1930s. They were "the guiding force" of a Hudson group called "Invisible Eye of Labor." It was, he added, a Klan offshoot, a "'white shirt' outfit or a hooded one." The Hudson local, the UAW leader asserted, "had many Southern employees from the hills, the real rabid people who would go for that type of organization."[47]

The Hudson hate strike began when sixteen hundred workers walked out "to protest against the hiring of eight Negroes as machine operators." When Frankensteen arrived at the plant gates, he discovered that Hudson defense "workers were on strike" and "were sitting down in the plant." He faced an angry crowd of workers who were "yelling, catcalling, and chanting all through the department." As the UAW leader walked through the plant to see where the strike began, chanting started: "'Nigger lover, Nigger lover, Nigger lover' all the way through." The Hudson workers sat down because two African

American men had been upgraded "from sweepers to machine operators." When Frankensteen attempted to explain the UAW wartime policy on non-discrimination: "There was dead silence, not a word."[48]

Although forceful UAW opposition drove the Packard Ku Klux Klan underground in 1942, its organizers continued to operate on the shop floor among the more racist or more conservative craft unionists, the Coughlin supporters, and the white southerners in the plant. As federal officials and black leaders pressured employers to include more black men and women and to utilize their skills in the war effort, Detroit erupted in venomous hate strikes in defense plants around the city in 1943 and later.

Increasingly, African American men and women responded to employment discrimination and to the developing hate strikes in what might best be described pride strikes in support of up-graders. Especially concerned about the discriminatory abuse of black women, African American men defended the dignity of black womanhood. So outraged was the *Michigan Chronicle*, the state's African American news weekly, that in February 1943 it called for a demonstration in support of the employment of "Negro" women and their upgrading in Detroit's war-production plants. The newspaper noted that a major complaint was the assignment of black women who trained for skilled work but were put to work as janitors, sometimes in men's washrooms and at men's heavy janitorial duties. For example, Chrysler Highland Park plant officials hired women trained for skilled war work but paid little attention to their new work skills. After they were hired, "the majority of them end[ed] up as janitors, or sweepers, both of which include[d] heavy work even for robust men." As janitors, they were expected to "handle barrels of metal chips and shavings weighing up to 250 pounds." They also had to wield "industrial type" mops and brooms sometimes "too heavy even for men." At the same time, white women in the same Chrysler department became clerical workers or messengers.[49]

A week later, the black newspaper offered more specific details on African American women's grievances at the Chrysler Highland Park plant. Complaining about the hard work of "pulling steel, running jitneys, and heavy mopping," one woman noted: "Many of us were hired as elevator operators but have never run an elevator at the plant because the men on the elevators refuse to transfer to the work we are doing. They say the work is too hard for them." Another reiterated that white women could turn such jobs down, while black women were told "they must do *these jobs* or ring their cards and go home." Another black women complained: "When we first went to the plant they gave us separate toilets—far from our work—and we were told we would have to eat our lunch in these rest rooms." It contained a low table between two benches. "We don't know," she added, "what they were used for before we were hired." She also recounted an incident where an African American woman dared to use the white women's restroom. She had "the buttons . . . cut off her coat and her galoshes cut to threads."[50]

Among Chrysler's African American men a "rising tide of resentment" resulted in a wildcat strike against the indignities African American women endured. Their principal complaint: "We are tired of seeing our women being pushed around." Many of the instigators received seven- to ten-day disciplinary layoffs for their strike in support of black women. After discussing the women's grievances, they unsuccessfully appealed to union committeemen and to Chrysler management. Their collated grievances included allowing "properly trained" women to have a chance working at machines, not assigning women to "too heavy work," a job quota for African American workers, a raise for low-paid work, and seniority as consideration for transfer and promotion. Since white unionists did not agree with the proposals, management refused to consider them. Eugene Carter led an evening strike and received a thirty-day layoff, reduced to ten days. But the "flame" that he had ignited started a second walkout of black men and women when they realized that "the union was not going to fight their cause."[51]

In the midst of the Chrysler turmoil, Walter Hardin, chair of the UAW's Interracial Committee, announced that he would quit his "job with the UAW-CIO and go back into the shop unless some of the Negro's labor problems are solved." African American workers were trapped due to wartime labor policy that kept workers at their jobs to prevent labor turnover in war-production plants. They were locked in "a labor pool enslaving Negro workers who are forced to remain on jobs from which they cannot be upgraded and cannot be released." Before transferring from janitorial positions to production jobs, they were "forced to give away their seniority." Defense employers, Hardin and others believed, made African Americans "slaves" of the wartime "labor pool."[52]

At Packard, two short work stoppages over the upgrading of African American women in mid-February and early March preceded the huge hate strike in late May. In February, Packard officials assigned "three colored women" as "drill press operators," traditionally white men's work. If black men on white men's jobs proved too much for Packard's white men to accept, black women surely exasperated and angered them. After the upgrades, Packard officials informed the three women that "they must not use any toilet facilities except one being reserved for their exclusive use." Packard officials accepted and enforced white fears about unclean African Americans and the need for separate facilities. The designated toilet for the black women was "formerly condemned as unsanitary and one only fitted for the use of males." A FEPC official felt that such "social discrimination" was not under his jurisdiction and urged the district War Man Power Commissioner to use "his influence so that wildcat stoppages will not cause the Packard company to cease employing Negro women of skill" due to the severe Detroit labor shortages.[53]

On March 18 another strike at Packard occurred over the upgrading of four black women to production work. National and local officials were "unable to prevail upon the strikers to immediately return to their jobs." Government and union leaders believed that "the Packard Motor Company, the UAW and all government agencies were challenged by this 'master race' strike." Colonel George E. Strong, the Air Corps industrial-relations officer, and union officials "with characteristic forcefulness" got the strikers back to work by the next morning. Packard employment manager C. E. Weiss, a southerner who sympathized with the hate strikers, had guards placed at the entrance to the floor where the four new women worked to prevent disrupters from entering. According to Weiss, "some smart ninnies . . . started the trouble" and "the Negroes themselves have caused the most trouble." Two days after the initial stoppage, another one occurred over the "same issue" where the original three black women had been working for some time in a different department. On March 24 the four women worked "unmolested" and the other three worked with "general acceptance." According to the union, this small strike involved an estimated twenty-three hundred workers.[54]

Two months later the huge Packard hate strike erupted, beginning with small stoppages at midnight on May 24 and erupting into a twenty-five-thousand-worker strike on June 3. The main issue was "the upgrading of three Negro workers to the assembly line," another privileged white job. Black Packard workers also walked out when the white workers refused to accept black assembly line workers. After three hundred white workers in the motor department refused to work on the line, black workers also left; "protesting discrimination, [they] stayed away from their jobs." The African American strikers soon returned to work and awaited a union meeting to discuss "the whole question of upgrading of Negroes to the production line." At the May 30 union membership meeting, R. J. Thomas, the UAW president, and Colonel Strong "spoke (or tried to speak) to those present. Both men were heckled by the white workers." Thomas emphasized the CIO's policies of nondiscrimination and that "the white workers would have to accept Negroes at all levels of skill." If the strike continued, Strong threatened to fire the "ringleaders."[55]

That evening, the three black workers reported to the production line for their new jobs. Catering to white southern worker sentiments, C. E. Weiss, Packard's labor-relations director, met the black workers and said that he "would not put the Negroes on the higher skill jobs unless they were acceptable to the white workers, regardless of what the union or the government thought about the matter." Weiss, recalled union official Poplawski, "seemingly recruited a lot of Southern boys." Present at the incident, Strong's representatives noted the black workers were "ordered out of the plant and even jostled by company representatives."[56]

Two days later R. J. Thomas "denounced Weiss and other Packard officers as instigators of racial strife and called for their resignation." When the three workers again tried to work on the production line that midnight, some white workers walked off their jobs at 1:00 A.M., and others continued to leave through the midnight shift. The strikers prevented day-shift workers from going to work. Other black workers reported for work, "but the entire plant closed down." Thomas condemned Packard officials for "inciting racial strife." Weiss, he said, urged "the men to refuse to work with Negroes." Somewhat disingenuously, some white strikers claimed that there was "no dispute over the promotion of Negro workers, but there is an implied [white worker] demand the they be segregated in [different] departments." The strike, the *Detroit News* later reported, "was over the issue of whether white men would work shoulder to should with Negroes."[57] Such arrangements as black workers in "segregated departments" and not working on an equal basis "shoulder to shoulder" certainly suited white southern sensibilities about industrial work.

Although the strikers briefly returned to work, they hit the pavement again on June 3. Despite the renewed War Labor Board threats, Packard workers continued their resistance. The next day, the strikers said that "they would not resume production until three Negro workers are removed from assembly lines." Some of the UAW local's stewards even sympathized with the strikers. About 95 percent of Packard workers struck. Despite the prodding of international, regional, and local union officials (including the new Packard Local president Norman Mathews), Weiss, Strong, and WLB executive director Carl R. Schedler appealed for the workers to return to their jobs. Outside on the picket line, Packard workers steadfastly refused to return to their jobs and booed union leaders with sound trucks at the gates and also booed black workers entering the plant.[58] Government officials "agreed that there are organized Klan movements behind the strike." They also determined that no "organized subversive movements" existed among African American workers.[59]

The following day, after a conference with federal, union, and company officials, UAW president Thomas reiterated his support of the African American union members. They paid the same dues as any other union member and "have fought and will fight in the future of this union." Earlier he gave his "strongest ultimatum" to the strikers, and now he said that he would be "even stronger." Thomas warned: "Even if it requires that large numbers of white workers out there lose their jobs . . . that's just what will happen if this strike continues." On Saturday a union and WLB-organized back-to-work movement gained momentum as around one-third of the workforce returned to their jobs.[60]

On Saturday evening military officials promised an investigation of the strikes and "punishment for those responsible." At the same time, the motor-repair department workers who refused to work with African American men and women voted to return to work. By Sunday night Packard war production had approached "near normalcy," as about 80 percent of workers in the aircraft-engine division returned to production. This followed Thomas's announcement that he had "'absolute evidence' that the Packard strike was promoted by the Ku Klux Klan." One piece of evidence was a formal invitation for Packard Klansmen to attend a special April meeting; another was a transcript of a phone conversation between a UAW member posing as a Klansman and a Klan member at its Forest Avenue headquarters. In the conversation, Charles Spare and Harvey Hanson were mentioned. WLB, FEPC, and other federal officials also conceded that "organized Klan movements" were "behind the strike." When asked about any "organized subversive movements" among black workers, FEPC officials responded that none existed. Subsequently, the *Detroit News* conducted a long-distance phone conversation with James A. Colescott, the KKK Imperial Wizard. Colescott claimed that his organization did not foment strikes against the national defense effort and that almost a year ago Charles Spare broke with the Klan and formed his own organization, the United Sons of America, in Detroit.[61]

Colonel Alonzo M. Drake, an Army Air Force district supervisor for procurement, announced: "As a result of an investigation by military authorities . . . white and colored instigators of the recent wildcat strike . . ., including a foreman, were suspended today from further employment with the company." A total of twenty-nine workers were suspended for the strikes. The Packard foreman allegedly "told white workers, they need not work with Negroes." In an apparent effort to appear equitable, some of the black workers who struck to defend the assembly-line up-graders were also suspended. All suspended workers would be allowed an opportunity to appeal and to defend of their actions. The UAW-CIO leaders and workers also gave assurances "that every effort will be made to increase production to offset the losses of the last two weeks." After Packard returned to normal production, the UAW local leaders insisted either on Weiss's suspension or that the suspended workers be put back to work.[62] Nevertheless, Weiss remained the Packard industrial-relations director.

After the strike ended, the FEPC received and heard thirty-one complaints from African American up-graders. After the hearings, Packard managers agreed that eleven complainants "had meritorious cases" and would be upgraded and allowed to move to upgraded jobs. The remainder would go through the regular union grievance process for their appeals in the presence of an FEPC representative. Nonetheless, referring to the Sojourner Truth housing incident of the previous year, the FEPC report ominously noted: "In view of the fact that adjustment of these cases is made difficult by the fear of more race riots, the Detroit area continues to be a very delicate one."[63]

Two weeks after the large Packard hate strike, Detroit exploded into a major race riot on June 20. At Detroit's Belle Isle Park, one hundred thousand Detroit residents, black and white, attempted to cool down on that hot early summer day. The overcrowded wartime recreational facilities erupted in brawls between black and whites seeking refuge from the heat. A large majority of those on Belle Isle were African American. The fights moved to the bridge that connected the island and the mainland, where about five thousand white and black men fought each other. Soon, rumors abounded: African Americans believed that whites threw a woman and her baby from the bridge to Belle Isle, and whites believed that black men were raping white women. Both white and black men fought because they thought they were defending black and white womanhood. The crowds then moved to nearby neighborhoods, including the black area ironically named Paradise Valley, in southeast Detroit. Blacks and whites "launched fierce attacks against passersby, streetcars, and property." Angry African Americans looted white-owned stores in Paradise Valley. Ten thousand whites gathered on Woodward Avenue near the black neighborhood and attacked any black who came near them. Police often sympathized with the white crowds, harassing, arresting, and brutalizing black participants and bystanders. The historian Thomas Sugrue concluded: "Over the course of three days, 34 people were killed, 25 of them black, 675 suffered serious injuries, and 1,893 were arrested before federal troops subdued the disorder."[64] Property losses due to looting, ransacked stores, burned autos, and other damage were an estimated $2 million. The two days of violence cost the nation more than one million man-hours of lost war production.[65]

The worst violence lasted only two days. Two contemporary analysts detailed the resulting mayhem and destruction: "Shootings. Beatings. Looting. Property destruction. Car-burnings. Maimed and wounded innocents. A terrified populace. A horrified minority, inadequately protected and besieged in an American City."[66] The bitter legacy of racial discrimination and hatred was costly to all Detroiters.

Detroit's explosive violence was a consequence of the earlier agitation of white southerners over housing and on the factory floor, and of the African American protests over housing and job discrimination. Detroiters endured working long hours, living in overcrowded housing, and playing in overused parks and recreational facilities. All rattled black and white nerves. Detroit newspapers proclaimed Detroit "a keg of powder with a short fuse." In the midst of the Packard strike, NAACP head Walter White predicted the consequences: "Let us drag out into the open what has been whispered throughout for months—that a race riot may break out here at any time."[67] Two weeks later, White's prediction came true.

Rather than delve into the real causes of and actual solutions to the racial problems that figured in the Detroit riots, investigators and commentators descended into a blame game. Almost everyone blamed the Detroit police force for their sympathetic treatment of white rioters and the harsh treatment of black ones. Police officials blamed African Americans for starting the riot. Liberals blamed the Klan and reactionary demagogues like Smith and Coughlin. Conservatives faulted liberals and Japanese and black agitators.[68]

Many attributed the riots to the recent migrations of both white and black southerners. U.S. Attorney General Francis Biddle wrote to President Roosevelt that rather than "Axis, or Fascist, or Ku Klux Klan incitement," the Detroit riots were due to a Detroit population increase of 485,000 in past three years and the resulting overcrowding of public transportation, housing in African American neighborhoods, and recreational facilities.[69]

Brigadier General William Gunther, who commanded federal troops during the riot, described the contention between young African Americans and young Americanized Poles. He observed: "There is bitter feeling between Negroes and the young hoodlum element of the Polish population in Detroit." On Detroit streets during the riots, he added: "This element on several occasions 'razzed' federal troops on patrol for intervening in the riot and have called the patrolling troops 'nigger lovers.'"[70]

A month after the riots, the reactionary demagogue Gerald L. K. Smith offered his southern solution to Detroit's trouble in his *The Cross and Flag*. He suggested the advantages of racial separation and segregation. Premised on white male fears of black male sexuality, Smith's writings vigorously condemned the "promiscuous mixture" of blacks and whites. In an appeal to white manhood, he targeted such promiscuity on public transportation, "where black men are permitted to sit down and crowd in close to white women" and with blacks and whites in factories, "where black men are mixed with white women closely in daily work." Smith's solution to Detroit racial problems was essentially the southern system of segregation.[71]

Despite a deeply divided rank and file, R. J. Thomas and the UAW played a positive role in the Detroit race riot as in the earlier hate strikes. Thomas, along with other UAW leaders, "supported the principle of equal opportunity for Negroes, but the sentiment was not shared by all the rank and file. Bigotry was more deeply ingrained than trade unionism among many of the men on the assembly line." After the Detroit riot subsided, Thomas called "an emergency meeting of the union's shop stewards" and later "a conference of all U.A.W. educational directors and chairmen" in order to "determine immediate steps for intensifying the union's educational program for building labor unity between men and women of all races." The goal was to emphasize "their common interests as workers who must stand together."[72]

Despite the troubles before the riots, the absence of black and white disturbances in Detroit factories demonstrated the UAW's positive role in race relations on the shop floor. Certainly, absenteeism, especially among black workers, due to fear of violence on the streets, lowered tensions. "It is extremely interesting," Attorney General Biddle wrote Roosevelt, "that there was no disorder WITHIN PLANTS where colored and white men worked side by side, on account of union discipline."[73] After the Detroit riots, G. James Fleming, the senior Detroit FEPC examiner, asked plant officials, military authorities, political leaders, and African American leaders about "the behavior of war workers inside the plants" during the racial troubles. Despite the turmoil and tumult on Detroit's streets, he discovered that although there was high absenteeism among Negro workers, during the height of the rioting there were, nevertheless, white and colored workers in plants every day, and there were not echoes of the rioting within these plants, so far as fights, rioting, and other conflict conduct were concerned. He attributed the peace inside factory gates to the fact "that these workers know each other better, have mutual interests and recognize their interdependence." Fleming further observed that during the Detroit riots such peace existed in integrated Detroit communities. "There were," he reported, "no fights or rioting in those sections of the city and in those blocks where Negroes and whites live as neighbors." Although arrests occurred in every city police precinct, only the area around Sojourner Truth, the former site of "bitter racial strife," had no arrests.[74]

Hate strikes persisted at Packard and other automobile plants and factories through the war years. A November 1944 Packard strike revealed the limited and local departmental character of such incidents. "In most cases," Shelton Tappes observed, "they were departmental walkouts and sometimes it would spread. If it was a key department this would cripple the whole plant." The reason for this strike, he said, was "the transfer of four Negro employees to the polishing department." Typically, the issue was the transfer of African Americans to jobs previously performed by European American workers. The UAW maintained its "nondiscriminatory policy," and after four days "70 percent of the workers returned to work." Indicative of plant-wide white support for African American workers, a penciled-in comment to a government report noted "Negro elected Vice Pres of local after strike."[75]

Though the Packard strike was the largest, the numerous racial strikes during World War II were much more than simply hate strikes. The wartime strikes took two forms, as the Packard incidents suggested. First, the actual hate strikes occurred where white workers forcefully objected to the upgrading of African American workers, both men and especially women, to jobs perceived as white. Second, the race strikes (or, better, the pride strikes) involved black workers proudly resisting and responding to the discriminatory behavior of their white shop mates. These reflected the growing awareness and increasing militancy of Detroit's African American community.

One issue that continued to exacerbate race relations on the shop floor was often the interplay of race and gender, or more specifically the social mixing of black men and white women. In July 1944 an incident at the Detroit Chrysler Tank plant exposed the latent racial tensions and fears. A white woman "alleged that a colored male employee put his arm around her." The woman could not identify her supposed assailant. Nonetheless, "feeling ran high in the department" and continued "rising until a noose was hung from one of the plant rafters, apparently to intimidate colored workers." Although the perpetrator was a UAW-CIO member, Chrysler management took "a firm stand [and] discharged the person thought responsible for the demonstration." In the end, tensions "subsided since the dismissal" of the man who hung the noose.[76]

The African American union activist Shelton Tappes remembered a Ford workplace grievance that touched on the sensitive issues related to race and gender. A foreman claimed to see a white woman ring out the time card of a black men alleged to be "her boyfriend." The two workers left the plant "almost arm in arm." Dismissed for their violation of plant rules, Tappes, as UAW shop representative, investigated their grievance cases. He discovered that the two "ate lunch together every day and she brought the lunch, a beautiful lunch, and she'd spread it out and they'd eat." They then would return to their respective jobs. Both were married to others, Tappes mentioned, "and they did leave the shop rather intimately, okay." But unnoted in the company investigation was "that this [black] fellow when he got out of the plant he deposited her in a car with her [white] husband." The problem for the two shop friends, Tappes recounted: her shopmate "was Black and she was White."

Also not mentioned, Tappes suggested, the black man and the white woman were friends since childhood. The two "had been kids in kindergarten," their mothers and fathers were close friends, and "the husband was just as much a friend of this guy as she was." The two families "even took their vacations together." Through the course of his investigation, Tappes "unraveled" the complex relationship and won the grievance case. Both the man and the woman were restored to their jobs with back pay. But the woman did not return to work, "because of the nasty stuff that was going on around about her among the other women."[77]

In contrast, white and black women, employers and workers generally accepted African American men in better jobs on the shop floor in the post–World War II years. They did so in the compliance with the union principle of seniority where, over time, a worker earned the right to an improved job. Moreover, the management purge of women from the male domain of the factory floor eliminated the racial and gendered threat and fears of the social mixing of black men and white women. Though new hires might grumble about the many whites privileged jobs, the union solidarity of white and black men eventually prevailed in the absence of women.

Conclusion

The More Things Change, the More They Stay the Same

Through the 1930s and 1940s, the automotive shop floor witnessed enormous changes. But despite incredible reshaping, the workplace problems of automobile workers after World War II remained much the same as existed at the time of the mass-production revolution. To be sure, the consolidation and acceptance of unions constituted the one really dramatic change that altered the relations between workers and their managers. In the postwar years, the problems of technology, race, and gender persisted and in some instances even got much worse. But—mass-production work remained degraded, repetitive, and monotonous. The speed-up endured as postwar improvements in mechanization and automation meant that workers had to match the pace of more sophisticated technology.

Most important, the shop floor once again became almost exclusively a male domain after World War II, often containing some of the worst elements of masculine culture as the presence of women diminished at the workplace. After the war, Ruth Milkman noted that women were "purged" from the automotive shop floor. During the war, she said, "the proportion of women in the automobile industry swelled from only 5 percent just before Pearl Harbor to 25 percent two years later." In the reconversion to civilian production, she added, a "typical pattern of collusion between male workers and management" excluded women from the automotive shop floor.[1] Despite the massive majority of women who desired to continue to work after the war, Dorothy Haener, a leader in the UAW Women's Department, noted they "dropped down to roughly 9 percent" after the war ended.[2]

At the same time, continuing racial tensions between black and white workers insured that black men would remain in the dirtiest and most laborious tasks in a highly racialized division of labor. Manufacturers willingly provided black men with relatively high union wages to perform the work that others refused to do. They had the opportunity to become providers in the immediate postwar years, but the tradeoff was awful and grueling work. Later, in the 1960s and 1970s, the civil rights and affirmative action revolutions reshaped the contours of workplace social relations. Black men rebelled against the demeaning racial slurs of supervisors who assaulted their manhood, and they protested continued assignment to the worst "man-killing" jobs in the automobile plants. More moved into assembly and machine operations, where they had to match pace with increasingly automated work processes. Debased and despised in the solidly male world, the few women who performed "male" work tasks increasingly faced sexual harassment and abuse.

In the immediate postwar years, industrial unions brought the most dramatic changes in the relations between workers and managers. The UAW leveled the playing field in the contest between labor and management. Maintenance of membership and the dues checkoff, acquired after the union's acceptance of the wartime no-strike pledge, strengthened the UAW membership base and deepened its financial pockets. Through the postwar economic boom, a strong UAW gained job security, improved wages, health insurance, and pension benefits for union members. UAW grievance procedures initially allowed some worker controls over the worst abuses of management.

The social configuration of union members and leaders also changed shortly after the war's end. Stanley Brams, an editor for *Ward's Automotive Reports*, recalled how much UAW rank-and-file leaders who attend the UAW conventions changed in the 1940s. Until the late 1940s, the conventions "were noisy and rowdy affairs. They were rough affairs. A fist fight on the floor was not unexpected. The fighting in the hotel lobbies was not unexpected." The "unlettered" convention delegates stood up, bellowing "their rights and telling their troubles and cursing out the management. This was the standard thing to do." The typical delegate "was a young man. He was a tough and hungry and fighting young man; he was lean." After 1949 the delegates changed "physically." The UAW delegates, Brams related, "were a few years older. They had put a few inches on their waistlines. They were inclined to holler just as loud, but not as profanely. They were less inclined to fist fights." The muscular disputes turned to verbal ones, or as Brams noted, "muscle had turned toward debating."[3]

By the late 1940s the typical convention delegate remained a man. Brams observed, he "is more cautious, he has bumped his head often enough that he would rather sit back and not bump heads any more." A different person from the years of union struggle and creation, the average delegate, Brams added, "has more gray hair, he has a bit of a paunch, and he walks a little slowly, he talks more quietly." Previously, the rank-and-file leadership was "in the hands of direct actionists." They were "the flying squadron members who went to the convention."[4] They were no longer the youthful and militant rebels but rather an old guard familiar with the bitter struggles of union building and secure with growing families, homes, automobiles, and the many benefits of the postwar economic boom. The new younger generation did not have the experience or knowledge of the earlier bitter struggles to form unions.

After World War II the production technology for automobiles remained essentially the same and gradually got much worse over time. Despite further mechanization and new automation techniques, work involved the same monotonous routine as in the prewar years. When Charles R. Walker and Robert H. Guest interviewed workers in the General Motors Framingham, Massachusetts, and Linden, New Jersey, plants shortly after World War II, the worker comments were similar to those of earlier generations of auto workers and could have been made in the 1910s, 1920s, and 1930s. The Framingham plant was a new plant with a young workforce; its 180 workers who were interviewed were "fairly well-educated," often married and largely World War II veterans. Their survey revealed that workers disliked "the mechanical pacing and repetitive character of their jobs" and the lack of time to "get quality" in their output. Most liked the pay and security of their jobs and most disliked their 'immediate jobs.'" Two-thirds favored the union; half thought poorly of the company.[5]

As with earlier generations of mass-production workers, those at Framingham expressed similar thoughts with a general theme that they traded high pay for rotten work. Noting the high level of labor turnover where new workers "would drop their tools their first day and walk out," a spot welder noted: "The general opinion of the fellows is that they wouldn't be there if the pay weren't higher than average." A steering column assembler reported: "There's nothing more discouraging than having a barrel beside you with 10,000 bolts in it and using them all up. Then you get another barrel with 10,000 bolts and you know that every one of those 10,000 bolts has to be picked up and put in exactly the same place as the last 10,000 bolts."[6]

Since Framingham was a new plant with many young workers, Walker and Guest wanted to discover how older workers felt about assembly-line work in the postwar years. They selected the older Linden plant and interviewed 202 workers with at least twelve years of seniority. The older Linden workers, the two concluded, "were not better adjusted and actually disliked their jobs more intensely than the [younger] Framingham workers."[7] A spray painter disliked the pace of the line and related that as he got older, he found "it more difficult to keep up with the line." The work was "OK when you are young," but a real problem for older workers. A clutch-and-brake assembler expressed his preference for a "non-moving line." A regular assembly line "really knocks you for a loop. It never stops! It tears the nervous system down to nothing."[8] These familiar comments echoed familiar refrains that persisted from the dawn of the mass-production era.

In the unionized postwar years, Stanley Brams found "jobs, content of jobs, how many [people] to work them, and seniority" were the principle causes of labor-management troubles. Union workers often grieved on these issues of production standards. Complaints about the job content involved how many tasks a worker performed as the work passed his workstation. It also involved the number of workers assigned to a particular task. Seniority became important because it permitted workers to move to softer and thus more favored jobs. Ironically, after unionization brought higher union wages, formerly despised janitorial work previously deemed as consisting of menial, low-wage tasks appropriate only for African Americans came into favor. With higher union wage, many desired the freedom from line work that it offered.[9]

Two decades later the young and rebellious generation of 1960s auto workers encountered the "Blue Collar Blues" in the General Motors Lordstown plant. If the postwar Linden and Framingham plants ran at line speeds of forty to forty-five cars per hour, the efficiency experts of the General Motors Assembly Division ramped the speed to the horrendous and intolerable speed of around one hundred per hour at Lordstown. At such line speeds, the Lordstown plant, with its "greatly increased degree of automation," came to symbolize in the popular mind and press the problems associated with work and industrial technology in advanced industrial society. Judson Gooding detected "new attitudes" that "cut across racial lines." Young black and young white workers now had "higher expectations of the jobs they fill and the wages they receive, and for the lives they will lead." The young rebellious Americans were "restless changeable, mobile, demanding." Their profound job dissatisfaction, he added, became "terribly clear twice each day when shifts end and the men stampede out the plant gates to the parking lots, where they sometimes actually endanger lives in their desperate haste to be gone."[10]

The "churning labor turmoil" of the late 1960s and early 1970s reflected the social turmoil of the Vietnam era and resulted in serious worker discontent. They expressed their shop-floor outrage in high rates of absenteeism, especially on Mondays and Fridays, and high rates of labor turnover—problems that plagued industrial managers since the inception of mass production. Earning relatively high wages, the youthful workforce revealed their indifference to the needs of efficient and high production. Lordstown workers also expressed their dissatisfaction with subversive and covert job actions. The labor turmoil, Gooding wrote, resulted in "wasted manpower, less efficiency, higher costs, a need for more inspections and repairs, more warranty claims—and grievous damage to company reputations." In some instances, worker discontent even led to "overt sabotage." The alienated young workers vented their anger on the automobiles that they built. Judson Gooding detailed some of the sabotage: "Screws have been left in brake drums, tool handles welded into fender compartments (to cause mysterious, unfindable, and eternal rattles), paint scratched, and upholstery cut."[11] In March 1972 the high line speeds and worker discontent resulted in a twenty-three-day strike and brought the blue-collar blues to the nation's attention. Continuous shorter wildcat strikes and stoppages persisted and bedeviled Lordstown production managers and shop supervisors.

In early 1972 Barbara Garson visited the Lordstown plant, which struck over the maddening pace of the assembly lines, and interviewed several young workers. Speaking about his wages, one auto worker said, "It pays good, but it's driving me crazy." Another welder noted that his father labored in auto plants for thirty-five years and "never talked about the job." At Lordstown, the young welder discovered why his father was so silent: "What's there to say? A car comes, I weld it. A car comes, I weld it. A car comes, I weld it. One hundred and one times an hour." A third worker from West Virginia facetiously said, "There's a lot of variety in the paint shop. . . . You clip on the color hose, bleed out the old color, and squirt. Clip, bleed, squirt, think; clip, bleed, squirt, yawn; clip, bleed, squirt, scratch your nose. Only now the Gee-Mads [the General Motors Assembly Division industrial engineers] have taken away the time to scratch your nose."[12] Despite years in the refinement of work reorganization and the development of new production technologies, automobile workers still despised their repetitive work tasks and work routines. Though they enjoyed their high wages, especially after unionization campaigns of the 1930s, few took pleasure in their work in American auto plants.

Shortly after the 1967 Detroit riots, the churning labor turmoil also appeared among young African Americans in the principle automobile plants in Detroit and elsewhere. The appearance of several Revolutionary Union Movements (RUM) black nationalist and Marxist products of 1960s radicalism revealed the deep discontents of African American auto workers and challenged the established and mainly white UAW leaders.[13] Since the World War II years, technology, degraded work, the racial division of labor, and the racist views of shop-floor supervisors culminated in widespread shop-floor discontent in Detroit and other plants. The result was hypermasculine posturing and protests against the supervisors who exploited them, the UAW leaders who seemed indifferent to their problems, the white workers who held desired factory jobs, and the black workers considered Uncle Toms. These groups first appeared in Chrysler's Dodge Main plant located in the largely Polish community of Hamtramck and then spread to other Chrysler plants and Detroit automobile factories, and to automobile plants in other American cities.

Through the 1950s and 1960s racial discrimination persisted in American automobile plants. The Chrysler plants were the eye of the storm of African American worker protests and wildcat strikes. For example, one Chrysler assembly worker and RUM leader, General Gordon Baker, asserted that in 1952, white workers resented the introduction of African American assembly-line workers and "stormed off the line refusing to work with black men," reminiscent of the wartime hate strikes at Packard and elsewhere. Gradually, however, black workers became the predominant component of the Chrysler workforce. In the mid-1960s, Heather Thompson noted, "Chrysler's four huge plants made it not only a 'major inner-city employer' but also *the* major employer of the city's African Americans." At the time, 60 percent of the Dodge Main plant's workers were African American. Through the 1960s Chrysler hired more and more young black men to labor in the worst jobs in the huge Dodge Main huge plant. Chrysler also managed to gain control over and to contain the UAW's militant and aggressive shop steward system, moving union power further away from shop floor, resulting in higher productivity and further degrading working conditions.[14]

Since the end of World War II, Detroit was a center of the urban civil rights movement. It had one of the largest chapters of the National Association for the Advancement of Colored People. It had a growing chapter of the Congress for Racial Equality. Within the UAW, veteran black unionists organized the Trade Union Leadership Conference to push for African American interests and concerns within the auto workers' union. The angrier and more militant young workers drifted toward black nationalist and Third World Marxist beliefs. In the radical 1960s many black students at Wayne State University cooperated with leftist militants and nationalists on the shop floor.

These shop-floor and community transformations produced the Dodge Revolutionary Union Movement (DRUM), an aggressively masculine reaction to the speed-up and automation of work and the racism of managers and shop supervisors in the huge Hamtramck Dodge plant. Black workers, Georgakis and Surkin noted, fulminated against "being forced to work harder and faster under increasingly unsafe and unhealthy conditions." The automobile firms, they noted, "called their methods automation; black workers in Detroit called them Niggermation."[15] Using radical rhetoric, DRUM railed against the racial and shop-floor exploitation—the privileged position of high-seniority white workers, the all-white shop and plant supervisors, and the mainly white UAW leadership. Despite the anti-white rhetoric, some white workers who suffered from the same exploitative conditions sometimes joined DRUM members and sympathizers in wildcat strikes against Dodge and other automobile plants.

For a few years, the black shop-floor rebellions disrupted production at the major automobile firms and challenged the UAW leadership. In May 1968 DRUM's first strike stopped production in the Dodge Main factory. Others wildcats followed. Soon, other revolutionary unions formed at Ford (FRUM), the Chrysler Eldon Avenue plant (ELRUM), the Cadillac plant (CADRUM), the Chrysler Jefferson Avenue plant (JARUM), the Chrysler Mound Road Engine plant (MERUM) in Detroit. RUMs also appeared in other automobile towns around the nation and eventually consolidated into the League of Revolutionary Black Workers. The actual RUM membership never numbered more than a few hundred, though their racially charged issues attracted a large number of black sympathizers and their critique of workplace—speed-ups, unsafe working conditions, and grievances—attracted white cohorts.

UAW officials and Chrysler management responded harshly to the young black militants on the shop floor. Fearing the internal union challenge at the workplace, the UAW leaders treated the black radicals the same as it earlier dealt with the communist internal threat. They stressed their Marxist rhetoric and red-baited them and physically intimidated them on the shop floor, at plant gates, and in the union halls. They attempted to use moderate veteran black unionists to oppose them. In contrast, the Chrysler corporation eliminated the most blatant racial discrimination, promoting African Americans to low-level supervisory positions, adopting more equitable and race-neutral disciplinary procedures, and reducing the racism of shop supervisors. The combination of the hard line of the UAW and the revised corporate policies reduced the militant threat as the RUM numbers dwindled. By 1973 the threats to smooth production and to UAW legitimacy eased, and the revolutionary union organizations drifted to factional leftist oblivion.

With so few women in the automobile plants in the postwar years, the dense masculine culture of the shop floor remained and also deepened and solidified. Auto workers continued their gambling, drinking, fighting, goofing off at work, cursing, and sex talk. Soon they began actively harassing women who were competitors for male jobs. Ben Hamper, who adopted the nickname Rivethead from his work task, labored in a Flint General Motors plant from the late 1970s to the mid 1980s and detailed the sometimes almost inane male world of work.[16] For Rivethead and his workmates, a major goal was to avoid work. His sometimes madcap and crude account was studded with examples of in-plant misbehavior—the shop floor games, illicit loafing, and escapes from the plant during working hours.

After World War II, Frank Marquart observed that "doubling-up" had become a common practice in unionized American automobile plants. Managers felt that workers were not doing the jobs that they were paid for, but for workers, doubling up was simply "a chance to escape at intervals from the monotony of the hated assembly line."[17] For Ben Hamper, his work goal involved the almost constant quest to find a work partner so they could learn each others' jobs and double-up, "a time-honored tradition throughout the shop that helped alleviate much of the boredom."[18] When he first doubled up, Hamper would sit at the shop floor picnic bench and read paperbacks to his working partner. He said: "It was like being paid to attend the library." As he and his workmate got better at the extra tasks, he managed to read "two newspapers, a magazine and a good chunk of a novel every evening." Learning to double-up and doing a particularly demanding work task, Hamper believed, was "very hale and manly . . . once you got the hang of it." Over time, he and his work partner became more adventurous, often leaving the department to explore the plant and even escaping the factory to spend the second half of the evening at his favorite tavern, Mark's Lounge. Near the end of his tenure at General Motors, the efforts of managers and supervisors to force him to work full shifts resulted in something of a nervous breakdown, forcing him to quit.

In order to make work more tolerable, Hamper and his workmates also created numerous diversions to alleviate the horrible monotony and deadening boredom of their work. They developed all sorts shop-floor pranks and games as their means of salvation. Two tricks were the "crucified wallet" and the charging tarantula. The former involved nailing a wallet to the floor with an exposed $20 bill sticking out; the latter a folded bill on the floor near a rubber spider attached to a string. In both instances, an unsuspecting passerby would be startled attempting pick up the wallet or bill. Their games included Rivet Hockey, where workers attempted to kick rivets into the ankles and shins of fellow workers, or Dumpster Ball, where an empty box was kicked into a garbage container. Other diversions involved "racing to the water fountain and back, chain-smoking, feeding Chee-tos to mice, skeet shooting Milk Duds with rubber bands, punting washers into the rafters, and spitting contests."[19]

Drink and, later, other mind-altering substances were quite common in Hamper's plant. Hamper recalled an "old guy" Louie, who worked at repair station at end of his line. He had a "great little racket goin' for himself. He peddled half pints of Canadian Club and Black Velvet up and down the line," charging "three bucks a bottle." Louie was a repairman not tied to a production line and he "delivered right to your bench" Not all workers cared about "[d]rinking right on the line," but, Hamper related, "plenty did, and the most popular [time] to go snagging for gusto was the lunch break." During lunchtime, Hamper and his partner often escaped to a pickup truck in the parking lot. There, his workmate would pull out "enormous joints," but Hamper stuck to his beer, conveniently located in the back.[20] Alcohol and marijuana provided an escape from the line for many of Hamper's auto-worker colleagues, sometimes in the parking lot and sometimes even on the assembly line.

The horrible treatment of the few women who remained in automobile plants revealed the breadth and depth of masculine culture in automobile plant. They often suffered major indignities through physical and sexual harassment. After World War II, Maryanne Van Daele, who worked at Studebaker, remembered that there were "an awful lot of men that resented women working in the factories." Women "were good enough during the war to fill in but after it was over, we had no business there as far as they were concerned."[21] When Walker and Guest studied and interviewed hundreds of General Motors workers at the Linden and Framingham, plants they significantly did not interview a single woman worker.[22]

One auto worker remembered just how deeply embedded the masculine and sexualized culture became in the Studebaker plant in the 1950s. Overstaffed since the war years, the plant had a reputation for much worker idleness and many workplace sexual encounters, though not necessarily with women who worked in the plant. Since the factory had two or three workers for every job, its workers engaged in all sorts of irregular and illicit activities. The appalled new worker recalled his initiation into its male culture: "You'd look out the window, and there [would] be people coming and going all day long through the gates." He remembered: "In the stackings" of the Studebaker shops, "they'd go back in there, and everything was going on, *everything*." The male workers even created private hideaways on the shop floor:

> ... in the middle you see, people would set up like little homes in the boxes, you know. They had everything in there, I mean they had booze, they had women was going there, they had *everything*—the men sleeping there. This is no joke, this is God's fact.

Such unauthorized behavior, he concluded, "had been going on for years since the war."[23]

In the 1960s after attitudes and behaviors about sex and sexuality shifted and became more public, workers, union officials, managers, and labor arbitrators simply presumed the shop floor was a thoroughly masculine world as they handled grievances dealing with relations between men and women. Women who ventured onto the male terrain did so at their peril. Workers, union officers, and industrial arbitrators often questioned the character of women who visited masculine space. One labor arbitrator described an office worker who visited the men on the shop as "playful" and "a vivacious, enthusiastic young lady with the proper tape measurement credentials." As she and a male shop worker engaged in several days' interpersonal banter and play, he tried to kiss her and she ran away, "yelling and screaming." The union defended the laid-off shop worker and filed a grievance in his case. Concluding that this was a "minor case" and not a "serious violation," the arbitrator observed that the office worker "was a provocative girl who consciously or unconsciously hoped that men would not only notice her . . . but make a 'pass,' as long as they did not go too far."[24] In the arbitrator's eyes, the woman, not the man, was the guilty party.

Similarly, another incident also demonstrated the male biases of those involved in the shop culture. The arbitrator questioned the discharge of a man involved in "lewd and obscene" conduct. The discharged male worker gave an envelope to a nineteen-year-old cashier in the cafeteria. It contained an "Application for a Date" with questions "related to intercourse." Managers discharged the harasser; the union defended him. The union's defense did not question the behavior of the man but rather the reputation of the woman, citing her tendency "to invite ribaldry" and her "friendly rakish banter with other men" in the cafeteria. The arbitrator agreed and determined "discharge was an excessive measure of discipline." Even though the man was clearly "guilty of misconduct," his prior record of good behavior should not deny "him the opportunity to redeem himself by future good conduct." The man's intention was "humorous." The woman "had created an atmosphere conducive to the ribald expressions by men" who used the cafeteria. The UAW revealed its assessment of the harassment case in the title of its arbitration note: "Little Girls that Play with Fire, etc."[25]

In both cases, managers acted on behalf of the woman, but the union officials and impartial arbitrators assumed that the culture and terrain of the shop floor was profoundly masculine. Moreover, the character of the women shaped how they viewed the case. And, despite the men's participation in the incident and their provocation of the women, the UAW and arbitrators defended or justified actions of the men.

A few years later, the Civil Rights Act's provisions against employment discrimination of women resulted in their return to the automotive shop floor in greater and greater numbers. No longer comrades in the war effort, these new Rosies met with a completely different situation and confronted brutal sexual harassment and abuse from some supervisors and some union "brothers." They now confronted a dramatically different masculine shop culture than in earlier years—coarser, grosser, and more violent. In the past, shop supervisors were the main harassers and abusers, but now co-workers also engaged in the harassment and abuse of women.

In the late 1960s and 1970s, women needed to fight off and to resist the sexual aggressions of shop supervisors and workmates alike. Typically, shop supervisors wielded enormous power over women, especially those working through their probationary period of employment. Refused sexual propositions often meant transfers to increasingly difficult jobs and ultimately terminations. Female workers endured the inappropriate language and touching and the degrading and humiliating treatment their workmates meted out. At the same time, the shop floor was a man's world, and upper-level managers, local union officials, and industrial arbitrators could not understand or were indifferent to the plight of women.

In their resistance, women turned to federal and state institutions for relief, engaged in lawsuits and public exposure of their abusive shop conditions, and eventually turned to sympathetic local and national UAW officials. In 1978 the Michigan Employment Security Commission allowed a Chrysler woman to receive unemployment insurance after "voluntarily" quitting because she "suffered severe sexual harassment" in a "noxious work environment." She asserted that her male co-workers made "obnoxious and insulting advances" and "constant and humiliating and degrading remarks" to her. One shop supervisor almost daily "touched her across the chest" and made repeated obscene comments and gestures to her. In another instance, "several rather degenerate men" would take turns accompanying her to her car and simply enter and sit in the car. One man, "Whiskey Mike," even showed her his new loaded pistol. After reporting the incidents to a foreman and a union steward, nothing happened.[26] Since an employer tax funded the unemployment insurance system, such rulings gradually convinced the automobile firms to begin to take a harder line on sexual harassment and abuse.

Around the same time, women also began to sue their harassers and abusers. In 1979 two women charged and sued their assembly-line foreman in a Detroit Cadillac plant, Ronald Mobely, for sexual harassment in 1976. They charged that he "used his supervisory position to pressure the women to have sex with him." Both said that the foreman "regularly rubbed his body against theirs in a sexual manner" and one even asserted that he "masturbated in front of her." When the women refused to cooperate, the foreman gave them "undesirable assignments" and wrote "bad reports" about their job performance. When General Motors failed to take action against the foreman, the women filed their legal suit against the foreman and the company, claiming damages for their "extreme nervousness" and "mental distress."[27]

Another woman sued Michael Gerskey, a general foreman in the General Motors Hydramatic Division. He told her that "the top half of her reminded him of Dolly Parton." When they were in an empty office, he grabbed her, kissed her, and "squeezed" her breasts. Then he told her that "if she would perform an oral sex act, she would pass her 90-day probation period." She refused, ran from the room, and left him "with his pants down." She immediately reported the incident to another foreman, who told her not to report it or she would lose her job. After she moved to another job, she was fired by a third foreman for having an "uncooperative attitude."[28]

In 1976 one woman who proudly became one of the few who managed to enter the GM skilled-trade apprentice program described the "hell of sexual harassment" to Mike Duffy, a *Detroit News* reporter. "The anguish," she told him, "began for her on day one." She attributed this to "jealousy from the male workers." She cataloged a long record of abuses to Duffy:

The unwanted pinches, pats and hugs from both supervisors and co-workers.
The promises of "going easy on you if you'll sleep with me" from supervisors.
The repulsive, obscene catcalls. The out-loud guesses about her bust size.

And the gynecological overkill of Hustler centerfolds and pictures of female genitalia plastered on toolboxes and held up to [her] face.

When she complained to her supervisor and to her union steward about the "pornographic photos" on the toolboxes, she said that they both replied: "If you want to work in a man's shop in a man's job, those pictures go along with it.[29]

In May 1979, major change finally came for women auto workers when the Michigan Department of Labor conducted several hearings on sexual harassment in the workplace, including one at the UAW headquarters in Solidarity House. Michigan women, especially auto workers, offered a comprehensive catalog of their harassment and abuse. A Grand Rapids Fisher Body production worker testified that she began her work in 1958 and ended it in 1978. She stated: "Sexual harassment in the work place is [a] degrading and intimidating power play utilized by men to keep women down." Such harassment, she said, "becomes a condition of employment and a woman receives treatment she wouldn't have as a man." She suffered through "repeated unwanted sexual comments, looks and suggestions or physical contacts" of her male supervisors and coworkers. During her first six weeks a manager walked by her and said, "I like those boobs"; a skilled tradesman inappropriately touched her; and an "intoxicated production worker" repeatedly said "I'd like to fuck you." When she protested, she received nastier and more difficult jobs, received complaints and reprimands about her work, underwent repeated job transfers, and endured harassing telephone calls. She "suffered emotional stress" and "became physically ill from the tension." After twenty years, she left her job receiving workmen's compensation.[30]

At the Solidarity House hearings, men and women testified about the futility of using the union grievance process to deal with harassment and abuse. Wilton Cain, the local union president of a Chrysler gear and axle plant, testified: "The grievance procedure is outdated and outmoded and requires approximately a month or two months in order to do anything about it." Often, in this time frame, the woman lost her job. Jeanne Tai, a Ford UAW Local 900 committee person, agreed when she testified that "the grievance procedures are too long and tedious." The woman was "out of work," while the foreman "continues to draw a salary."[31]

After the Detroit harassment hearings UAW women convinced the male leaders finally to act on sexual harassment and abuse in the automobile plants. Two days after the hearings Edith Van Horn, a UAW Community Action Program (CAP) leader, wrote to three male CAP leaders about the

hearings attended by 150 in Solidarity House. She noted a "direct relationship between the growing percentage of women in the work force and the
increasing incidents of sexual harassment" and offered some advice to the
men. She especially feared "repercussions" against some women "who had
the courage to testify" and suggested that the UAW "help 'protect' them from
any such possibilities." She advised the UAW to tell management that "we will
intensify our vigilance and will not tolerate such physical and psychological
abuse." Van Horn also insisted that the UAW address the issue "within our
own ranks." She noted that, just as in the pre-union era, when management
extorted "personal favors" from workers, harassment was "a form of extor-
tion" of "sexual favors" from women. Noting the testimony on the inadequacy
of the grievance procedure, she suggested "contract language" to offer a harassment "shortcut" for grievances. In the current grievance process, such
grievances required a "stricter standard of truth and evidence" than other
grievances. Often, the victim was not believed. The grievance participants
often expressed "boys will be boys" and "she asked for it" excuses for the
harassers. She suggested also that special educational efforts among women
union members on harassment be put in place and that the UAW Community Action Program lobby for Michigan legislation on sexual harassment.[32]

Apparently, the male UAW leaders listened and eventually acted. About a
year later, Douglas A. Fraser, the UAW president, issued a forceful adminis-
trative letter to all local unions about the elimination of sexual harassment
at the workplace. "Sexual harassment of workers by members of supervision or co-workers," it began, "should not be tolerated at any workplace
organized by the UAW." It was "conduct unbecoming a union member" and
a "serious obstacle" to "full employment opportunity" for all workers, men
and women. Fraser directed all international staff and local union leaders
to "commit their efforts to its elimination." Citing the Michigan Task Force
on Sexual Harassment, his letter defined it as "*unwanted* sexual attention,"
either "verbal abuse" or "physical contact."[33]

Fraser added that the problems of sexual harassment were grievable "as
a form of *sex discrimination* under the contract's anti-discrimination clause
and/or equal application clause." Despite problems cited by local union leaders in the 1979, Fraser suggested that harassment "can best and most speed-
ily be remedied through the grievance procedure." Though he recognized
the problems of credibility with the he-said–she-said testimony, he offered
only that "additional evidence, while *not* necessary, is desirable." Moreover,
the UAW president mentioned that in the 1979 Big Three negotiations, the
UAW negotiators had a "frank and open discussion with management" that

resulted in the establishment and distribution of "a statement against sexual harassment to plant supervision." And the UAW obtained contract language with Ford and Chrysler that "identified sexual harassment as a subject for National and Local Equal Application Committees." At the end of his letter, the UAW president asserted: "Sexual harassment violates the fundamental principles of fairness and equity for which the union has fought so hard."[34]

Once the UAW made its commitment to end the abusive male behavior, changes gradually came, and the tone of arbitration rulings shifted dramatically. By the mid-1980s two issues of the UAW *Arbitration Services News Notes* alerted local union officials to the new situation for women in the auto grievance process. Titled "Sexual Harassment," or "sexual deviancy in the work place," the arbitration newsletters signaled the transformation of the way arbitrators ruled in harassment cases. Two important arbitration decisions revealed the intolerance for supervisor and co-worker harassment.[35]

One decision involved the issue of a Douglas Aircraft woman "demoted from a higher pay grade to a lower pay grade" for "a continuing history of poor workmanship and excessive absenteeism."[36] In this case the union acted on behalf of the woman and claimed management demoted her because she refused "to succumb to the sexual advances of her General Foreman" and the assistant foreman. The reason for her "her nervousness and absences were a direct result of sexual harassment." The union also maintained that it had informed labor relations officials of earlier cases of the general foreman's actions, yet they had refused to act. After detailing the various forms of harassment, the arbitrator asserted, "Finally and emphatically, any suggestion or implication that an employee's hope for job security or promotion might be greater if he or she were 'friendlier,' or that any complaint's might jeopardize his or her job is most definitely and flagrantly harassment."[37] The arbitrator also pointed to witnesses testimony on the inappropriate behavior of the general foreman: his "unwelcome comments about various parts of a female employee's body in her presence," "routinely" putting "his arm around women employees" often "in the vicinity of their breasts," hugging them, and offering women "repeated invitations for drinks" with him.[38] Calling for the reinstatement of the woman and the restoration of her seniority and pension time, the arbitrator provided the basis for future grievance cases that involved managers and supervisors.

The second arbitration case dealt with a local union's defense of a male worker who attempted to undress and assault a female co-worker in the parking lot. Several incidents occurred in a remote section of the plant complex over the course of an evening. Among other actions, the worker approached and "appeared to unzip his pants," later he "grabbed her shoulder" and "insisted that she kiss him," and in her car became "very forceful" and "got physical with her." Later he again tried to kiss her, putting his tongue in her ear. As she fought to free herself, he "grabbed her clothes and unzipped her coveralls," forcing "his hand into her bra" and then "his hands toward her underpants." She struggled to get herself free, ran back to the building, and encountered her supervisor. The supervisor reported the incident. After an investigation, the company discharged the worker.[39]

The UAW local chose to defend the woman's discharged co-worker and claimed she "came to the case with 'dirty hands.'" Blaming the victim, the union claimed that her "common sense discretion would have certainly averted any misdoings." Moreover, forgetting that the grievance involved an attempted rape, the union maintained that "the industrial capital punishment [of discharge] is too severe for this incident."[40]

The arbitrator strongly disagreed and upheld the discharge, citing the Civil Rights Act of 1964 and maintaining that management had "the responsibility to protect employees from sexual harassment on the job." Once it knew about the incident, despite the woman's "reticence" to formally protest, the company had to act in accordance with the law. Unless discharged, the fear existed that the man "might make another employee a victim of his harassment."[41]

Both cases revealed how much attitudes had changed in a few short years. No longer was the factory floor a male bastion where predatory men, either supervisors or workers, could mistreat and abuse women at will. Supervisors were finally accountable for their exploitation of vulnerable women. No longer could men maintain that the shop floor was male terrain that women had to adapt to the "boys will be boys" justification for outrageous behavior toward women. Though some men might continue to harass women, they would be outliers who often suffered the consequences. The 1970 rulings on sexual harassment finally brought significant changes to the overly masculine industrial terrain.

Though the UAW and the American automobile firms considerably reduced the overt sexual harassment and abuse, the next major incident of such a nature arrived on American soil with a Japanese industrial transplant, the Mitsubishi plant in Illinois. With management indifference, male workers again became aggressive predators who consistently harassed women workers. In the early 1990s, for example, when women workers encountered sexual harassment at the plant, the Equal Employment Opportunity Commission claimed that they entered "a workplace saturated with sexuality, most of it demeaning to women."[42] In time, the aberrant male misbehavior resurfaced as a vulgar and brutal shop-floor norm, as one commentator noted, "a misogynous mix of sexist Japanese management practice and American blue-collar, bully-boy machismo." The National Organization of Women mobilized a national boycott of Mitsubishi products and labeled the firm a "Merchant of Shame." At the time, the female Mitsubishi assembly-line workers, *Time* magazine disclosed,

> reported obscene, crude sketches of genital organs and sex acts, and names of female workers scratched into unpainted car bodies moving along the assembly line. Women were called sluts, whores, and bitches and subjected to groping, forced sex play, and male flashing. Explicit sexual graffiti such as KILL THE SLUT MARY were scrawled on the rest-area and bathroom walls. In a particularly egregious case, a worker put his airgun between a woman's legs and pulled the trigger. Declared a line supervisor: "I don't want any bitches on my line. Women don't belong in the plant."[43]

Despite the legal sanctions and UAW monitoring of shop floor harassment, such incidents and complaints recurred when plant management tolerated abusive behavior.

Despite the numerous changes through the end of twentieth century, much remained the same in American automobile plants. In 2009 Marvin Powell, who entered a Pontiac assembly plant in 1996, recalled his thirteen years' work experience with the firm to a *New York Times* reporter. A committed Christian, the black worker was "taken aback" by the illicit, if not immoral, activities in his deeply male workplace. The Pontiac Assembly Center, the reporter related, "was a world of temptations unto itself, with drugs, alcohol, numbers runners, bookies and even 'parking-lot girls' who would come to the plant during lunch breaks to service male workers." Some behaviors persisted through the years; some even got worse. Powell concluded: "Anything you can find outside the plant, you can find inside the plant. You either got caught up in it, or you stay apart from it."[44]

The Great Recession had a devastating impact on male workers, especially the older ones, desiring employment. For prime-aged men between twenty-five and fifty-four years old, the *New York Times* recently reported the tripling of the unemployment rate, "since the late 1960, to 16 percent." The "Vanishing Male Worker" no longer had a fundamental site for the expression of manhood—his job at his workplace. One skilled and proud forty-nine-year-old electrical worker lived on his wife's part-time income and a small but diminishing inheritance from his mother to support his wife and two children. Unemployed for two years in 2012 after he lost work, he took on a job at Home Depot, only to be fired after he failed to greet a corporate spot-ter posing as a shopper. After drawing unemployment benefits, he worked for Peapod loading groceries on delivery trucks and lost his job when he asked for "a vacation day . . . to care for his dying mother." Through his low-employment period, he depleted his union pension account and ran up a huge credit card debt. After this, he refused an undignified $10 per hour job in a fast food restaurant to support his wife and two children. Committed to his union and the prospect of its small pension, he maintained his union membership and as a result cannot get non-union work as an electrician.[45]

Since the 1950s and 1960s, through decades of automation, plant reloca-tions, de-industrialization, de-unionization, and globalization, working-class men of America's industrial heartland have lost a fundamental element of their manhood—their jobs that allowed them to fulfill their roles as respon-sible and respectable providers for their families. All that remained were paths to rough manliness—the anger of their sexism and racism expressed in their negative attitudes toward women and ethnic others. Through this period, the rough manhood also appeared in the male attraction to rough and violent sports, such as football, basketball, hockey, boxing, or mixed marshal arts. They participated in the rough sporting culture, not acting and doing, but through watching mainly with other men in front of televisions while drinking at sports bars and in their dens or man caves. Other than soothing male egos, such a rough manhood served neither a social nor an economic end. At least the earlier version of rough manhood brought the social and economic advantages of unionism and involved struggles with management to achieve the respectable status of family provider or manly control over work space.

Abbreviations for Archives
and Newspapers

Archives

ALB—Automobile Labor Board, National Recovery Administration Records, RG 9, NA.

ALHUA—Archives of Labor History and Urban Affairs, Reuther Library, Wayne State University.

BFRC—Benson Ford Research Center, The Henry Ford, Dearborn, Michigan.

BHLUM—Bentley Historical Library, University of Michigan

CGP—Catherine Gelles Papers, ALHUA

CMAP—Chris and Marti Alston Papers, ALHUA

EAWP—Edward A. Wieck Papers, ALHUA

ECP—Ely Chinoy Papers, ALHUA

ELP—Edward Levinson Papers, ALHUA

EVHP—Edie Van Horn Papers, ALHUA

FEPC—Fair Employment Practices Commission, RG 228, NAS

HBP—Heber Blankenhorn Papers, ALHUA

HKP—Henry Kraus Papers, ALHUA

HSP—Harry Shulman Papers, Manuscripts and Archives, Yale University Library

JBP—Joe Brown Papers, ALHUA

JLP—James Lindahl Papers, ALHUA

MSP—Maurice Sugar Papers, ALHUA

MSUA-LSOH—Michigan State University Auto-Lite Strike Oral Histories, ALHUA

NA—National Archives, Washington, D.C.

NAS—National Archives, Suitland, Maryland

OHRC—Oral Research History Center, Indiana University

PPS—Records of the War Department General and Special Staffs: Plant Protection Section, RG 165, NAS

PSTP—Paul Schuster Taylor Papers, Bancroft Library, University of California–Berkeley

RLP—Rensis Lickert Papers, BHLUM

RWDP—Robert W. Dunn Papers, ALHUA

SHSW—State Historical Society of Wisconsin

SLP—Staughton Lynd Papers, SHSW

UAWCDR—UAW Chrysler Department Records, ALHUA

UAWGMDR—UAW General Motors Department Records, ALHUA

UAWL9R—UAW Local 9 Records, ALHUA

UAWL75R—UAW Local 75 Records, ALHUA

UAWL121P—UAW-CIO Local 121, Janesville, Wisconsin, Papers, SHSW

UAWL174R—UAW Local 174 Records, ALHUA

UAWL212R—UAW Local 212 Records, ALHUA

UAWL400R—UAW Local 400 Records, ALHUA

UAWL650R—UAW Local 650 Records, ALHUA

UAWR1R—UAW Region 1 Records, ALHUA

UAWR1BR—UAW Region 1B Records, ALHUA

UAWR2R—UAW Region 2 Records, ALHUA

UAWR8R—UAW Region 8 Records, ALHUA

UAWWDHR—UAW Women's Department Haener Records, ALHUA

WMLP—William M. Leiserson Papers, SHSW

UMFLHP—University of Michigan-Flint Labor History Project, Genesee Historical Collections Center, Thompson Library

WMC—Records of the War Manpower Commission, Record Group 211, NAS

WPB—War Production Board, RG 179, NAS

YSPC—Yale Student Papers Collection (RU 331), Manuscripts and Archives, Yale University Library

YTSC—Yale Technology and Society Collection (RU 472), Manuscripts and Archives, Yale University Library

Newspapers

AW—Auto Worker

AWN—Auto Workers News

DFP—Detroit Free Press

DN—Detroit News

DT—Detroit Times

FAW—Flint Auto Worker

MC—Michigan Chronicle

NYT—New York Times

UAW—United Automobile Worker

WSJ—Wall Street Journal

Notes

Introduction

1. For the women's critiques of labor historians, see especially Ava Baron, *Work Engendered: Toward a New History of American Labor* (Ithaca, N.Y.: Cornell University Press, 1991); Elizabeth Faue, *Labor History: Special Issue* 34 (1993): 167–341; and Alice Kessler-Harris, *Gendering Labor History* (Urbana: University of Illinois Press, 2007).

2. Baron, "Gender and Labor History: Learning from the Past, Looking to the Future," in *Work Engendered*, 30 and 20.

3. Peter N. Stearns, *Be A Man! Males in Modern Society* (New York: Holmes and Meier, 1979), 86.

4. Frank Marquart, *An Auto Worker's Journal: The UAW Crusade to One-Party Union* (University Park: Pennsylvania State University Press, 1975), 11–12.

5. On manhood and working-class manhood, see Michael S. Kimmel and Michael A. Messner, eds., *Men's Lives* (New York: Macmillan, 1989), and Paul Willis, *Learning to Labor: How Working Class Kids Get Working Class Jobs* (New York: Columbia University Press, 1981).

6. Stan Gray, "Sharing the Shop Floor: Women and Men on the Assembly Line," *Radical America* 18, no. 5 (September-October 1984): 77.

7. David Montgomery, "Workers' Control of Machine Production in the Nineteenth Century," in *Workers' Control in America: Studies in the History of Work, Technology, and Labor Struggles* (New York: Cambridge University Press, 1979), 13; and David Montgomery, *The Fall of the House of Labor: The Workplace, the State, and American Labor Activism, 1865–1925* (New York: Cambridge University Press, 1987), 58.

8. Andrea Graziosi, "Common Laborers, Unskilled Workers, 1880–1915," *Labor History* 22 (Fall 1981): 513, 516, 533, 516–18.

9. Frank Tobias Higbie, *Indispensable Outcasts: Hobo Workers and Community in the American Midwest, 1880–1930* (Urbana: University of Illinois Press, 2003), 19.

10. Whiting Williams, *What's on the Worker's Mind: By One Who Put on Overalls to Find Out* (New York: Scribner's, 1920).

11. Graziosi, "Common Laborers," 519 and 527.

12. Joshua B. Freeman, "Hardhats: Construction Workers, Manliness, and the 1970 Pro-War Demonstrations," *Journal of Social History* 26 (June 1993): 725 and 732.

13. Steven Maynard, "Rough Work and Rugged Men: The Social Construction of Masculinity in Working Class History," *Labour/Le Travail* 23 (Spring 1989): 161.

14. Peter Way, *Common Labor: Workers and the Digging of North American Canals, 1780–1860* (Baltimore, Md.: Johns Hopkins University Press, 1993), 135 and 162.

15. James R. Barrett, *The Irish Way: Becoming American in a Multiethnic City* (New York: Penguin, 2013), 119–22.

16. Way, *Common Labor*, 146, 162, and 165–76.

17. Williams, *Worker's Mind*, 5, 11, 20, and 29.

18. Ibid., 108, 211, and 226.

19. Ibid., 21 and 193.

20. Parker cited in Graziosi, "Common Laborers," 544.

21. Freeman, "Hardhats," 727 and 728.

22. Wayne A. Lewchuk, "Men and Monotony: Fraternalism as a Managerial Strategy at the Ford Motor Company," *Journal of Economic History* 53 (December 1993): 827 and 833.

23. P. J. Conlon, "Memories of the Past," *Machinists' Monthly Journal* 34 (April 1922): 337.

24. H. Dubreuil, *Robots or Men? A French Workman's Experience in American Industry* (New York: Harper, 1930), 51 and 52.

25. Dubreuil, *Robots or Men?* 50.

26. Harold M. Groves, "The Machinist in Industry: A Study of the History and Economics of His Craft," Ph.D. diss., University of Wisconsin, 1927; and Montgomery, *House of Labor*, chapter 4.

27. Maynard, "Rough Work and Rugged Men," 160.

28. Michael S. Kimmel, *Manhood in America* (New York: Free Press, 1996), 101–2.

29. Maynard, "Rough Work and Rugged Men," 166 and 160.

30. Lisa Fine, "'Our Big Factory Family': Masculinity and Paternalism at the Reo Motor Car Company of Lansing, Michigan," *Labor History* 34, no. 2–3 (1993): 280.

31. Lewchuk, "Men and Monotony"; Fine, "'Our Big Factory Family.'"

32. Freeman, "Hardhats," 727 and 731.

33. John Lippert, "Sexuality as Consumption," in Jon Snodgrass, ed., *For Men against Sexism: A Book of Readings* (Albion, Can.: Times Change, 1977), 209.

Chapter 1. Lost Manhood

1. "Detroit Hearings: Dr. I. W. Raskin," December 16, 1934, 392, box 186, RG 9, Records of the Automobile Labor Board, NA.

2. Ibid., 393–95.

3. David A. Hounshell, *From the American System to Mass Production, 1800–1932* (Baltimore, Md.: Johns Hopkins University Press, 1984).

4. Ely Chinoy, "Manning the Machines—The Assembly-Line Worker," in Peter Berger, The Human Shape of Work: Studies in the Sociology of Occupations (New York: Macmillan, 1964), 51.

5. Peter F. Drucker, *The Concept of the Corporation* (New York: New American Library, 1983), 149.

6. Charles R. Walker, *Steeltown: An Industrial Case History of the Conflict between Progress and Security* (New York: Harper, 1950), 51.

7. Chinoy, "Manning the Machines," 51.

8. Stephen Meyer, *The Five Dollar Day: Labor Management and Social Control in the Ford Motor Company, 1908–1921* (Albany, N.Y.: State University of New York Press, 1981), chapters 2 and 3.

9. Julian Street, "Detroit the Dynamic," *Collier's* 53 (July 4, 1914): 24.

10. E. McCluny Fleming was one of fourteen Yale University students (among possibly dozens over the years) who spent their summer working in Detroit's recently mechanized automobile factories between 1925 and 1932 and who wrote essays about their experiences. The majority of these Yale Industrial Group students seemed to have worked in the Ford Highland Park and River Rouge plants. Some of these mainly middle- and upper-class American students wrote essays, which they submitted for the Yale Industrial Research Contest prize. (The essay writers also included an African American, an African student, and a Chinese student.) Their essays depicted their personal confrontations with the routinized and monotonous work in Detroit's mass-production automobile machine shops and assembly rooms. The students' essays also detailed their individual encounters with middle- and upper-class migrants and offered a view into the lives and cultures of Detroit's working class. One student, Oliver Zendt, noted that Jerome Davis, a Yale Divinity School professor who apparently organized the industrial program, said that one purpose of the Yale project was to have students "rubbing elbows with reality." See, Zendt, "Henry Ford—The Virtues of the Man and his Industry," 1930, 40, folder 104, box 11, YSPC.

11. E. McCluny Fleming, "A Summer in Detroit Industry," n.d, 4, folder 111, box 11, YSPC.

12. "Is Ford a Genius?" *AWN*, September 1928, 2.

13. "Sleepers," *AWN*, May 1928, 4.

14. Walter Edward Ulrich, *On the Belt* (New York: League for Industrial Democracy, 1929), 7.

15. Robert L. Cruden, "The Worker Looks at Ford: Speed Is Henry's God," *Labor Age*, June 1928, 3, in folder 2.9, box 2, RWDP.

16. Sawyer R. Brockunier, "Industrial Relations at the Ford Plant," 7, 1932, folder 103, box 11, YSPC.

17. Everett F. S. Davies, "Harsh Symphony: A Brief Paper on Industrial Relations," 25–26, 1930, folder 101, box 11, YSPC.

18. Ibid., 19.

19. Kemper A. Dobbins, "Facts about the Ford Worker," 3, 1930, folder 120, box 11, YSPC.

20. P. A. Raymond, "Program for Automobile Industry," c. 1929, 2, folder 5, box 1, HKP.

21. Robert W. Dunn, "Speed-up Real Boss of Detroit Auto Workers," *AWN*, July 1928, 1.

22. Marquart, *Auto Worker's*, 13.

23. Fleming, "Summer in Detroit," 5.

24. C. N. Li, "A Summer in the Ford Motor Company, Detroit Michigan," 11–12, n.d., folder 109, box 11, YSPC.

25. Davies, "Harsh Symphony," 15.

26. Zendt, "Henry Ford," 11.

27. Dobbins, "Ford Worker," 4–5.

28. Davies, "Harsh Symphony," 16.

29. George Zalkan, "A Worker Looks at Organized Labor," 32, n.d., folder 99, box 11, YSPC.

30. Andrew Steiger, "Autos and Jobs," *Nation* 126 (May 2, 1928): 506.

31. Horace J. Cobb, "What Is the Matter with the Machinists Trade?" *Machinists' Monthly Journal* 36 (May 1926): 226.

32. "Detroit Hearings: Charles Madden," December 15, 1934, 92, box 186, ALB.

33. Ulrich, *On the Belt*, 7.

34. Robert L. Cruden, "'No Loitering: Get Out Production,'" *Nation*, June 12, 1929, in folder 2.19, box 2, RWDP.

35. David Moore in the PBS Great Depression series, "A Job at Ford."

36. John F. Leheney, "Industrial Inferno," unpublished paper, 1929, 1 and 5, folder 2.32, box 2, RWDP.

37. Fred M. Wolff, "Ford—Rouge—A1016," 1, n.d., folder 9, box 11, YSPC.

38. "Sleepers."

39. Dobbins, "Ford Worker," 5–6.

40. Interview No. 37, 1–27–47, 6, folder: Thesis Interviews, box 3, ECP.

41. Davies, "Harsh Symphony," 16.

42. Dobbins, "Ford Worker," 2.

43. Wolff, "Ford—Rouge," 5.

44. "Ford Speed-up Maims Worker," *AWN*, November 1929, 1.

45. "Loss of Fingers Must Not Interfere with Production at Ford Pl.," *AWN*, March 1928, 2.

46. Ibid.

47. Jack W. Skeels, interviewer, "Oral History Interview of Roy H. Speth," March 4, 1963, 3, ALHUA; and "Going through the Mill at the Chevrolet Plant," *AWN*, July 1928, 2.

48. Erskine Caldwell, "The Eight-Finger City," in *Some American People* (New York: McBride, 1935), 164, 166–67, 169, and 172.

49. Wolff, "Ford—Rouge," 7.

50. Raymond, "Program for Automobile Industry," 2–3.

51. Jack W. Skeels, interviewer, "Oral History Interview of Kenneth F. Bannon," February 28, 1963, 2–3, ALHUA.

52. "More about Hudson's," *AWN*, May 1927, 3.

53. "Young Workers Most Militant in Oakland Fight," *AWN*, June 1929, 3; notecard, Young worker, folder: Young Workers, Research Notes, box 1, RWDP; and Robert Dunn, *Labor and Automobiles* (New York: International, 1929), 72.

54. "Cleveland Hearings: W. Mortimer Testimony," January 5, 1935, 51, box 188; and Harry Weiss to Leon Henderson, "Preliminary Report on Conferences on Regularizing Employment and Otherwise Improving the Conditions of Labor in the Automobile Industry," January 7, 1935, 28, folder 22, box 662, ALB.

55. "Toledo Hearings: Elias Keiser," December 23, 1934, 93, box 188, ALB; John B. Wolford, interviewer, "Oral History Interview of Joe Meszaros," June 27, 1984, 13, OHRC; notecard, Young men, folder: Young Workers, Research Notes, box 1, RWDP; notecard, Young workers—Jones—Flint, folder: Young Workers, Research Notes, box 1, RWDP; and Dunn, *Labor and Automobiles*, 72; Jack W. Skeels, interviewer, "Oral History Interview of Harry Ross," July 10, 1961, 13–14, ALHUA; and Cruden, "'No Loitering."

56. "Detroit Hearing: Forest Brown," December 15, 1934, 188–89, box 186, ALB; and P. Z., "Ford Believes in the Man to Man Policy! Why?" *AWN*, October 1927, 3.

57. Zendt, "Henry Ford," 19; notecard, Youth—Chalmers, folder: Young Workers, Research Notes, box 1, RWDP; and "South Bend Hearings: R. F. Houston," January 2, 1935, 33, box 188, ALB.

58. "Auto Worker Correspondent," ca. December 1933, folder 13, box 1, HKP.

59. Ibid.

60. Montgomery, "Workers' Control."

61. "Toledo Hearings: George Powers," December 24, 1934, 53, box 188, ALB; and "Doing Time at Briggs," *AWN*, September 1928, 3.

62. "A Modern 'Simon Legree,'" *AWN*, September 1927, 3; "Spanish Royalty Lives Off Sweat of Packard Workers," *AWN*, January 1929, 3; and "Milwaukee Hearings: Eugene Osmond," December 30, 1934," 165, box 188, ALB.

63. "Bad Conditions in Fisher Body Plant," *AWN*, March 1928, 1; Kenneth B. West, interviewer, "Oral History Interview of Gus Morley," August 24, 1979, 1, UMFLHP; and Jack W. Skeels, interviewer, "Oral History Interview of John W. Anderson," February 17, 1960–May 21, 1960, 4–5, ALHUA.

64. Bill Meyer, interviewer, "Oral History Interview of Leo Connelly," March 6, 1980, 2, UMFLHP; Kenneth West, interviewer, "Oral History Interview of Raymond Zink," March 4, 1980, 31, UMFLHP; and "Kenneth F. Brannon," 3.

65. Meyer, "Interview of Connelly," 2; Kenneth West, interviewer, "Oral History Interview of Mrs. Jerry Aldred," March 13, 1980, 1, UMFLHP; Neil Leighton, interviewer, "Oral History Interview of Cloyse Crane," February 27, 1980, 17, UMFLHP; and "St Louis Hearings: Leonard Lutz," December 28, 1934, 88, box 188, ALB.

66. "St Louis Hearings: Martin Henry Hartman," December 28, 1934, 85–86, box 188, ALB.

67. "Conditions in the Peninsular Products," *AWN*, December 1927, 4.

68. "A Cog Writes of Working Conditions in Hudson Motor Co.," *AWN*, May 1928, 2.

69. "Speeding Up at Hudson's," *AWN*, September 1927, 3.

70. Dubreuil, "Robots or Men?"; and "Cog Writes of Working Conditions."

Chapter 2. Reclaiming Manhood

1. James C. Scott, *Weapons of the Weak: Everyday Forms of Peasant Resistance* (New Haven, Conn.: Yale University Press, 1985).

2. Daniel Nelson, *Managers and Workers: The Origins of the New Factory System in the United States, 1880–1920* (Madison: University of Wisconsin Press, 1975), 161–69.

3. Meyer, *Five Dollar Day*, 83.

4. Meyer, *Five Dollar Day*, 80–85.

5. Frederick W. Taylor, *Principles of Scientific Management* (New York: Norton, 1967), 18–19.

6. Taylor, *Principles of Scientific Management*, 20–21.

7. Montgomery, *Worker's Control*, 12–13.

8. Stanley B. Mathewson, *Restriction of Output among Unorganized Workers* (Carbondale: Southern Illinois University Press, 1969), originally published in 1931.

9. Ibid.

10. Mathewson, *Restriction of Output*, 146–47.

11. "Harmony?" in Mathewson, *Restriction of Output*, 127.

12. Arthur E. Morgan, "Introduction," 3, folder "Mathewson, Stanley, 1915–1942," box 26, WMLP.

13. Marquart, *Auto Worker's Journal*, 11.

14. Ibid., 24.

15. Montgomery, *House of Labor*, 135.

16. John Anderson, "The Worker; His Job; His Pay; His Work Place; His Boss," 1, folder 4, Anderson, John W.—Writings: Articles and Outlines, box 1, SLP.

17. Marquart, *Auto Worker's Journal*, 31.

18. Tony Lane, "A Merseysider in Detroit," *History Workshop Journal* 11 (Spring 1981), 145.

19. Bill Meyer, interviewer, "Oral History Interview of Joe Fry," July 27, 1979, 13–14, UMFLHP.

20. Kenneth West, interviewer, "Oral History Interview of Irving King," March 26, 1980, 16–17, UMFLHP.

21. W. A. Logan, "The Union Man," *Official Journal of the Carriage, Wagon, and Automobile Workers Industrial Union*, June 1915.

22. "The Union Man's Duty," *AW*, August 1924, 3.

23. Editorial, "Manhood," *AWN*, October 1927, 4.

24. Ibid.

25. Federated Press cartoon, *AW*, January 1920, 1.

26. "A Little Walkout at Packards," *AWN*, May 1928, 2.

27. Clipping, "My Father Was a Man," folder: Labor in Literature—Poetry, box 14, JBP.

28. Kolb cited in Montgomery, *House of Labor*, 202.

29. Footnote 69 in Montgomery, *House of Labor*, 202.

30. "Fisher Two Side Glances," *FAW*, April 29, 1937.

31. Gene Richards, "On the Assembly Line," *Atlantic Monthly* 159 (April 1937): 425.

32. Richards, "Assembly Line," 428.

33. Howard P. Chudacoff, *The Age of the Bachelor: Creating an American Subculture* (Princeton, N.J.: Princeton University Press, 2000).

34. Morris L. Marcus, "What Price Industry?" 6–7, 8, 12–13, and 15–16, 1928, folder 106, box 11, YSPC.

35. Thomas B. Mimms, "My Adventure in Industry," n.p., 1915, folder 107, box 11, YSPC.

36. Fleming, "Summer in Detroit Industry," 14, 16, and 18.

37. Zendt, "Henry Ford," 32–33, and Ackley, "Our Industrial System at Its Best," n.p., folder 112, box 11, YSPC.

38. H. W. Russell, "Boarding Houses," *Association Boys* 8 (October 1910): 210.

39. Mimms, "My Adventure in Industry," n.p., and Fleming, "A Summer in Detroit Industry," 6.

40. Ackley, "Our Industrial System," n.p.

41. C. N. Li, "Second Summer in the Ford Motor Company, Detroit Michigan," 2, 22, and 23, box 11, and "A Summer in the Ford Motor Company, Detroit Michigan," 9, box 11, YSP.

42. Ackley, "Our Industrial System," n.p.

43. Charles Madison, "My Seven Years of Automotive Servitude," *Michigan Quarterly Review* 19 and 20 (Fall 1980 and Winter 1981): 446 and 447.

44. Meyer, *Five Dollar Day*, 73.

45. Ibid., 131.

46. Watkins, "Labor Situation in Detroit," *Journal or Political Economy* 28 (December 1920): 841.

47. Coleman Young and Lonnie Wheeler, *Hard Stuff: The Autobiography of Coleman Young* (New York: Viking, 1994), 20–21.

48. Fleming, "Summer in Detroit Industry," 19, 20, and 24, and Mimms, "My Adventure," n.p.

49. A. A. Jameson, "Social Evil," *Association Boys* 8 (October 1910): 266–67.

50. H. T. Powers, "Amusements: The Survey of the Boyhood of Detroit," *Association Boys* 8 (October 1910): 207; and E. H. Lerchen, "Obscene Literature: The Survey of the Boyhood of Detroit," *Association Boys* 8 (October 1910): 217.

51. Frank H. Ritchie, "The Saloon and Tobacco: The Survey of the Boyhood of Detroit," *Association Boys* 8 (October 1910): 234–35 and 235–36.

52. Glen S. Taylor, "Prostitution in Detroit," 29, unpublished manuscript, [ca. 1933], Hatcher Library, University of Michigan, Ann Arbor.

53. Taylor, "Prostitution in Detroit," 27.

54. "Detroit, Michigan . . . Report on Prostitution, the Police, the Law, and the Courts," 77, Series 7.2, Surveys, 1919–21, American Social Health Association Records, 1905-1990, *Social Welfare History Archives*, Elmer L. Andersen Library, University of Minnesota, Minneapolis. Hereafter cited as "Detroit Report on Prostitution."

55. Taylor, "Prostitution in Detroit," 64.

56. "Detroit Report on Prostitution," 18, 25, and 8.

57. Ibid., 8–9.

58. Ibid., 75.

59. Ibid., 77.

60. Mimms, "My Adventure," n.p.; "Detroit Report on Prostitution," 10; and Helen McGowan, *Motor City Madam* (New York: Pageant, 1964), 153.

61. Taylor, "Prostitution in Detroit," 32 and 101; "Detroit to Clean up Vice," *NYT*, July 8, 1926.

62. Taylor, "Prostitution in Detroit," 115–16; "Detroit Report on Prostitution," 77.

63. "Detroit Report on Prostitution," 9 and 75.

64. Robert C. Jones, "Field Notes: Mexican, Michigan Ave," September 13, 1928, n.p., "Field Notes: Mexican on Michigan near 1st St.," July 29, 1928, n.p., and "Field Notes: Auguilera, White, Speaks some English," August 23, 1928, n.p., folder 70, carton 11, PSTP.

65. Taylor, "Prostitution in Detroit," 82–83 and 101.

66. Ibid., 83–4.

67. Ibid., 98.

68. Ibid., 101 and 118.

69. Ibid., 98; "Detroit Report on Prostitution," 56.

70. Taylor, "Prostitution in Detroit," 99, 100, 98, and 111.

71. Erskine Caldwell, "The School of Prostitution," in *Some American People* (New York: McBride, 1935), 174.

72. Ibid., 179.

73. Ibid., 180–81.

Chapter 3. "Rats, Finks, and Stool Pigeons"

1. "Beware of This Spy," *Carriage and Wagon Workers Journal* 7 (January 1906): 104.

2. E. C. Davison, "Labor Spies and Others," *Machinists' Monthly Journal* 38 (January 1926): 13.

3. Jack W. Skeels, interviewer, "Oral History Interview of Harold Cranefield," May 17, 1963, 9–12 and 14, ALHUA.

4. "Blankenhorn Testimony," April 10, 1936, 5–6, Hearings before a Senate Subcommittee on Education and Labor, Violations of Free Speech and Assembly and

Interference with the Rights of Labor, 74th Congress, 2nd session. Hereinafter cited as La Follette Committee.

5. "Blankenhorn Testimony," April 11, 1936, 64, La Follette Committee.

6. "Capitalist Weapons: An Organization of Spies, Scabs, and Cutthroats, to Harm Organized Labor," *Carriage and Wagon Workers' Journal* 4 (June 1903): 7.

7. This represented an enormous incentive to work as an industrial spy: adjusting for inflation, $100 in 1906 would be worth almost $2,600 in 2014. See "The Inflation Calculator" at http://www.westegg.com/inflation.

8. "Beware of This Spy," 104.

9. Owen W. Bombard, interviewer, "The Reminiscences of Mr. W. C. Klann," September 1955, 138 and 141, *Accession 65*, BFRC.

10. Ibid., 138 and 142.

11. Meyer, *Five Dollar Day*, 173–94.

12. Edmund Leigh, Chief, Plant Protection Section, Military Intelligence Division, "Memorandum of the Value of Detective Agencies," ca. October or November 1918, 10, folder: Detective Agencies, box 7, entry 104, PPS, NAS.

13. Ibid., 1.

14. On War Plans White, see Joan M. Jensen, *Army Surveillance in America, 1775–1980* (New Haven, Conn.: Yale University Press, 1991), 177–210; and Alan Dawley, *Changing the World: American Progressives in War and Revolution* (Princeton, N.J.: Princeton University Press, 2003), 273–76.

15. S. L. Newman, "Report of Our Business Agents: Akron, Ohio," *Machinists' Monthly Journal* 33 (January 1921): 54–56.

16. W. A. Logan, "The 'Company Union,'" *AW*, October 1922.

17. James S. Martin to Edward Levinson, May 2, 1944, folder: Correspondence, January–May 1944, box 7, ELP.

18. Jim Keeney and Herbert Hill, interviewers, "Oral History Interview of Nick DiGaetano," June 17, 1968, 3, ALHUA.

19. "Golden Rules," *AW*, January 1922, 1.

20. Ibid.

21. Ibid.

22. Ibid.

23. "Suggestions for Reports," folder: Espionage—Labor, box 9, JBP.

24. Ibid.

25. Louis Stark, "Terror Charged by Auto Workers," *NYT*, December 16, 1934; "Statement Made to Jack Beck by Ralph Rimar on October 19, 1939," 22, folder 54–9, box 54, MSP; Neil Leighton, interviewer, "Oral History of Ingvald Bjaland and James O'Hara," March 7, 1980, 12, UMFLHP; and Lane, "Merseysider in Detroit," 151.

26. "St. Louis Hearings: Frank Alexander Testimony," December 28, 1934, 196, box 188, ALB; and Jack W. Skeels, interviewer, "Oral History Interview of Louis Adkins," August 16, 1951, 8, ALHUA.

27. "Summary of Senate Sub-Committee's Report on Use of Espionage in Industry," *NYT*, December 22, 1937.

28. Ibid.

29. Jack W. Skeels, interviewer, "Oral History of Leonard E. Klue," May 19, 1961, 7, ALHUA.

30. Jack W. Skeels, interviewer, "Oral History of Hugh Thompson," March 28, 1963, 18, ALHUA; and Skeels, "Interview of Cranefield," 9–10.

31. "Use of Espionage," 22.

32. "Detroit Hearings: Maurice Sugar," December 16, 1934, 253–56, ALB.

33. Skeels, "Interview of Cranefield," 16 and 17.

34. Jack W. Skeels, interviewer, "Oral History Interview of Stanley J. Gregory," March 4, 1963, 3–4; Jack W. Skeels, interviewer, "Oral History Interview of F. R. Palmer," July 23, 1960, 7; Jack W. Skeels, interviewer, "Oral History Interview of Ed Lee," April 20, 1961, 16–17; Jack W. Skeels, interviewer, "Oral History Interview of Patrick J. O'Malley," July 25, 1961, 9, ALHUA.

35. Clayton W. Fountain, *Union Guy* (New York: Viking, 1949), 49.

36. Jack W. Skeels, interviewer, "Oral History Interview of Dan Gallagher," January 26, 1960, 28–29, ALHUA.

37. "J. H. Smith and Dan G. Ross Testimony," January 27, 1937, 1251–54 and 1258, La Follette Committee; and Jack W. Skeels, interviewer, "Oral History Interview of Richard Frankensteen," October–December 1961, 16, ALHUA.

38. "Richard Truman Frankensteen Testimony," January 27, 1937, 1262–64 and 1267, La Follette Committee.

39. Ibid.; and Skeel, "Interview of Frankensteen," 16.

40. "Frankensteen Testimony," January 27, 1937, 1264–69.

41. Clipping, *DN*, January 27, [1937], folder: Labor Spies, box 14, JBP.

42. Clipping, *UAW*, April 7, 1937, folder: Espionage-Labor, box 9, JBP; and "Success Story," *Fortune* 12 (December 1935): 115–16, and 118.

43. "Success Story," 118 and 120; clipping, *DT*, December 1, 1935; and clipping, *Detroit Federation of Labor*, November 1, 1935, folder: Factory Spies, box 14, JBP; and Stark, "Terror Charged," 5.

44. Clippings, *DN*, March 30, March 31, and April 1, 1937, folder: Factory Spies, box 14, JBP.

45. Clippings, *DN*, March 30 and April 1, 1937, folder: Factory Spies, box 14, JBP.

46. Harold D. Lewis, "Trial Board Hearing [author's title]," March 20, 1937, 1–2, folder: Correspondence, January–June 1937, box 1, UAWL121.

47. Ibid., 2.

48. Ibid., 2–3.

49. Ibid., 4; and "Pinkerton Letters [author's title]," February 5–April 19, 1936, folder: Correspondence, 1936, January–June, box 1, UAWL121.

50. "Pinkerton Letters," February 5, 1936.

51. Ibid., February 8, 18, 20, and 21, 1936, and March 15, 1936.

52. Ibid., February 18, 21, and 28, 1936, and March 7, 10, 18, and 25, 1936.

53. Ibid., March 16 and 28, 1936, and April 9, 1936.

54. Ibid., March 3 and 26, 1936.

55. Ibid., March 3, 4, and April 6, 1936.

56. Ibid., February 20, 1936, and March 7, 25, and 31, 1936.

57. Ibid., February 20, 1936; March 30, 1936; and April 10, 1936.

58. "Trial Board Hearing," 2–3 and 13.

59. Ibid., 5 -10.

60. Executive Board Local Union 121 to Harold D. Lewis, February 13, 1937, folder: Correspondence, January–June 1937, box 1, UAWL121.

61. "Trial Board Hearing," 12.

62. Recording Secretary Local Union #121 to Harold Lewis, April 16, 1937, folder: Correspondence, January–June 1937, box 1, UAWL121.

63. Jack W. Skeels, interviewer, "Oral History Interview of Elmer Yenny," April 27, 1961, 10, ALHUA.

64. Clipping, *UAW*, April 7, 1937.

65. William A. Sullivan, interviewer, "Oral History Interview of Nick DiGaetano," April 29, 1959, and May 7, 1959, 24, ALHUA.

66. Keeney and Hill, "Interview of DiGaetano," 57–58.

67. Jack W. Skeels, interviewer, "Oral History Interview of John A. Zaremba," 17, ALHUA.

68. Kenneth B. West, interviewer, "Oral History Interview of Archie Jones," August 20, 1979, 31, 32, and 43, UMFLHP.

69. Neil O. Leighton, interviewer, "Oral History of Maynard (Red) Mundale and Georgia Baldwin," July 22, 1980, 57–58, UMFLHP.

70. Leighton, "Interview of Bjaland and O'Hara," 8.

71. Skeels, "Interview of Cranefield," 18.

Chapter 4. Fighting to Provide

1. "Why Men Quit Work" *AWN*, January 1929, 4.

2. "New She-Town," *AWN*, September 1927, 3.

3. Irving Bernstein, *Turbulent Years: A History of the American Worker, 1933–1941* (Boston: Houghton Mifflin, 1971), 501.

4. Stephen H. Norwood, *Strikebreaking and Intimidation: Mercenaries and Masculinity in Twentieth Century America* (Chapel Hill: University of North Carolina Press, 2002), 196.

5. On the Briggs strike see Joyce Shaw Peterson, *Automobile Workers, 1900–1933* (Albany: State University of New York Press, 1987), 139–48; and Sidney Fine, *The Automobile under the Blue Eagle: Labor, Management, and the Automobile Manufacturing Code* (Ann Arbor: University of Michigan Press, 1963), 27–30.

6. Samuel Romer, "The Detroit Strike," *Nation* 136 (February 15, 1933): 167.

7. For the Toledo strike, see Bernstein, *Turbulent Years*, 219–29; Fine, *Blue Eagle*, 274–83; and Philip A. Forth and Margaret R. Beagle, *I Remember Like Today: The Auto-Lite Strike of 1934* (Lansing: Michigan State University Press, 1988).

8. Fine, *Blue Eagle*, 278–79; Bernstein, *Turbulent Years*, 222–23; and "Troops in Toledo to Check Rioting, Workers Besieged," *NYT*, May 24, 1934.

9. Fine, *Blue Eagle*, 279; Bernstein, *Turbulent Years*, 223–24; "Two Slain, Score Injured, as National Guard Fires on Toledo Strike Rioters," *NYT*, May 25, 1934; and "Six Thousand in Battle," *NYT*, May 25, 1934.

10. For details on the incident, see Margaret Beegle, interviewer, "Oral History Interview of Margaret Byrd," 13–14, 1973; and Philip Korth, interviewer, "Oral History Interview of Carl Leck," 1973, 16, MSUA-LSOH. To view the unedited photograph with a shorter tie, see Sol Dollinger and Genora Johnson Dollinger, *Not Automatic: Women and the Left in the Forging of the Auto Workers' Union* (New York: Monthly Review Press, 2000), following p. 120.

11. Philip Korth, Margaret Beegle, and Claude Kazanski, interviewers, "Oral History Interview of William and Hildegarde Lockwood," 1973, 18, MSUA-LSOH.

12. Claude Kazanski and Margaret Beegle, interviewers, "Oral History Interview of John Toczynski," 1973, 7–8, MSUA-LSOH.

13. Fine, *Blue Eagle*, 281–83.

14. See especially, Sidney Fine, *Sit-Down: The General Motors Strike of 1936–1937* (Ann Arbor: University of Michigan Press, 1969); Bernstein, *Turbulent Years*, 509–54; Henry Kraus, *Many and the Few: A Chronicle the Dynamic Auto Workers* (Urbana: University of Illinois Press, 1985); *Heroes of Unwritten Story: The UAW, 1934–1939* (Urbana: University of Illinois Press, 1993); and Genora Dollinger, "Striking Flint," in Dollinger and Dollinger, *Not Automatic*, 123–60.

15. Victor G. Reuther, *The Brothers Reuther and the Story of the UAW: A Memoir* (Boston: Houghton Mifflin, 1979), 157.

16. Fine, *Sit-Down*, 331.

17. Norwood, *Strikebreaking and Intimidation*, 172.

18. Heber Blankenhorn, "Case VII-C-148 (FORD PLANTS, ROUGE, LINCOLN AND HIGHLAND PARK) Outline of Status of Investigation March 8, 1941," 1–2 and 9, folder 2-4, box 2, HBP.

19. Ibid.,10.

20. Ibid., 9.

21. Ibid., 10.

22. Ibid., 10.

23. Ibid., 10–11.

24. Judith Stepan-Norris and Maurice Zeitlin, *Talking Union* (Urbana: University of Illinois Press, 1996), 82.

25. "Detroit Hearings: Sugar," 254.

26. Jack W. Skeels, interviewer, "Oral History Interview of Martin Jensen," November 27, 1959–November 1, 1960, 10, ALHUA.

27. Jack W. Skeels, interviewer, "Oral History Interview of James Couser," November 19, 1960, 13, ALHUA.

28. Jack W. Skeels, interviewer, "Oral History Interview of Carl Haessler," November 27, 1959–October 24, 1960, 64, ALHUA.

29. Alex Baskin, "The Ford Hunger March—1932," *Labor History* 13 (Summer 1972): 335–38.

30. Ibid., 339 and 345–46.

31. Ibid., 347–50; and "Ford Riot Victims Buried with Red Rites," *NYT*, March 13, 1932.

32. Stepan-Norris and Zeitlin, *Talking Union*, 61.

33. UAW Press Release, May 18, 1937, folder 16-2, box 16, HKP.

34. UAW Publicity Department, "For Immediate Release," May 26, 1937, folder: UAW—Organizing Activities, Ford 1937, JBP. A copy of the organizational leaflet was printed in the *Daily Worker*. See Clipping, *Daily Worker*, May 27, 1937, folder 7-2, box 7, MSP.

35. Clipping, *DN*, May 26, 1937, folder 7–3, box 7, MSP; and "In the Matter of Ford Motor Company and International Union, United Automobile Workers of America, Case No. C-199, Decided December 22, 1937," in National Labor Relations Board, *Decisions and Orders of the National Labor Relations Board* 4 (Washington, D.C., 1938), 632–33 (hereinafter cited as NLRB Case No. C-199). The NLRB later discovered that the Miller Road overpass was actually public property.

36. Clipping, *DN*, May 27, 1937, folder 7-3, box 7, MSP.

37. Clipping, *DN*, May 27, 1937; and NLRB Case No. C-199, 629.

38. UAW Press Release, May 26, 1937, folder 16-2, box 16, HKP.

39. NLRB Case No. C-199, 629, 634, 635, and 643.

40. "List of Men and Women Hurt" [author's title], undated, folder 16-2, box 16, HKP; and NLRB Case No. C-199, 631.

41. Clipping, *DFP*, May 28, 1937, folder 7–3, box 7, MSP.

42. "List of Men and Women Hurt"; and Case No. C-199, 631–32 and 636.

43. Clipping, *DN*, May 26, 1937, folder 7–3, box 7, MSP.

44. Clipping, *DN*, May 28, 1937, folder 7-3, box 7, MSP.

45. Clipping, *DN*, May 26, 1937.

46. Clippings, *DFP*, May 28, 1937; *DT*, May 28, 1937; and *DN*, May 29, 1937, and June 1, 1937, folder 7-2, box 7, MSP.

47. NLRB Case No. C-199, 644–45 and 676–78.

48. UAW Press Release, October 1, 1940, folder: UAW—Organizing Activities, Ford 1940, box 32, JBP; and Clipping, *Sunday Worker*, ca. October 7, 1940, folder: Percy Lewellyn—2, box 10, Small Personnel Collections. The *Detroit Times* (April 2, 1941) described the "vigorous, stocky" Widman.

49. "CIO Union Asks Ford Labor Poll," *NYT*, December 12, 1940; and "Conciliator Adjusts Union-Ford Dispute," *NYT*, December 21, 1940.

50. Clipping, *DT*, April 2, 1941, folder 58-5, box 58, MSP.

51. "U.S. Orders Ford Sign Pact with CIO and Rehire 142," *UAW*, March 1, 1941, 1.

52. Clipping, *Ford Facts*, March 19, 1941, folder 58-1, box 58, MSP.

53. *Clipping, *Daily Worker*, April 1, 1941, folder 58-1, box 58, MSP.

54. Ibid.

55. Ibid.

56. Clippings, *DFP*, April 2, 1941; and *Daily Worker*, April 2, 1941, folder 58-3, box 58 and *DN*, April 2, 1941, folder 58-2, box 58, MSP.

57. Clipping, unidentified and undated, ca. April 2, 1941, folder 58-2, box 58, MSP.

58. Clipping, *DN*, April 2, 1941.

59. Clipping, unidentified and undated, ca. April 2, 1941, folder 58-2, box 58, MSP.

60. William A. Sullivan, interviewer, "Oral History Interview of Mr. DiGaetano," 61, April 29 and May 7, 1959, ALHUA.

61. Clipping, *DN*, April 2, 1941.

62. Clippings, *DN*, April 2, 1941; *DFP*, April 2, 1941; and *DT*, April 2, 1941, folder 58-3, box 58, MSP.

63. Clippings, *DFP*, April 2, 1941; *DN*, April 2, 1941; and *DT*, April 2, 1941, folder 58-3, box 58, MSP.

64. Clipping, *DN*, April 2, 1941.

65. Ibid.

66. Clipping, *DFP*, April 2, 1941; and *DN*, April 2, 1941.

67. Clipping, unidentified and undated, ca. April 2, 1941; and *Ford Facts*, April 5, 1941.

68. Clippings, *DN*, April 3, 1941; and *DFP*, April 3, 1941, folder 58-4, box 58, MSP.

69. Clippings, *DN*, April 3, 1941, and April 4, 1941; and *DFP*, April 3, 1941, folder 58-4, box 58, MSP.

70. Clipping, *DN*, April 3, 1941; and Clipping, *DFP*, April 4, 1941, folder 58-6, box 58, MSP.

71. "Charles Harp, 2126 Canniff, Hamtramck, Michigan," April, 6, 1941, 1, folder: Ford Motor Company, box 1, ELP; and Clipping, *DN*, April 7, 1941, folder 58-10, box 58, MSP.

72. "Charles Harp," 2; and Clipping, *DN*, April 7, 1941.

73. "Charles Harp," 2–3; and Clipping, *DN*, April 7, 1941.

74. "Charles Harp," 3–4; and Clipping, *DN*, April 7, 1941.

75. "Charles Harp," 2–3 and 4–5; and Clipping, *DN*, April 7, 1941.

76. "Charles Harp," 5; and Clipping, *DN*, April 7, 1941.

77. "Charles Harp," 4; and Clipping, *DN*, April 7, 1941.

78. "Charles Harp," 1; and Clipping, *DN*, April 7, 1941.

79. For a description on how the UAW won over the Detroit black community, see August Meier and Elliott Rudwick, *Black Detroit and the Rise of the UAW* (New York: Oxford University Press, 1979), 78–107.

80. "Negro Organization at Fords," undated, 1, folder 1-20, box 1, Catherine Gelles Papers, ALHUA.

81. Ibid.

82. Herbert Hill, interviewer, "Oral History Interview of Hodges Mason," November 28, 1967, 28, ALHUA.

83. Ibid., 28–29.

84. Clippings, *DFP* and *DN*, April 6, 1941, folder 58-8, box 58; and *DN*, April 7, 1941, folder 58-10, box 58, MSP.

85. Ford Organizing Committee—UAW-CIO, press release, April 6, 1941, folder: Strikes and Lockouts—Ford Motor Co.—1941, box 21, JBP; and Clipping, *DN*, April 7, 1941, folder 58-19, box 58, MSP.

86. NLRB, "Cases Nos. R-2425 and R-2426: Supplemental Decision and Certification, June 41, 1941," *Decisions of the National Labor Relations Board* 32, 1002.

87. "CIO Sweeps Rouge and Lincoln," *UAW*, July 7, 1941, 1.

88. Skeels, "Interview of Bannon," 8.

89. Harry Shulman, "Opinion A-1: 'Discipline of Employees for Assault and Mass Disturbance,'" June 3, 1943, box 137, UAWR1R. Additional details of this incident are found in the military interrogations of UAW members and plant protection men in box 1791, entry 473, WMC.

90. "Statement of Lawrence Yost to Captain Thomas J. Sullivan," March 15, 1943, WMC; and Shulman, "Opinion A-1."

91. Shulman, "Opinion A-1."

92. Ibid.

93. Ibid.

94. "Statement of Paul Ste. Marie to Captain Thomas J. Sullivan," March 16, 1943, WMC, NAS.

95. Shulman, "Opinion A-1."

96. Ibid.

97. Harry Shulman, "Opinion A-2," June 17, 1943, box 137, UAWR1P.

98. Harry Shulman, "Opinion A-31," November 23, 1943, and "Opinion A-16," September 23, 1943, folder 179, box 9, HSP.

99. Stepan-Norris and Zeitlin, *Talking Union*, 121 and 120.

Chapter 5. Fashioning Dense Masculine Space

1. Philip Korth and Margaret Beegle, interviewers, "Oral History Interview of Charles Rigby," 1973, 25, MSUA-LSOH; and Skeels, interviewer, "Oral History Interview of Stanley Brams," November 23, 1959, 11–12.

2. Clipping, Local 212 edition UAW, 1-17-40, folder: UAW—Flying Squadrons, box 31, JBC.

3. Dollinger and Dollinger, *Not Automatic*, 82–83; and Clipping, *MESA Educator*, November 1938, folder: UAW—Flying Squadrons, box 31, JBC.

4. Clipping, Local #2 issue UAW, 12–27–39, folder: UAW—Flying Squadrons, box 31, JBC.

5. Clipping, Local #154 Edition UAW, 9-1-40, folder: UAW—Flying Squadrons, box 31, JBC.

6. Walter P. Reuther, "The United Automobile Workers: Past, Present, and Future," *Virginia Law Review* 50 (January 1964): 87.

7. On the operation of the grievance systems, see Stephen Meyer, *Stalin Over Wisconsin: The Making and Unmaking of Militant Unionism, 1900–1950* (New Brunswick, NJ: Rutgers University Press, 1992), 105–46; and Steve Jeffreys, *Management and Managed: Fifty Years of Crisis at Chrysler* (New York: Cambridge University Press, 1986), 74–75 and 85–86.

8. David Brody, "The Uses of Power I: Industrial Battleground," *Workers in Industrial America: Essays on the Twentieth Century Struggle* (New York: Oxford University Press, 1980), 173–214.

9. See Sidney Pollard, "Factory Discipline in the Industrial Revolution," *Economic History Review* 16, no. 2 (1963): 254–71; and Edward P. Thompson, "Time, Work Discipline, and Industrial Capitalism," *Past and Present* 38 (December 1967): 56–97.

10. Thompson, "Time, Work Discipline, and Industrial Capitalism," *Past and Present* 38 (December 1967): 57.

11. Paul Thompson, "Playing at Being Skilled: Factory Culture and Pride in Work Skills among Coventry Car Workers," *Social History* 13, no. 1 (1988): 58.

12. Alf Leudtke, "Cash, Coffee Breaks, Horseplay: Eigensinn and Politics among Factory Workers circa 1900," in Michael Hanagan and Charles Stephenson, eds., *Confrontation, Class Consciousness, and the Labor Process* (Westport, Conn.: Greenwood, 1986), 80 and 82.

13. "Board of Review on Umpire Appeals," Case E-65, December 18, 1947, and Case F-197, September 25, 1950, folder: GM Board of Review Decisions, vol. 1, box 1, UAWGMDR.

14. "Discharge Hearing for C. W. Clouse, 21B, and William Hornyak, 165," September 30, 1943, folder: Discharge Hearings, 1943, box 12, UAWL9R.

15. "Notice of Appeal, Case L-91," October 27, 1965, folder: L Series, box 169, UAWR8R.

16. "Complaint No. I-647," March 14, 1940, folder: Grievances, Mack Ave, 1940, box 10, UAWL212R.

17. "Complaint Record, No. 64," August 16, 1937, folder: Grievances—Mack Ave. (2), box 2, UAWL212R.

18. "Petition," October 24, 1941, folder: Grievances, Mack Ave, 1941 (2), box 11, UAWL212R; and "Recommendations on Horseplay," August 16, 1944, folder: Shop Rules, box 21, UAWL75R.

19. Unsigned, Union Brief, undated, folder: Umpire Cases; and "Disciplinary Hearing Held Wednesday, February 20, 1957, Carl Leonard," Reports of J. O. Reynolds, Ted Reitz, William D. Fort, and D. W. Starner, folder: Board of Review, box 5, UAWR2R.

20. Michael Burawoy, *Manufacturing Consent: Changes in the Labor Process under Monopoly Capitalism* (Chicago: University of Chicago Press, 1979), 51. In the auto indus-

try, management structured its piece-rate systems around masculine competitiveness. One hundred percent was allegedly the work pace in number of pieces produced that allowed a normal worker to achieve an expected daily income. "Making out" involved earning as much as possible with the least effort and avoiding a rate cut.

21. Burawoy, *Manufacturing Consent*, 81–82.

22. M. E. Stone to Harry Shulman, Complaint No. 17758, February 16, 1949, folder Umpire Cases, 1949, box 58, UAWL9R.

23. M. E. Stone to Harry E. Shulman, Complaint No. 15339, February 16, 1949, folder Umpire Cases, 1949, box 58, UAWL9R.

24. John Lippert, "Sexuality as Consumption," in Snodgrass, ed., *For Men against Sexism*, 208.

25. Edward L. Cushman, "Decision of the Impartial Chairman, Grievance No. 54," March 31, 1954; "Management Brief," Grievance 54, Joe Brzak, Disciplinary Discharge," n.d.; "Union Brief," March 9, 1954; and "Union Exhibit G," folder Umpire Decisions, n.d., box 20, UAWL650R.

26. George W. Taylor, "Umpire Decision No. A-77: Disciplinary Layoff Followed by Discharge," June 3, 1941, folder 13, box 72, UAWGMDR. Emphasis added.

27. Ralph T. Steward, "Umpire Decision C-329: Discharge for Assaulting a Supervisor," March 6, 1945, folder 7, box 72, UAWGMDR.

28. "Strikers Fired," *Business Week*, March 18, 1944, 90.

29. Early Reynolds to R. W. Conder, March 16, 1944; and "Grievance #279: Management Statement," 1–2, folder 6, box 101, UAWCDR.

30. "Grievance #279," 2.

31. G. Allan Dash, "Umpire Decision No. C-150: Disciplinary Layoff of 145 Employes," December 14, 1943, 501–2, box 3, UAWL174R.

32. Ibid.

33. Ibid.

34. Ibid.

35. G. Allan Dash, "Opinion C-33: Appeal of Nine Discharges," April 20, 1943, 108, folder 12, box 12, UAWGMDR.

36. Ibid., 108 and 109.

37. Ibid., 111.

38. G. Allan Dash, "Opinion C-199: Disciplinary Layoff," April 14, 1944, 650–51, folder 11, box 72, UAWGMDR.

39. "Complaint Record, No. A-340," October 4, 1938, folder Grievances—Mack Ave, 1938, (12), box 5, UAWL212R.

40. George W. Taylor, "Umpire Decision A-151: Disciplinary Layoff," September 2, 1941, folder 13, B 72, UAWGMDR.

41. G. Allan Dash, "Umpire Decision B-141: Appeal of Discharge," April 16, 1942, folder 13, box 72, UAWGMDR.

42. George W. Taylor, "Umpire Decision B-26: Disciplinary Layoff," November 16, 1941, folder 13, box 72, UAWGMDR.

43. For a detailed examples of these shop-floor struggles, see Meyer, *"Stalin Over Wisconsin,"* 82–97.

44. George W. Taylor, "Umpire Decision A-169: Disciplinary Layoff," September 17, 1941, folder 13, box 72, UAWGMDR.

45. G. Allan Dash, "Umpire Decision C-161: Disciplinary Layoff," January 11, 1944, folder 11, box 72, UAWGMDR.

46. Harry Shulman, "Opinion A-122: Assault on Fellow Employee," July 5, 1944, box 137, UAWR1R.

47. George W. Taylor, "Umpire Decision No. A-74: Discharge of Employe," June 2, 1941, folder 13, box 72, UAWGMDR.

48. G. Allan Dash, "Umpire Decision No. C-228: Appeal of a Discharge," June 19, 1944, folder 13, box 72, UAWGMDR.

49. G. Allan Dash, "Umpire Decision No. B-124: Disciplinary Layoff of a Committeeman," March 18, 1942, folder 13, box 72, UAWGMDR.

50. Ralph T. Seward, "Umpire Decision No. C-238: Discharge for Using Abusive Language to Supervisors," September 5, 1944, folder 7, box 72, UAWGMDR.

51. Harry Shulman, "Opinion A-174: Discharge for Striking a Foreman," January 27, 1945, box 137, UAWR1R.

52. Shulman, "Opinion A-174."

53. George W. Taylor, "Umpire Decision No. B-41: Protest of Employe Discharge," December 2, 1941, folder 13, box 72, UAWGMDR.

54. Harry Shulman, "Opinion A-132: Assault on Foreman Outside the Plant," July 31, 1944, box 131, UAWR1R.

55. Shulman, "Opinion A-132."

56. Harry Shulman, "Opinion A-49: Discipline for Assault on Foreman: Case No. 121 (Local No. 249)," January 11, 1944, box 137, UAWR1R.

57. Ibid., emphasis added.

58. Ibid.

59. Ibid.

Chapter 6. The Female "Invasion"

1. On women auto workers, see Ruth Milkman, *Gender at Work: The Dynamics of Job Segregation During World War II* (Urbana: University of Illinois Press, 1987); Nancy F. Gabin, *Feminism in the Labor Movement: Women and the United Auto Workers, 1935–1975* (Urbana: University of Illinois Press, 1990); and Pamela H. Sugiman, *Labour's Dilemma: The Gender Politics of Auto Workers in Canada, 1937–1979* (Toronto: University of Toronto Press, 1997).

2. "Industry's Petticoat Army," *Management Review* 32 (March 1943): 101, "Table 4. Female and Total Employment in the Auto and Electrical Industries, 1940 to 1944—Production Workers Only," in Milkman, *Gender at Work*, 51; and Gregory W. Chester, *Women in Defense Work during World War II: An Analysis of the Labor Problem and Women's Rights* (New York: Exposition, 1974), 68.

3. W. G. Guthrie, "Why We Like Women in Our Shop," *Factory Management and Maintenance* 101 (February 1943): 80; and Ray Sanders, "Benefits that Follow the Hiring of Women," *Factory Management and Maintenance* 101(July 1943): 294.

4. "Conditioning Women to Factory Work," *Management Review* 31 (October 1942): 348.

5. Sugiman, *Labour's Dilemma*, 65 and 66.

6. Ibid., 73.

7. Ibid., 73–84, 86–87, 93, and 95.

8. Karen L. Gatz, interviewer, "Oral History Interview of Naomi J. Wilson," February 19, 1982, 21, OHRC.

9. Kenneth B. West, interviewer, "Oral History Interview of Elizabeth Pichotte," March 4, 1980, 7–8, UMFLHP.

10. Lyn Goldfarb, Lydia Kleiner, and Christine Miller, interviewers, "Oral History Interview of Dorothy Haener, United Automobile Workers," ca. 1978, 24, BHLUM.

11. George Romney, "Automotive Council Statement," March 9, 1945, in United States Senate, Hearings before the Special Committee Investigating the National Defense Program, Part 28 (Washington, 1945), 13563 and 13591.

12. Karen Anderson, *Wartime Women: Sex Roles, Family Relations, and the Status of Women during World War II* (Westport, Conn.: Greenwood, 1981), 52–3, "Morals: Production Problem," *Management Review* 32 (August 1943): 80; and Montgomery Mulford, "Girls in Plants," *Personnel Journal* 21 (April 1943): 356–57.

13. Lowell Juilliard Carr and James Edson Stermer, *Willow Run: A Study of Industrialization and Cultural Inadequacy* (New York: Harper, 1952), 148.

14. "Morals: Production Problem," 80.

15. Jack W. Skeels, interviewer, "Oral History Interview of William H. Oliver," March 5, 1963, 4, ALHUA, and Ruth Meyerowitz, interviewer, "Oral History Interview of Mildred Jeffrey," August 13, 1976, 55, BHLUM.

16. Skeels, "Interview of Oliver," 4.

17. Ibid., 4; and Meyerowitz, "Interview of Jeffrey," 55.

18. Harry Shulman, "The Case of the Lady in the Red Slacks," Opinion A-117, June 30, 1944, in UAW-Ford Umpire Decisions: Harry Schulman: Opinions A-1-A-284: Decisions M-1-M399: Issued by National Ford Department, Ken Bannon, Director, in Box 142, Accession 512, UAWRiB and "REPORT OF THE GRIEVANCES OF LOCAL 400 AS HAVE BEEN SUBMITTED TO THE UMPIRE FOR THE PERIOD OF 1942–43–44," folder 6, box 51, UAWL400R.

19. Shulman, "Violation of Safety Rule, Case Nos. 76 and 77 (Local 683)," Umpire Opinion A-43, December 23, 1943, in binder titled "UAW-Ford Umpire Decisions: Harry Schulman: Opinions A-1- A-284: Decisions M-1 - M399: Issued by national Ford Department, Ken Bannon, Director" in box 142, accession 512, UAWRiBR.

20. Shulman, "Violation of Safety Rule."

21. Ibid.

22. Ibid.

23. Ibid.

24. Sugiman, *Labour's Dilemma*, 73.

25. "Fashion Invades the Factory," *Personnel Journal* 19 (January 1943): 593–94.

26. Skeels, "Interview of Anderson," 4–5.

27. "Conditions in the Studebaker Plant," *AWN*, June 1927, 1; "Fisher Union Growing," *FAW*, October 1936; "Milwaukee Hearings: Anna Glatowski," December 30, 1934, 263, box 188, ALB; Kazanski and Beegle, " Interview of Toczynski," 18.

28. "Muskegon Hearings: Joseph J. Belland," December 20, 1934, 153–54, box 188, ALB, NA.

29. Marquart, *Auto Worker's Journal*, 138.

30. Ibid., 72

31. Jack W. Skeels, interviewer, "Oral History Interview of Mr. Dan Gallagher," January 26, 1960, 2–3, ALHUA.

32. Sherna Berger Gluck, interviewer, "Oral History Interview of Bette Murphy," *Rosie the Riveter Revisited*, vol. 28, 85, ALHUA; and Ruth Meyerowitz, interviewer, "Oral History Interview with Caroline Davis," July 23, 1976, 107, BHLUM.

33. Bill Meyer, interviewer, "Oral History Interview of Gilbert Rose," August 13, 1979, 69, UMFLHP.

34. "Morals: Production Problem," 287.

35. UAW Local 833, "TANK ARSENAL PLANT, Grievance No. 36," December 12, 1944, "AFFIDAVIT OF MRS. O. THOMAS," August 26, 1944, folder 18, box 98, UAWCDR; W. Van den Bossche, "LABOR RELATIONS SUPERVISOR'S ANSWER," undated; and E. J. Reis, "PLANT MANAGER'S DESIGNATED REPRESENTATIVE STATEMENT," undated, "TANK ARSENAL PLANT, Grievance No. 36," December 12, 1944, folder 18, box 98, UAWCDR.

36. Clayton W. Fountain, *Union Guy* (New York: Viking, 1949), 27–28.

37. Cindy Cleary, interviewer, "Oral History Interview of Mary Luna," *Rosie the Riveter Revisited*, vol. 20, 46, ALHUA.

38. "Discharge for Passing Obscene Note to Female Employee, Case No. 454, H. Booker, Motor Building—Local 600, H. Booker (B-2137)," August 19, 1944, Case M-80, UAW-Ford Umpire Decisions: Harry Schulman . . . Issued by National Ford Department, Ken Bannon, Director Binder of Ford Umpire Decisions, box 142, UAW-R1BR.

39. "Discharge on complaint of female employee, Case No. 390, J. Q. Shaw (BK-653), Willow Run—Local 50," August 21, 1944, Case M-82, UAW-Ford Umpire Decisions: Harry Schulman . . . Issued by National Ford Department, Ken Bannon, Director, in box 142, UAWR1BR.

40. Cindy Cleary, interviewer, "Oral History Interview of Mildred Eusibio," Rosie the Riveter Revisited, vol. 11, 37, ALHUS.

41. Jan Fischer, interviewer, "Oral History Interview of Vera Hunter," *Rosie the Riveter Revisited*, vol. 17, 59; Cindy Cleary, interviewer, "Oral History Interview of Helen Struder," *Rosie the Riveter Revisited*, vol. 41, 77; and Jan Fischer, interviewer,

"Oral History Interview of Mary Pollard," *Rosie the Riveter Revisited*, vol. 34, 44, ALHUS.

42. Jack W. Skeels, interviewer, "Oral History Interview of Sam Sage," July 18, 1960, 32–33. ALHUA.

43. Ralph T. Seward, "Appeal of Discharges for 'Unsatisfactory Conduct Off Plant Property and Outside of Working Hours,'" Umpire Decision No. C-278, November 27, 1944, 867 in folder 7, box 72, UAWGMDR.

44. Allan Dash, "Appeal of Two Discharges," 735, Umpire Decision No. C-231, June 19, 1944, 735 in folder 7, box 72, UAWGMDR.

45. Dash, "Appeal of Two Discharges," 735 and 736.

46. On the "moral police," see Thomas Dublin, *Women at Work: The Transformation of Work and Community in Lowell, Massachusetts, 1826-1860* (New York: Columbia University Press, 1979).

47. Seward, "Appeal of Discharges," 868.

48. Dash, "Appeal of Two Discharges," 736.

49. Ibid., 736 and 737.

50. Ibid.,737.

51. Seward, "Appeal of Discharges," 867–68.

52. Ibid., 868–69.

53. Ibid., 870.

54. Anderson, *Wartime Women*, 47; Cleary "Interview of Struder," 82; and Jan Fischer, interviewer, "Oral History Interview of Norma Central," *Rosie the Riveter Revisited*, vol. 5, 42, ALHUA.

55. Jack W. Skeels, interviewer, "Oral History Interview with John K. McDaniel," May 26, 1961, 11; and Fischer "Interview of Pollard," 34.

56. Cindy Cleary, interviewer, "Oral History Interview of Lupe Purdy," *Rosie the Riveter Revisited*, vol. 41, 45; and Jan Fischer, interviewer, "Oral History Interview of Genevieve Roesch," *Rosie the Riveter Revisited*, vol. 36, 51, ALHUA.

57. Cindy Cleary, interviewer, "Oral History Interview of Annie Strangeland," *Rosie the Riveter Revisited*, vol. 40, 64, ALHUA ; and Fischer "Interview of Pollard," 38.

58. Kenneth West, interviewer, "Oral History of Irving King," March 26, 1980, 52, UMFLHP; and Dollinger and Dollinger, *Not Automatic*, 151–53.

59. Cleary, "Interview of Eusibio," 34; Cleary, "Interview of Struder," 67.

60. Jan Fischer, interviewer, "Oral History Interview of Mildred Owen," *Rosie the Riveter Revisited*, vol. 32, 60, ALHUA.

61. Ralph T. Seward, "Umpire Decision C-242: Discharge for Fighting," September 5, 1944, folder 7, box 72, General Motors Department Collection, ALHUA.

62. Linda Cleary, interviewer, "Oral History Interview of Eva Lowe," *Rosie the Riveter Revisited*, vol.19, 31–32, ALHUA.

63. "Genevieve Roesch," 45; and Jan Fischer, Interviewer, "Oral History Interview of Isabel Orwin," *Rosie the Riveter Revisited*, vol. 31, 53–4, ALHUA.

64. Fischer, "Interview of Hunter," 59,

65. Likert Survey No. 143, folder: Study S-72, box 25, RLP.

66. Likert Survey No. 154, folder: Study S-72, box 25, RLP.

67. Likert Survey No. 027, Likert Survey No. 198, and Likert Survey No. 082, folder: Study S-72, box 25, *RLP*.

68. Milkman, "Rosie the Riveter Revisited: Management's Postwar Purge of Women Workers," in Meyer and Lichtenstein, *On the Line*, 129; and Robbin Zeff, interviewer, "Oral History Interview of Maryanne Van Daele," August 23, 1985, 12, OHRC.

69. John Bodnar, interviewer, "Oral History Interview of Clifford MacMillan," May 11, 1984, 34–35, OHRC.

Chapter 7. The Challenge to White Manhood

1. Anthony Luchek to Joseph D. Kennan, memorandum on "Degrees of Utilization of Negro Workers in War Industries in the Detroit Industrial Area . . .," July 14, 1943, 8, folder: Labor, box 317, entry 3, WPB.

2. "March-on-Washington Movement among Negroes," May 12, 1942, 3, folder 9-7, OWI Reports and Memoranda, RLP.

3. James N. Gregory's *The Southern Diaspora: How the Great Migrations of Black and White Southerners Transformed America* (Chapel Hill: University of North Carolina Press, 2005) forces us to consider the interplay between black and white migrants. John Hartigan's *Racial Situations: Class Predicaments of Whiteness in Detroit* (Princeton, N.J.: Princeton University Press, 1999) explores the subsequent social impact of white migrants in Detroit.

4. Joe Brown to Ed[ward Wieck], August 20, 1942, folder: Brown, Joe—Correspondence, 1935–44, box 10, EAWP.

5. William A. Sullivan, interviewer, "Oral History Interview of John Panzner," April 20, 1959, 5, ALHUA.

6. Charles Denby (Matthew Ward), *Indignant Heart: A Black Worker's Journal* (Boston: South End, 1978), 31.

7. Christopher Alston, "CCA Tape Transcripts, 11/18/90 Interview with Charlotte Zwerlin & Tom Spann—PBS," 1, folder 1-8, box 1, CMAP.

8. In *The Wages of Whiteness: Race and the Making of the American Working Class* (London: Verso, 1991), 12–13, David R. Roediger borrows W. E. B. Dubois's phrase about the "psychological wages of whiteness" to describe the social and economic advantages achieved by those considered "white." In one sense, the Americanization of immigrant workers was one step toward whiteness.

9. Young and Wheeler, *Hard Stuff*, 17.

10. Neil Leighton and Kenneth West, interviewers, "Oral History Interview of Henry Clark," August 13, 1979, 16–17, and 102, UMFLHP; and Michael Marve, interviewer, "Oral History Interview of Roger Townsend," May 1979, 1, UMFLHP.

11. Hill, " Interview of Mason," 1 and 12.

12. Robert C. Weaver, "The Negro Comes of Age in Industry," *Atlantic Monthly* 172 (September 1943): 55.

13. Anthony Luchek to Joseph D. Kennan, memorandum on "Degrees of Utilization of Negro Workers in War Industries in the Detroit Industrial Area," July 14, 1943, 7, folder: Labor, box 317, Entry 3, WPB.

14. Marve, "Interview of Townsend," 3.

15. Ibid., 2–3.

16. Erdmann Doane Beynon, "The Southern White Laborer Migrates to Michigan," *American Sociological Review* 3 (June 1938): 336.

17. Lewis M. Killian, "The Adjustment of Southern White Migrants to Northern Urban Norms," *Social Forces* 32 (October 1953): 67; and Louis Adamic, "The Hill-Billies Come to Detroit," *Nation* 140 (February 13, 1935): 177.

18. Marquart, *Auto Worker's Journal*, 31; and Adamic, "Hill-Billies," 178.

19. Herbert Hill, interviewer, "Oral History Interview of Frank Marquart," July 24, 1968, 4; and Herbert Hill, interviewer, "Oral History Interview of Shelton Tappes, #1, Part 1," October 27, 1967, 2, ALHUA.

20. James Lindahl, "Processes of Decision-Making in a UAW-CIO Local Union," master's thesis, Wayne State University, 1954, 22–24, folder 7, box 5, JLP. Before attending Wayne State University, James Lindahl was the recording secretary of UAW Local 190 in the early 1940s. Typical of industrial sociology at that time, he masked the firm's name as the "Deluxe Motor Car Company." However, the internal evidence indicates that the firm he described was Packard.

21. Ibid.; and Jack Skeels, interviewer, "Oral History Interview of Mr. Adam Poplawski," May 2, 1960, 3–7 and 9, ALHUA.

22. Ibid., 9, 12, 14–15, and 19.

23. Lindahl, "UAW-CIO Local Union," 24–25.

24. Ibid., 25–26.

25. Ibid., 26–28.

26. "Packard Called for Plane Engines," *NYT*, June 17, 1940; "Packard Assumes Rolls Royce Job," *NYT*, July 4, 1940; and "Packard Begins on Air Engines," *NYT*, August 3, 1941.

27. "Accuse Agents of Sabotaging War Industry," *MC*, March 6, 1943, 1 and 2.

28. Chester L. Quarles, *The Ku Klux Klan and Related American Racialist and Anti-Semitic Organizations* (Jefferson, N.C.: McFarland, 1999), 78–81; and Michael Newton and Judy Ann Newton, *The Ku Klux Klan: An Encyclopedia* (New York: Garland, 1991) 125.

29. "KKK Seeks Recruits from Packard Employes," *UAW: Local 190 Packard Edition*, September 13, 1939, 3. Lindahl was editor of this issue.

30. These UAW Klan spy reports and KKK organizational letters, mainly undated or only partially dated from 1940 and 1941, make it difficult to recreate the specific sequence and dates of the informant's or the KKK activities. "KU KLUX KLAN: Letters to members during parts of 1940 and 1941," folder 9, box 5, JLP. The reports are cited as "Klan Reports and Letters."

31. Ibid., undated.

32. Ibid.

33. Ibid.

34. "What Does the Klan Stand For?," folder 9, box 3, JLP.

35. George Addes to Curt Murdoch, January 1942, copy published in *UAW: Packard Local 190 Edition*, February 15, 1942, 1. The Addes letter suggests that the Klan spy was reporting to national UAW leaders.

36. "Klan Reports and Letters," undated; "Packard Local Fights KKK," *UAW: Packard Local 190 Edition*, February 15, 1942, 1–2; leaflet, "Membership Double-Crossed by Murdock," undated, folder 4, box 1; and leaflet "The Truth Behind the K.K.K. Forgery," undated, folder 23, box 3, JLP; and "Sample Ballot," *UAW: Packard Local 190 Edition*, February 15, 1942, 2.

37. "Detroiters in Riot on Negro Project," *NYT*, March 1, 1942; and "Detroit Riot Issue Put Up to Capital," *NYT*, March 2, 1942.

38. "Detroit Riot Issue Put Up to Capital," *NYT*, March 2, 1942, "Detroit Housing Unit Won't Be Opened Now," *NYT*, March 3, 1942; and "Government to Investigate Klan Activity in Detroit," *The Hour*, March 7, 1942.

39. "800 Soldiers Protect 12 Families Moving In," *NYT*, April 30, 1942; and "Detroit Michigan," folder: Tension Areas Report, box 389, FEPC.

40. "In the matter of Preferment of Charges against Frank Buehrle by Curt Murdock President of Packard Local U.A.W.-C.I.O. No. 190 held at the local headquarters of the local at 6111 Mt. Elliot Avenue in the city of Detroit, Mich, Commencing March 31st 1942 at 7-00 P M, Books 1–4, March 31–April 3, 1944," folder 10-11, box 5, JLP, For reports on the trial to local union members, see *UAW: Packard Local 190 Edition*, April 15, 1942.

41. "Poplawski Testimony—Charges against Frank Buehrle, Book 3, April 2, 1942," 75; and "Murdock Testimony—Charges against Frank Buehrle, Book 4, April 2, 1942," 57; and "Lindahl Testimony—Charges against Frank Buehrle, Book 4, April 2, 1942," 49.

42. "Lindahl Testimony," 50–51; and "Poplawski Testimony," 71–72.

43. "Report of the Trial Board," undated, folder 11, box 2, JLP.

44. "Lindahl Testimony," 50–51.

45. Report, Lester A. Walton to Adolf Berle, July 1942, 1–2, folder: Reports A–C, box 227, FEPC.

46. Lester A. Walton to Adolf Berle, July 1942.

47. "Halt Naval Work Over Negro Issue," *NYT*, June 19, 1942; and "Workers Return to Their Jobs at Hudson Naval Arsenal," *WSJ*, June 20, 1942, 2; and Skeels, "Interview of Frankensteen," October 10 and 23, 1959, and November 6, 1959, December 7, 1961, 78–79, ALHUA.

48. "Workers Return to Their Jobs at Hudson Naval Arsenal," *WSJ*, June 20, 1942, 2; and Skeels, "Interview of Frankensteen," 79–80.

49. "War Workers Used for Janitor Work," *MC*, February 20, 1943, 1 and 3.

50. "Inside Story of Chrysler Plant Strike," *MC*, March 27, 1943, 1 and 2.

51. "Inside Story of Chrysler Strike," 1 and 2.

52. "Believe Walkout Led By Klan Element," *MC*, March 27, 1943, 3.

53. G. James Fleming to George M. Johnson, "Detroit Progress Report," March 5, 1943, folder: Reports 1, Fleming, G. James, box 228, FEPC.

54. Memorandum, Jack B. Burke and Michael R. Donovan to G. James Fleming, "Walkout at Packard Motor Company . . .," March 24, 1943, folder: Reports 1, Fleming, G. James, box 228, FEPC.

55. "Wildcat Strike Shuts Packard," *DN*, June 3, 1943, 1; and G. James Fleming to Lawrence W. Cramer and George M. Johnson, "Continued Work Stoppage at Packard Motor Company . . .," June 3, 1943, folder F, box 63, FEPC.

56. Skeels, "Interview of Poplawski," 23; and "Fleming to Cramer and Johnson."

57. "Fleming to Cramer and Johnson"; "Packard Strikers Defy UAW," *DFP*, June 4, 1943, 1; "25,000 Ignore Pleas to Return at Packard," *DN*, June 4, 1943, 2; and "U.S. to Punish Leaders of Packard Strike," *DN*, June 6, 1943, 1.

58. "Strikers at Packard Ignore WLB Order," *DFP*, June 5, 1943, 1 and 14.

59. "Fleming to Cramer and Johnson."

60. "Strike Probe at Packard Is Pledged," *DFP*, June 6, 1943, 2.

61. "U.S. to Punish Leaders of Packard Strike," *DN*, June 6, 1943, 1; "Packard Men Start Back," *DFP*, June 7, 1943, 1; "Fleming to Cramer and Johnson"; and "Klan Out of Detroit, Says Chief," *DN*, June 10, 1943, 1.

62. "Packard Men Start Back," 1 and 3; "27 Strike Leaders Suspended at Packard," *DN*, June 7, 1943 1; "Packard Plant Returns to Normal Production: Strike Leaders Ousted," *DFP*, June 8, 1943, 1.

63. "Packard Motor Company-Detroit, Michigan," undated, folder: Strike Data, box 404, FEPC.

64. Thomas J. Sugrue, *The Origins of the Urban Crisis: Race and Inequality in Postwar Detroit* (Princeton, N.J.: Princeton University Press, 1996), 26. Other accounts include: Harvard Sitkoff, "The Detroit Race Riot of 1943," *Michigan History* 53 (Summer 1968): 183–206; Alfred McClung Lee and Norman Daymond Humphrey, *Race Riot* (New York: Dryden, 1943); and Robert Shogan and Tom Craig, *The Detroit Race Riot: A Study in Violence* (Philadelphia: Chilton, 1964).

65. Shogan and Craig, *Detroit Race Riot*, 89.

66. Lee and Humphrey, *Race Riot*, 2.

67. Sitkoff, "Detroit Race Riot," 188; and Shogan and Craig, *Detroit Race Riot*, 8.

68. Sitkoff, "Detroit Race Riot," 198.

69. Lee and Humphrey, *Race Riot*, 60.

70. Shogan and Craig, *Detroit Race Riot*, 88.

71. Lee and Humphrey, *Race Riot*, 63.

72. Ibid., 32.

73. Shogan and Craig, *Detroit Race Riot*, 32; and Lee and Humphrey, *Race Riot*, 61.

74. G. James Fleming to William Maslow, "Progress Report: Rioting and War Workers," July 9 1943, 2, folder: Reports, I Fleming, G. James, box 228, FEPC, NAS.

75. Hill, "Interview of Tappes," 76; and "For Tension File: From Region V, Detroit Suboffice, November 11, 1944," folder: Tension Data, box 404, FEPC, NAS.

76. "From Swan's Report, July 22[, 1944]," folder: Strike Data, box 404, FEPC, NAS.

77. Unknown interviewer, "Oral History Interview of Shelton Tappes," September 1983, 4.3–4.5, ALHUA.

Conclusion

1. Milkman, "Rosie the Riveter Revisited," 135 and 145–46.

2. Dorothy Haener, testimony before Michigan Department of Labor, "A Public Hearing on Sexual Harassment in the Work Place, Volume 2, May 9, 1979, Detroit, Michigan," 53, folder 28-10, box 28, UAWWDHR.

3. Skeels, "Interview of Brams," 38.

4. Ibid., 39.

5. "Guide to the Technology and Society Collection, RU 472," compiled by Daniel Hartwig, May 2008, Manuscripts and Archives, Yale University Library.

6. Study Questionnaire, folder 81, box 13; and Study Questionnaire, folder 67, box 12, accession 1985-A-066, series 3, YTSC. Each folder contained the questionnaire for a single worker.

7. "Guide to the Technology and Society Collection."

8. Study Questionnaire, folder 259; and Study Questionnaire, folder 260, box 23, YTSC.

9. Skeels, "Interview of Brams," 32.

10. Judson Gooding, "Blue-Collar Blues on the Assembly Line," *Fortune* (July 1970), 69.

11. Ibid., 70.

12. Barbara Garson, "Luddites in Lordstown: It's Not the Money, It's the Job," *Harper's* 244 (June 1972): 68–69.

13. On the RUMs, see Dan Georgakis and Marvin Surkin, *Detroit: I Do Mind Dying* (New York: St. Martin's, 1975); David M. Lewis-Colman, *Race against Liberalism: Black Workers and the UAW in Detroit* (Urbana: University of Illinois Press, 2008), 90–111; Steve Jefferys, *Managers and Managed: Fifty Years of Crisis at Chrysler* (Cambridge: Cambridge University Press, 1986), 168–87; and Heather Ann Thompson, *Whose Detroit? Politics, Labor, and Race in a Modern American City* (Ithaca, N.Y.: Cornell University Press, 2001).

14. Georgakis and Surkin, *Detroit*, 21–22; Thompson, *Whose Detroit?* 58–60; and Jeffries, *Managers and Managed*, 156–60.

15. Georgakis and Surkin, *Detroit*, 85.

16. Ben Hamper, *Rivethead: Tales from the Assembly Line* (New York: Warner, 1992).

17. Marquart, "The Auto Worker" in *Voices of Dissent* (Freeport, N.Y.: Books for Libraries, 1969), 144.

18. Hamper, *Rivethead*, 35.

19. Ibid., 48, 49, 150–51, and 95.

20. Ibid., 54, 56, and 40–41.

21. Robbin Zeff, interviewer, "Oral History Interview of Maryanne Van Daele," August 23, 1985, 12, OHRC.

22. Framingham interviews in boxes 11–14 and Linden interviews in box 23, both in series 3, YTSC. Although the Walker and Guest interviews formed the basis for their 1952 book, *The Man on the Assembly Line,* the absence of a single woman interviewee is stunning and may well reveal the complete absence of women in these GM plants.

23. John B. Wolford, interviewer, "Oral History Interview of Joe Panzica," September 11, 1984, 8, OHRC.

24. "Playful Prank Not a 'Serious Violation,'" *UAW Arbitration Services: News Notes,* February 1968.

25. "Little Girls that Play with Fire, Etc.," *UAW Arbitration Services: News Notes,* October 1968.

26. *Debra A. Valentic v. Chrysler Corporation,* Appeal No. B78-10917 and Appeal No. B78-53236, [1978], folder 35-14, box 35, UAWWDHR.

27. "GM Sued for Sex Harassment," *Detroit Times* clipping, folder 35-14, box 35, UAWWDHR.

28. Clippings: "Sex Charge Filed against GM Foreman"; "GM Sex Case Continues"; "Sex Case Foreman 'Railroaded,'" all *Ypsilanti Press,* March 21, 1979, April 15, 1979, and undated, folder 27–10, box 27, UAWWDHR.

29. Clipping, "The Hell of Sexual Harassment," *DFP,* May 18, 1980, 1H and 8H, folder 1, box 3, EVHP.

30. "Sally Jackson Testimony before Michigan Department of Labor," vol. 1, May 9, 1979, 47–49.

31. "Wilton Cain Testimony before Michigan Department of Labor," vol. 1, May 9, 1979, 35–36; and "Jeanne Tai Testimony before Michigan Department of Labor," vol. 1, May 9, 1979, 30.

32. Memorandum, Edie Van Horn to Hank Lacayor, Irv Bluestone, and Sam Fishman, "Hearings—Sexual Harassment on the Job—Solidarity House," May 11, 1979, folder in box 13, EVHP.

33. Douglas A. Fraser to All Local Unions, "Policy on the Elimination of Sexual Harassment," ca. 1980, 1, folder 31–11, box 31, UAWWDHR. See also "The Hazards of Sexual Harassment," from *Solidarity,* March 1981, folder 1, box 13, EVHP.

34. Fraser, "Elimination of Sexual Harassment," 2–5.

35. "Sexual Harassment (Sexual Deviancy in the Work Place)," *UAW Arbitration Services News Notes* 21 (First Quarter 1985): 1–7.

36. Ibid., 1.

37. Ibid., 2–3.

38. Ibid., 3.

39. Ibid., 4–5.

40. Ibid., 5.

41. Ibid., 6.

42. "Mitsubishi Will Pay $34 Million," *Chicago Tribune*, June 12, 1998, 1 and 20.

43. "Assembly-Line Sexism?" *Time* 147 (May 6, 1996): 56–58.

44. Jonathan Mahler, "G.M., Detroit, and the Fall of the Black Middle Class," *NYT Magazine*, June 28, 2009, 33.

45. "The Vanishing Male Worker, Waiting It Out," *NYT*, December 12, 2014.

Index

absenteeism, 33, 189, 196, 206; reasons for, 34–35
Acciacca, Archie, 111
Ackley, Ernest, 46, 47
ACTU (Association of Catholic Trade Unions), 179
Addes, George, 177
Adkins, Louis, 65–66
AFL. *See* American Federation of Labor
African American Community, 101–2, 165, 190; UAW and, 100, 104–6; wartime attitudes, 180–81
African American workers, 165–66, 169–74, 182–84, 190, 197–98; AFL and CIO appeals to, 100–102, 105; caste system for, 169; challenge racial boundaries, 11; demeaned, 33, 170; discrimination, 166, 170, 181, 183; Ford loyalists, 95, 101, 102–3, 104; foundry, 96, 102–4; manhood, 49–50, 166, 193; man-killing jobs, 25, 172, 193; Midwest, 180–81; migrants, 170; Packard, 172, 173–74; postwar jobs, 193; segregated work, 170, 172; shared social space, 166, 169; UAW loyalists, 104–5; UAW policy, 105; up-graders, 180–84, 187; white jobs, 170, 172; white worker reaction to, 166, 171, 172; women's work, 182–83. *See also* Revolutionary Union Movements; Trade Union Leadership Conference
ALB. *See* Automobile Labor Board
Alston, Christopher, 105, 168
American Federation of Labor, 95–96, 101–2, 106–7, 172; Federal Union of Automobile Workers, 66; Packard, 167. *See also* UAW-AFL
American Social Hygiene Association, 51
Anderson, John W., 30, 38, 149
Anderson, Karen, 145
Andrews, John C., 70–71
Arbitration Services News Notes, 206
assembly line, 13–18, 34; symbol of modern industrialism, 12; transformation of shop traditions, 13
Association of Catholic Trade Unions, 177, 179
Automation, 121, 192, 194, 195, 198, 209
Automobile Labor Board, 28, 65, 66; hearings, 26, 27, 68, 72, 150
Automotive Council, 145
Automotive Industrial Workers Association, 69, 70, 173
Auto Worker, 40, 63; "union man," 40; "a union man's duty," 40–41
Auto Workers News, 21, 22, 23, 25, 29, 62, 62, 82; "What Is Manhood?" 41
Auto Workers Union, 16, 23, 25, 41, 62, 63
AWIA. *See* Automotive Industrial Workers Association
AWU. *See* Auto Workers Union

bachelor culture, 44, 46–47, 49
Baker, General Gordon, 197
Bannon, Ken, 24, 107
Baron, Ava, 1

"Battle of the Overpass," 89, 91–94, 97, 99, 100

"Battle of the Running Bulls," 86

Bennett, Harry, 61, 94–96, 104; Ford Service Department, 87–91; spy system, 81; worker attitudes toward, 107, 109, 110

Bernstein, Irving, 83

Biddle, Francis, 188

Bjaland, Ingvald, 65

black bottom, 49, 67

Black Legion, 167, 171, 181

black workers. *See* African American workers

Blankenhorn, Heber, 59, 87–89

"Bloody Monday," 90

"bloody riot," 107–10

"Blue Collar Blues," 195

Borawoy, Michael, 122

Boy-like male behavior, 44, 118–19, 132, 135, 154, 205

Brams, Staley, 193, 195

breadwinner, 28, 58, 84, 112. *See also* family provider

Brockunier, Sawyer, 16

Brody, David, 115

brothels, 47, 48. 49, 52, 53, 153

Brown, Joe, 167

Brzak, Joe, 124

Buehrle, Frank, 177; trial, 179–80

Caldwell, Erskine, 56–57; "eight fingered city," 23

CAP. *See* UAW Community Action Program

Carr, Lowell Julliard, 145

Carriage and Wagon Workers' Union, 59

Carter, Eugene, 183

Chester, Gregory W., 142

Chinoy, Ely, 12, 13

CIO. *See* Congress of Industrializations

CIO Klan informant, 175–76, 235n30

Clark, Henry, 169

Colescott, James A., 175, 176, 177, 186

commercialized leisure, 48, 49, 50, 51, 57

communists, 101, 167, 174, 175, 177

Congress for Racial Equality, 197

Congress of Industrial Organizations, 81, 94–98, 107, 112, 167, 181, 183–84. *See also* UAW-CIO

Conlon, P. J., 7

control, 6, 16, 20, 33, 35, 161; conveyor, 17, 18, 19; machine cycle, 17, 19

Conveyor, 77

Corkum, Gerald, 69, 71–73

Coughlin, Father Charles, 167, 173–74, 177, 179, 182, 188

Coulthard, Stan, 39, 65

craft traditions, 3, 5–8, 10, 13, 15, 25

Cranefield, Harold, 59, 67, 68, 81

Crawford, Rev. John W., 100

crisis in masculinity, 9

Cross and Flag, 189

Cruden Robert, 16, 20, 26

cursing, 44, 115, 160, 193, 199

Cushman, Edward, L., 124, 126

Dash, G. Allen, 156, 158, 159, 160

Davies, Everett, 16, 19, 21

Davis, Carolyn, 151

Denby, Charles, 168

dense male space, 34, 111, 143, 146, 199

detective agencies: Corporations Auxiliary, 60, 63, 66–67, 69, 70–71; Pinkerton, 63, 65–67, 73–79; Railway Audit, 63, 67; Sherman, 63; Thiel, 59

Detroit: "Mecca for prostitutes," 51; red-light district, 2, 51

Detroit Federation of Labor, 101

Detroit Free Press, 99

Detroit House of Corrections, 54–55

Detroit News, 98, 99, 100, 101, 185, 186, 203

Detroit race riots: 1943, 187–90; 1967, 197

Detroit Times, 72, 99

division of labor: ethnic, 166; racial, 193, 197

Dobbins, Kemper, 16, 19, 21

Donelli, John, 108

Dorosh, Walter, 111

doubling up, 199

Drake, Col. Alonzo M., 186

drinking, 5–6, 46–47, 108, 119, 156–58, 199–200, 209

Drucker, Peter, 13

Dubreuil, Hyacinthe, 7–8, 38

dude employee, 48, 49

Dunn, Robert, 17, 25, 26, 27

Egbert, Mark, 77

Evans, Hiram Wesley, 175

factionalism, 81, 94, 173, 174. *See also* UAW-AFL or UAW-CIO

factory culture, 13

factory spies, 11, 58, 65; fear, 68; Ford, 60–62, 85; hooking, 67, 73–74; information gathered, 67; negative manhood of; 58; rules and reports, 63–65, 74–77; worker retribution, 78–79. *See also* detective agencies

Fair Employment Opportunity Commission, 207

Fair Employment Practices Commission, 165, 180, 184, 186, 187, 189

family provider, 11, 40, 41, 56, 83, 84, 193, 209; Fighter and, 42. *See also* breadwinner

family wage, 6, 25, 33, 57, 111

fatigue, 20–21

female space, 141, 143–45

fighting, 1–2, 80, 82–84, 108–9, 112–14, 133, 138; with foremen, 134–35, 136, 137–38; interethnic, 133–34; interracial, 134, 137; with woman, 161–62; words, 29, 139

Five Dollar Day, 48

Fleming, E. McCluny, 15, 45, 50

Fleming, G. James, 189–90

Flint Auto Worker, 44

flying squadrons, 93, 112–14, 194

Ford, Henry, 13, 48, 61. 72. *See also* Fordism

Ford Facts, 94, 105

Ford Hunger March, 90–91, 111

Fordism, 9, 116

Ford organizational drive: 1937, 91–94; 1940–41, 94–106

Ford Service Department, 20, 61, 87–88, 104, 106, 108–10; organization, 88–89

Ford Sociological Department, 41, 61

Ford Times, 48

foremen, 18, 119–21; female abuse, 149–50, 203–4, 206; worker abuse, 22, 28–30

Fortune, 71

Fountain, Clayton, 69, 153

Frankensteen, Richard, 69–71, 91–93, 99, 181, 182

Frankowski, William, 72, 73

Fraser, Douglas A., 205–6

Freeman, Josh, 4, 6, 10

Fry, Joe, 39

Gallagher, Dan, 150–51

gambling, 5, 64, 103–4, 117–18, 144–45, 199

gangsters, 59, 61, 88–89, 102

Garson, Barbara, 196

gender: despite absence of women, 1; identity and work, 9; stereotyped jobs, 141

Gilder, Frank, 108–9

Gillman, John, 101

Gooding, Judson, 195, 196

Gray, Stan, 2–3

Graziosi, Andrea, 3–4; rough laborers, 4

Great Depression, 17, 27, 56, 57, 82–83, 85, 83

Great Recession, 208

Green, William, 95, 101

grievances, 107–10, 114–15; community customs, 138–39; fail for women, 201, 204, 205, 206; female dress, 146–49; fighting, 109–10, 111; goosing, 124–26; male culture, 117–40; party girls, 153–61; report foremen's harassment, 152–53; up-graders, 187

Guest, Robert H., 194, 200

Haener, Dorothy, 144, 192

Haessler, Carl, 90

Hamper, Ben ("Rivethead"), 199–200

Hanson, Harvey, 176, 177, 186

Hardin, Walter, 104, 183

Harp, Charles, 102–4

health and safety, 12, 21–26, 118, 119, 172, 198; loss of fingers, 22–23; sanitary conditions, 31; speed-up, 18, 32, 35; statistics, 24

he-man, 42, 139, 140

HIA. *See* Hudson Industrial Association

Higbie, Tobias, 4

hillbillies. *See* southern white migrants

horseplay, 116, 127–28, 199–200; fighting, 133; holiday, 132; homoeroticism, 124–26; safety, 118–19; women, 162. *See also* pranks

howling, 43–44

Hudson Industrial Association, 42

humiliation, 21, 28–30, 85, 144, 202–3

"hungry bastards," 37, 38

IAM. *See* International Association of Machinists

industrial jurisprudence, 115

International Association of Machinists, 7, 62

Iron Age, 43, 142

Jeffrey, Mildred, 146, 147

Jeffries, Edward J., 178

Jensen, Martin, 90

Johnson, Genora, 160

Jones, Archie, 80

Kanter, Robert, 91

Kennedy, J. J., 91

King, Irving, 39–40

Klann, William C., 60–61

Knights of Labor, 7

Kolb, Alfred, 43

Ku Klux Klan, 167, 168, 171, 174–82, 186, 188; Michigan, 176; organizing auto workers, 176–77; Packard, 177–80

labor turnover, 33, 194, 196; reasons for, 34, 194

La Follette Civil Liberties Committee, 59, 66, 68, 70, 78, 81

Leheney, John, 20

Leigh, Edmund, 61–62

leisure, 5, 50; preindustrial, 115; industrial, 116–17, 119

Lenz, Arnold, 83

Leonard, Carl "Tex," 119–22

Leudtke, Alf, 116

Levinson, Edward, 63

Lewis, Harold D., 69, 73–78; confession and trial, 77–78

Li, C. N., 18–19, 47

Lindahl, James, 172, 173, 174, 179, 180, 235n20

Lippert, John, 10, 124

Logan, W. A., 40, 62

McCoy, Charles "Kid," 89

McCrea, Duncan C., 93

McGowan, Helen, 53

McKie, Bill, 65

machines: automatic, 9, 13, 14, 16–17, 24, 25; cycle and control, 17; semiautomic, 17; single purpose, 17; specialized, 14, 17

machinists, 6, 7–8, 20, 32, 58, 62

Machinists' and Blacksmiths' International Union, 7

making out, 122–23, 228n20

manhood, 2, 41, 123; pride and honor, 131. See also respectable male culture; rough male culture

man-killing jobs, 19, 25, 165, 172, 193

"manly bearing," 3, 28, 122, 131

March on Washington, 165, 180

Marcus, Morris L., 44–45

Marinovich, Frank, 93

Marquardt, Frank, 150, 171–72, 199; mass production, 18; worker control, 37–39; youth, 1–2

Marquis: S. S., 60

Marshal, Donald T., 101

Martel, Frank X., 101

Martin, Homer, 77, 81, 91, 93, 94, 101, 113, 173, 176, 177

Martin, John S., 62–63

Marx, Karl, 19

masculine culture, 1–5, 112; Great Depression and, 83; language, 135; male bonding, 123; mass production workers, 9–10; new forms, 115–18; persistence of, 199; women and, 200. See also respectable male culture; rough male culture

Mason, Hodges, 105–6

mass production, 1, 9, 10, 11, 14–21, 34, 38; human costs, 12; loss of dignity, 20; loss of manhood, 20, 57; madness, 14–15, 17; manhood, 19–20; origins, 14; speed-up, 18; young workers favored, 25

Mathews, Norman, 185

Mathewson, Stanley B., 35–37; Restriction of Output among Unorganized Workers, 36

Maynard, Steven, 4, 9

Mechanics Educational Society of America, 113

Merriweather, William, 93

MESA. See Mechanics Educational Society of America

Meszaros, Joe, 26

Michigan Chronicle, 182

Michigan Department of Labor: sexual harassment hearings, 204

Michigan Employment Security Commission, 202

Milkman, Ruth, 164, 192

Miller, Carolyn, 146–47

Miller, George, 60

Mimms, Thomas, 45, 46, 50

Mitsubishi plant, 207–8

Montgomery, David, 3, 28, 38, 43

Moore, David, 20, 90–91, 111; loss of manhood, 20

Moore, Ray, 72

moral police, 43, 157

Morgan, Arthur E., 36–37

Mortimer, Wyndham, 26, 66, 94; Great Depression, 27–28; older workers, 25–27

Mundale, Red, 80

Murdock, Curt, 177–80

Murphy, Bette, 152

Murphy, John, 101

National Association for the Advancement of Colored People (NAACP), 102, 188, 197

National Industrial Recovery Act, 59, 173

National Labor Relations Act, 81, 87, 91

National Labor Relations Board, 59, 92,

93–95, 106–7, 130, 165, 170; Ford election, 94, 106–7
National Organization of Women, 208
National Union for Social Justice, 167
necktie cutting, 126–28
Newman, S. L., 62
New Woman, 43, 52, 54
New York Times, 208
NIRA. *See* National Industrial Recovery Act
NLRA. *See* National Labor Relations Act
NLRB. *See* National Labor Relations Board
Norris, Frank, 175
Norwood, Stephen H., 83, 87

O'Hara, James, 81
Oliver, William H., 146–48
output restriction, 33, 35–37, 122; class struggle, 37; manhood, 37; reasons, 36; skilled workers, 35; women, 161

Panzner, Joseph, 167–68
Parker, Carlton H., 5
paternalism, 9, 41, 147, 161
patriarchal behavior, 3, 6, 25, 38, 41, 139, 153
Poplawski, Adam, 177, 179, 185
Powderly, Terence V., 7
pranks, 44, 115, 128–29, 132, 152, 162, 199–200. *See also* horseplay
Progressive Caucus, 94, 173, 174
prostitution, 47–48, 50–57; child, 56–57; Dixon's Regulations, 52; economic situation of women, 55–56; Great Depression, 56; investigators, 51, 53, 54; social profile, 54–55

race mixing, 189, 190–91
Randolph, A. Philllip, 165
Raskin, Dr. I. W., 12, 20
rate busters, 37. *See also* hungry bastards
rats, 11, 38, 42, 54, 66, 79, 80. *See also* factory spies
Raymond, Phil, 16–17, 23
reconversion, 164, 192
relief, 30–31, 117, 135. *See also* toilets
re-masculinization, 9, 10, 42
respectable male culture, 5–11, 25, 131, 209; autonomy, 6; control, 6; dress, 5–7; family wage, 6; features of, 3; origins, 5–6; skilled workers, 3, 6; unionism and, 40–42; values, 6–9
Reuther, Roy, 83
Reuther, Victor, 86

Reuther, Walter, 88, 91–94, 99, 114
Revolutionary Union Movements, 197–99
Richards, Gene, 44
Rimar, Ralph, 65
Rockefeller Foundation, 42, 51, 53, 54
Romney, George, 145
Roosevelt, Franklin D., 95, 165, 188, 189
rough male culture, 10–11, 112–14, 117, 119, 209; anti-unionists, 80, 85; features, 1–5; Ford and, 49; laborers, 3–5; women and, 141–44, 161, 164
RUM. *See* Revolutionary Union Movements

sabotage, 196
Sanford, Rev. Raymond Prior, 92
Schedler, Carl L., 185
Scott, James C., 33
Seward, Ralph T., 156
sexual assault/harassment, 153–55, 200–208; Civil Rights Act, 202; failure of grievance process, 204; grievances, 201–2, 206–7; indifference to, 201; Mitsubishi, 207–8; officials favor harasser, 154, 155, 201–2; supervisors and co-workers, 150–53, 202
sexuality, 1, 2, 5, 6, 10, 11, 43–48; 1960s attitudes, 201. *See also* prostitution
Shirt-Tail Parade, 129–30
shop stewards, 98, 107, 114, 119, 128, 179, 185, 189, 197, 204
shop talk, 3, 44, 110, 136
Shulman, Harry, 107, 108–10, 122–23, 147–49, 154–55
Shutok, Joseph, 72
skill: dilution, 9, 15, 17, 174; mental and manhood, 17; redefinition of, 9; separation mental from manual, 9
Smith, Gerald L. K., 175, 188, 189
Smith, John W., 53
smoking demonstrations, 130–31
Sojourner Truth housing, 172, 187, 190; riots, 178–79
soldiering, 33, 35, 122; systematic, 35
southern white migrants, 168–71, 172, 174–75, 177, 181; anti-union attitudes, 171; cultural baggage, 173; suitcase brigade, 171
Spare, Charles, 176, 186
speed-up: Great Depression, 17–18
Speth Roy, 23
stealing a trade, 33, 38–40; pathway to skilled work, 38; specialized production, 38

Stearns, Peter N.: rough manhood defined, 1
Ste. Marie, Paul, 109
Street, Julian, 15
strikes: Auto Lite strike, 83, 84–85; Briggs strike, 84; Chevrolet Toledo, 76; Chrysler sit-down, 73; Dodge sit-down, 78; Ford River Rouge strike (1941), 96–106; General Motors Flint sit-down, 85–87; hate, 166, 167, 172, 180 190; Hudson hate, 181–82; "master race," 184; Packard hate, 171, 180–87, 190; "pride," 166, 172, 182, 183, 190; wildcat, 197, 198
Strong, Col. George E., 184
Sugar, Maurice, 67–68, 89–90
Sugiman, Pamela, 143–44, 149
Sugrue, Thomas, 187–88
suitcase brigade, 46, 51, 171

Tappes, Shelton, 105–6, 172, 190, 191
Taylor, Frederick W., 13, 35. See also Taylorism
Taylor, Glen S., 51, 52, 53–56
Taylor, Sam, 102, 103
Taylorism, 9, 116
Thomas, R. J., 81, 94, 181, 184–86, 189
Thompson, Edward P., 116
Thompson, Heather, 197
Thompson, Paul, 116
Time, 208
time-study men, 37
toilets, 30, 31–32, 89, 117–18, 170; sand piles, 178; segregated, 182–83; shop trough, 144. See also relief
tools, 7–8, 38, 39, 40, 80; tool box, 7
Townsend, Roger, 169
Trade Union Leadership Council, 197
Travis, Robert, 66
Trescott, Arthur, 124

UAW-AFL, 94, 96, 107, 133, 171, 173, 176
UAW-CIO, 94, 96–98, 106, 107, 130, 133, 173, 176, 187
UAW Community Action Program, 204–5
UAW. See United Automobile Workers Union
UAW Fair Practices Committee, 146
UAW-Ford contract, 107
UAW Women's Auxiliary, 91
UAW Women's Bureau, 146
United Automobile Worker, 79, 175

United Automobile Workers Union, 42, 71–73, 79, 83, 85–87, 193–94; Detroit riot 1941, 189; factionalism, 81, 94, 173; Ford River Rouge strike, 91–103; Packard, 177–78; sexual harassment policy, 205–6; spies, 65–69
Unity Caucus, 94, 173, 174
up-graders. See under African American Workers
Ulrich, Walter, 20
union button campaign, 95–96

Van Horn, Edith, 204–5

Walker, Charles R., 13, 194
Walker, Glen, 72
Walton, Lester, 180–81
War Department: plant protection service, 61
Ward's Automotive Reports, 193
War Labor Board, 185
War Manpower Commission, 108, 142
War Plans White, 62
War Production Board, 169–70
Watkins, Myron, 49
Way, Peter, 4–5
"weapons of the weak," 33
Weiss, C. E., 184, 185, 187
Weiss, Harry, 26, 27
White, Walter, 188
white jobs, 166, 169–70, 172, 190
whiteness, 166–67, 168, 169; wages of, 171, 234n8
Widman, Michael F., 94, 97
Williams, Claude, 174–75
Williams, Whiting, 4–5; What's on the Worker's Mind, 4, 46
Wolff, Fred M., 21–22
Women's Emergency Brigade, 86
women workers, 10–11, 33–34, 141–64, 202–8; accommodation to men, 160–61; degradation of, 10, 11, 33, 46; dress, 146–49; hostility, 159–60, 164; male rough culture, 143; male space, 141, 143, 164; male work, 142; morals problem, 145–46; party girls, 155–59; postwar purge, 192; statistics, 142, 164, 192; teasing, 162; war changes views of, 163; war work, 142–43
work, 1; brawn and strength, 9; degradation, 22; machine control, 16; mass production,

19; mindless, 15, 16, 19; skilled, 8–9; slow-down tactics, 122–23; unskilled work, 4–5
workers: age, 193; 25, 26–27; assembly line, 12–15, 18, 43–44, 184–85, 194–96, 199; blend rough and respectable cultures, 9–10; complaints, 26–29; craftsmen, 2, 9, 14, 25, 33, 38, 172, 173; docile, 20, 29; dress, 7, 49; ideology, 174; immigrant 3–4, 9, 25, 39, 51, 52, 141, 167–68; Irish, 4–5; laborers: 3–5; Mexican, 54; production, 2, 9–10, 21, 28, 29, 36; resistance, 115; semiskilled, 8–10; social and political diversity, 167; Southern and Eastern European, 4–5, 96, 166–67, 169, 173, 170, 171; young, 25–26, 27, 43, 79, 83, 100

workplace: culture, 6; female invasion, 3, 11, 149, 157, 159; filth, 30, 32; "last sanctum of male culture," 3; noise, 16
workplace rule of law, 115

Yale student workers, 15, 44–47, 215n10; radicalized, 19
Yale Technology Project, 13
Yenny, Elmer, 77, 78
Yost, Lawrence, 108
Young, Colemn, 49, 167, 168; *Hard Stuff*, 49

Zalkan, George, 19
Zaremba, John, 79–80
Zendt, Oliver M., 19, 27, 46

STEPHEN MEYER is an emeritus professor of history at the University of Wisconsin—Milwaukee. His books include *The Five Dollar Day: Labor Management and Social Control in the Ford Motor Company, 1908–1921* and *Stalin over Wisconsin: The Making and Unmaking of Militant Unionism, 1900–1950.*

THE WORKING CLASS IN AMERICAN HISTORY

Worker City, Company Town: Iron and Cotton-Worker Protest in Troy
  and Cohoes, New York, 1855–84   *Daniel J. Walkowitz*
Life, Work, and Rebellion in the Coal Fields: The Southern West Virginia
  Miners, 1880–1922   *David Alan Corbin*
Women and American Socialism, 1870–1920   *Mari Jo Buhle*
Lives of Their Own: Blacks, Italians, and Poles in Pittsburgh, 1900–1960
  John Bodnar, Roger Simon, and Michael P. Weber
Working-Class America: Essays on Labor, Community,
  and American Society   *Edited by Michael H. Frisch and Daniel J. Walkowitz*
Eugene V. Debs: Citizen and Socialist   *Nick Salvatore*
American Labor and Immigration History, 1877–1920s:
  Recent European Research   *Edited by Dirk Hoerder*
Workingmen's Democracy: The Knights of Labor
  and American Politics   *Leon Fink*
The Electrical Workers: A History of Labor at General Electric
  and Westinghouse, 1923–60   *Ronald W. Schatz*
The Mechanics of Baltimore: Workers and Politics in the Age
  of Revolution, 1763–1812   *Charles G. Steffen*
The Practice of Solidarity: American Hat Finishers in the
  Nineteenth Century   *David Bensman*
The Labor History Reader   *Edited by Daniel J. Leab*
Solidarity and Fragmentation: Working People and Class
  Consciousness in Detroit, 1875–1900   *Richard Oestreicher*
Counter Cultures: Saleswomen, Managers, and Customers
  in American Department Stores, 1890–1940   *Susan Porter Benson*
The New England Working Class and the New Labor History
  Edited by Herbert G. Gutman and Donald H. Bell
Labor Leaders in America   *Edited by Melvyn Dubofsky and Warren Van Tine*
Barons of Labor: The San Francisco Building Trades and Union Power
  in the Progressive Era   *Michael Kazin*
Gender at Work: The Dynamics of Job Segregation by Sex
  during World War II   *Ruth Milkman*
Once a Cigar Maker: Men, Women, and Work Culture in
  American Cigar Factories, 1900–1919   *Patricia A. Cooper*
A Generation of Boomers: The Pattern of Railroad Labor Conflict
  in Nineteenth-Century America   *Shelton Stromquist*
Work and Community in the Jungle: Chicago's Packinghouse
  Workers, 1894–1922   *James R. Barrett*
Workers, Managers, and Welfare Capitalism: The Shoeworkers
  and Tanners of Endicott Johnson, 1890–1950   *Gerald Zahavi*
Men, Women, and Work: Class, Gender, and Protest in the New England
  Shoe Industry, 1780–1910   *Mary Blewett*

Workers on the Waterfront: Seamen, Longshoremen, and Unionism
    in the 1930s   *Bruce Nelson*

German Workers in Chicago: A Documentary History of Working-Class
    Culture from 1850 to World War I   *Edited by Hartmut Keil and John B. Jentz*

On the Line: Essays in the History of Auto Work
    Edited by Nelson Lichtenstein and Stephen Meyer

Labor's Flaming Youth: Telephone Operators and Worker Militancy,
    1878–1923   *Stephen H. Norwood*

Another Civil War: Labor, Capital, and the State in the Anthracite Regions
    of Pennsylvania, 1840–68   *Grace Palladino*

Coal, Class, and Color: Blacks in Southern West Virginia, 1915–32
    Joe William Trotter Jr.

For Democracy, Workers, and God: Labor Song-Poems
    and Labor Protest, 1865–95   *Clark D. Halker*

Dishing It Out: Waitresses and Their Unions in the
    Twentieth Century   *Dorothy Sue Cobble*

The Spirit of 1848: German Immigrants, Labor Conflict, and the Coming
    of the Civil War   *Bruce Levine*

Working Women of Collar City: Gender, Class, and Community
    in Troy, New York, 1864–86   *Carole Turbin*

Southern Labor and Black Civil Rights: Organizing
    Memphis Workers   *Michael K. Honey*

Radicals of the Worst Sort: Laboring Women in Lawrence,
    Massachusetts, 1860–1912   *Ardis Cameron*

Producers, Proletarians, and Politicians: Workers and Party Politics
    in Evansville and New Albany, Indiana, 1850–87   *Lawrence M. Lipin*

The New Left and Labor in the 1960s   *Peter B. Levy*

The Making of Western Labor Radicalism: Denver's Organized
    Workers, 1878–1905   *David Brundage*

In Search of the Working Class: Essays in American Labor History
    and Political Culture   *Leon Fink*

Lawyers against Labor: From Individual Rights to
    Corporate Liberalism   *Daniel R. Ernst*

"We Are All Leaders": The Alternative Unionism
    of the Early 1930s   *Edited by Staughton Lynd*

The Female Economy: The Millinery and Dressmaking
    Trades, 1860–1930   *Wendy Gamber*

"Negro and White, Unite and Fight!": A Social History of Industrial
    Unionism in Meatpacking, 1930–90   *Roger Horowitz*

Power at Odds: The 1922 National Railroad Shopmen's Strike   *Colin J. Davis*

The Common Ground of Womanhood: Class, Gender,
    and Working Girls' Clubs, 1884–1928   *Priscilla Murolo*

Marching Together: Women of the Brotherhood of Sleeping
    Car Porters   *Melinda Chateauvert*

Down on the Killing Floor: Black and White Workers in Chicago's
    Packinghouses, 1904–54   *Rick Halpern*
Labor and Urban Politics: Class Conflict and the Origins of Modern Liberalism
    in Chicago, 1864–97   *Richard Schneirov*
All That Glitters: Class, Conflict, and Community in Cripple Creek
    Elizabeth Jameson
Waterfront Workers: New Perspectives on Race
    and Class   *Edited by Calvin Winslow*
Labor Histories: Class, Politics, and the Working-Class Experience
    Edited by Eric Arnesen, Julie Greene, and Bruce Laurie
The Pullman Strike and the Crisis of the 1890s: Essays on Labor and Politics
    Edited by Richard Schneirov, Shelton Stromquist, and Nick Salvatore
AlabamaNorth: African-American Migrants, Community, and Working-Class
    Activism in Cleveland, 1914–45   *Kimberley L. Phillips*
Imagining Internationalism in American and British Labor,
    1939–49   *Victor Silverman*
William Z. Foster and the Tragedy of American Radicalism   *James R. Barrett*
Colliers across the Sea: A Comparative Study of Class Formation in Scotland
    and the American Midwest, 1830–1924   *John H. M. Laslett*
"Rights, Not Roses": Unions and the Rise of Working-Class Feminism,
    1945–80   *Dennis A. Deslippe*
Testing the New Deal: The General Textile Strike of 1934 in the
    American South   *Janet Irons*
Hard Work: The Making of Labor History   *Melvyn Dubofsky*
Southern Workers and the Search for Community: Spartanburg County,
    South Carolina   *G. C. Waldrep III*
We Shall Be All: A History of the Industrial Workers of the World
    (abridged edition)   *Melvyn Dubofsky, ed. Joseph A. McCartin*
Race, Class, and Power in the Alabama Coalfields, 1908–21   *Brian Kelly*
Duquesne and the Rise of Steel Unionism   *James D. Rose*
Anaconda: Labor, Community, and Culture in Montana's
    Smelter City   *Laurie Mercier*
Bridgeport's Socialist New Deal, 1915–36   *Cecelia Bucki*
Indispensable Outcasts: Hobo Workers and Community in the
    American Midwest, 1880–1930   *Frank Tobias Higbie*
After the Strike: A Century of Labor Struggle at Pullman   *Susan Eleanor Hirsch*
Corruption and Reform in the Teamsters Union   *David Witwer*
Waterfront Revolts: New York and London Dockworkers, 1946–61   *Colin J. Davis*
Black Workers' Struggle for Equality in Birmingham
    Horace Huntley and David Montgomery
The Tribe of Black Ulysses: African American Men
    in the Industrial South   *William P. Jones*
City of Clerks: Office and Sales Workers in Philadelphia,
    1870–1920   *Jerome P. Bjelopera*

Reinventing "The People": The Progressive Movement, the Class Problem,
    and the Origins of Modern Liberalism   *Shelton Stromquist*
Radical Unionism in the Midwest, 1900–1950   *Rosemary Feurer*
Gendering Labor History   *Alice Kessler-Harris*
James P. Cannon and the Origins of the American Revolutionary
    Left, 1890–1928   *Bryan D. Palmer*
Glass Towns: Industry, Labor, and Political Economy in
    Appalachia, 1890–1930s   *Ken Fones-Wolf*
Workers and the Wild: Conservation, Consumerism, and Labor
    in Oregon, 1910–30   *Lawrence M. Lipin*
Wobblies on the Waterfront: Interracial Unionism in Progressive-Era
    Philadelphia   *Peter Cole*
Red Chicago: American Communism at Its Grassroots, 1928–35   *Randi Storch*
Labor's Cold War: Local Politics in a Global Context
    Edited by Shelton Stromquist
Bessie Abramowitz Hillman and the Making of the Amalgamated Clothing
    Workers of America   *Karen Pastorello*
The Great Strikes of 1877   *Edited by David O. Stowell*
Union-Free America: Workers and Antiunion Culture   *Lawrence Richards*
Race against Liberalism: Black Workers and the UAW
    in Detroit   *David M. Lewis-Colman*
Teachers and Reform: Chicago Public Education, 1929–70   *John F. Lyons*
Upheaval in the Quiet Zone: 1199/SEIU and the Politics of Healthcare
    Unionism   *Leon Fink and Brian Greenberg*
Shadow of the Racketeer: Scandal in Organized Labor   *David Witwer*
Sweet Tyranny: Migrant Labor, Industrial Agriculture,
    and Imperial Politics   *Kathleen Mapes*
Staley: The Fight for a New American Labor Movement
    Steven K. Ashby and C. J. Hawking
On the Ground: Labor Struggles in the American Airline Industry
    Liesl Miller Orenic
NAFTA and Labor in North America   *Norman Caulfield*
Making Capitalism Safe: Work Safety and Health Regulation
    in America, 1880–1940   *Donald W. Rogers*
Good, Reliable, White Men: Railroad Brotherhoods, 1877–1917   *Paul Michel Taillon*
Spirit of Rebellion: Labor and Religion in the New Cotton South   *Jarod Roll*
The Labor Question in America: Economic Democracy
    in the Gilded Age   *Rosanne Currarino*
Banded Together: Economic Democratization in the Brass Valley   *Jeremy Brecher*
The Gospel of the Working Class: Labor's Southern Prophets
    in New Deal America   *Erik Gellman and Jarod Roll*
Guest Workers and Resistance to U.S. Corporate Despotism   *Immanuel Ness*
Gleanings of Freedom: Free and Slave Labor along
    the Mason-Dixon Line, 1790–1860   *Max Grivno*

Chicago in the Age of Capital: Class, Politics, and Democracy
    during the Civil War and Reconstruction   *John B. Jentz and Richard Schneirov*
Child Care in Black and White: Working Parents and the History
    of Orphanages   *Jessie B. Ramey*
The Haymarket Conspiracy: Transatlantic
    Anarchist Networks   *Timothy Messer-Kruse*
Detroit's Cold War: The Origins of Postwar Conservatism   *Colleen Doody*
A Renegade Union: Interracial Organizing and Labor Radicalism   *Lisa Phillips*
Palomino: Clinton Jencks and Mexican-American Unionism
    in the American Southwest   *James J. Lorence*
Latin American Migrations to the U.S. Heartland: Changing Cultural Landscapes
    in Middle America   *Edited by Linda Allegro and Andrew Grant Wood*
Man of Fire: Selected Writings   *Ernesto Galarza, ed. Armando Ibarra
    and Rodolfo D. Torres*
A Contest of Ideas: Capital, Politics, and Labor   *Nelson Lichtenstein*
Making the World Safe for Workers: Labor, the Left, and Wilsonian
    Internationalism   *Elizabeth McKillen*
The Rise of the Chicago Police Department:
    Class and Conflict, 1850–1894   *Sam Mitrani*
Workers in Hard Times: A Long View of Economic Crises
    Edited by Leon Fink, Joseph A. McCartin, and Joan Sangster
Redeeming Time: Protestantism and Chicago's Eight-Hour
    Movement, 1866–1912   *William A. Mirola*
Struggle for the Soul of the Postwar South: White Evangelical Protestants
    and Operation Dixie   *Elizabeth Fones-Wolf and Ken Fones-Wolf*
Free Labor: The Civil War and the Making of an American
    Working Class   *Mark A. Lause*
Death and Dying in the Working Class, 1865–1920   *Michael K. Rosenow*
Immigrants against the State: Yiddish and Italian Anarchism
    in America   *Kenyon Zimmer*
Fighting for Total Person Unionism: Harold Gibbons, Ernest Calloway,
    and Working-Class Citizenship   *Robert Bussel*
Smokestacks in the Hills: Rural-Industrial Workers in West Virginia   *Louis Martin*
Disaster Citizenship: Survivors, Solidarity, and Power
    in the Progressive Era   *Jacob A. C. Remes*
The Pew and the Picket Line: Christianity and the American Working Class
    Edited by Christopher D. Cantwell, Heath W. Carter, and Janine Giordano Drake
Conservative Counterrevolution: Challenging Liberalism
    in 1950s Milwaukee   *Tula A. Connell*
Manhood on the Line: Working-Class Masculinities
    in the American Heartland   *Stephen Meyer*

The University of Illinois Press
is a founding member of the
Association of American University Presses.

University of Illinois Press
1325 South Oak Street
Champaign, IL 61820-6903
www.press.uillinois.edu